Common Sense Book of COMPLETE CAT CARE

Common Sense Book of COMPLETE CAT CARE

Louis L. Vine, D.V.M.

QUILL
WILLIAM MORROW
New York

THE COMMON SENSE BOOK OF COMPLETE CAT CARE

ISBN 0-688-11618-3

Library of Congress cataloging-in-publication data has been requested.

LC 92-6149

Printed in the United States of America

First Quill Edition

1 2 3 4 5 6 7 8 9 10

To the Cat Lover

ACKNOWLEDGMENT

The author wishes to thank Norma C. Scofield for her tireless work in editing the myriad materials used in compiling this book. Without her help, this book would not have been possible.

Contents

Introduction

Not many years ago, the veterinarian was known as a horse doctor; today, he has to be physician, surgeon, and psychotherapist. The profession is becoming more sophisticated all the time and, as a result, the veterinarian has the obligation to keep the pet owner up to date on as much of the new information as will be useful to him in caring for his pets. While many of a cat's problems are similar to those of a human being—the physical ailments, psychosomatic illnesses, emotional problems—and often the treatment is similar, a cat is wholly dependent on your knowledge and understanding to communicate how it feels. My reason for writing this book is to help you to raise your cat to be a healthy, happy, and well-adjusted animal and to enable you to recognize the behavioral and symptomatic signs when there are problems. I have tried to keep the technical details and medical phraseology to a minimum, and have concentrated on describing your cat's health in everyday language and using common-sense knowledge. I have also tried to indicate when an operation or procedure is particularly risky; when it will prolong the life of the cat for only a short time; and when it is likely to be especially expensive. Since no two cats are alike, you must adapt what you read here to you and your pet, and not always accept the advice that I have given as hard and fast. Also, fortunately, under normal circumstances cats are remarkably capable of good care of themselves.

The early detection of any physical, emotional, or mental abnormality in your cat is vital to the maintenance of its health. No one knows better than you when your cat is not feeling well. Every cat has a personality of its own, and you alone will be familiar with the particular habits of your cat and able to spot any deviation from normal. This book is not meant to be used for diagnosis and treatment of all disorders occurring in cats. It should help you distinguish between those occasions when you yourself can correct the conditions causing the cat's discomfort and those times when it is essential that you take your cat to a veterinarian—usually as soon as possible. No matter how competent a veterinarian is, the earlier in any illness you can bring your pet to him, the better he can treat it.

Research in veterinary colleges in the United States and throughout the world, as well as research conducted by commercial drug and cat-food laboratories, has dramatically improved the standards of available veterinary medical treatment. Veterinary medicine is also benefiting greatly from the advancement of research in human medicine. As drugs and techniques improve, animals that not long ago were considered to be in hopeless condition are now routinely being saved in any good veterinary hospital. Service in an animal hospital is now comparable to that given in the most modern hospital for humans. Veterinarians employ the full range of medical knowledge, such as intravenous anesthetics and feeding, tranquilizers, antibiotics, and blood analysis. The latest in laboratory diagnostic equipment is available: heart ailments can be diagnosed with an EKG (electrocardiograph) machine; brain and spinal diseases can be diagnosed with an EEG (electroencephalograph) machine. Even open-heart surgery and other refined types of surgical operations are becoming more common. In feline dentistry the veterinarian uses high-frequency dental units to remove tartar from the teeth, and extraction of decayed and infected teeth and treatment of sore gums are routine in most veterinary hospitals. Many veterinarians are specialists, devoting their time solely to surgery, radiology, heart diseases, eye diseases, or other aspects of feline medicine.

As a result, many cats are living longer, and the relatively new field of veterinary geriatrics is gaining prominence. It is now possible to treat heart, liver, and kidney diseases and arthritis in aging cats, and many cats are now able to enjoy a longer life. Most veterinarians oppose euthanasia, or mercy killing, unless the animal is hopelessly ill. In the past, destroying a cat was the easy way out; today most veterinarians will work tirelessly to save your pet.

For your cat's well-being and your peace of mind you must have confidence in both your veterinarian and his staff. By cooperating with your veterinarian you can receive the full benefit of his knowledge, ability, and skills.

Today more than 55 percent of American families own some kind of pet, and these pets are a valued part of family life. Your obligation is to see that your pet goes through life healthy and contented—with the benefit of your affection and common-sense care and, when necessary, your veterinarian's special attention.

A cat has absolute honesty. Male or female, a cat will show you how it feels about you. People hide their feelings for various reasons but cats never do.

—ERNEST HEMINGWAY

Part 1
The Life Cycle of a Cat

1 · Selecting Your Kitten

Breeds · Selection Considerations · The Actual Selection

Cats come in such a variety of sizes, shapes, colors, hair lengths, temperaments—and prices—that choosing a kitten for the first time can be a confusing experience. Although a knowledge of basic breed characteristics is helpful, actually no one breed is smartest, cleanest, most affectionate, or best with children. Cats are what their owners make them, and most of all, they require love, time, effort, and patience.

Breeds

Most experts think that domestic cats first made their appearance in Egypt between four and five thousand years ago and resembled the present-day Tabby. Through the centuries cats have bred among themselves and also with their wild cousins. Today there are more than twenty pure breeds of cats and various crossbreeds and many mixed breeds. The ma-jority of cats in our households today are a combination of two or more breeds; there are probably ten mixed-breed cats to every purebred. The purebred kitten will usually grow up to resemble its parents and the rest of its breed in temperament as well as in appearance and size. Contrary to popular belief, the mixed breed is not superior to the purebred in health and intelligence. Although all cats are subject to the same diseases and ailments, actually far more purebreds survive than mixed breeds, simply because most breeders strive to eliminate hereditary diseases and congenital defects. But mixed breeds are as affectionate as any purebred, and when properly cared for, they return just as much devotion.

Although no two cats are alike, breed characteristics do prevail. Some breeds are more high-strung than others, but occasionally this tendency can be altered with proper environment and training. Cats are adaptable and they readily adjust to their environment, whether a one-room apartment or a big house with acres of surrounding land.

In determining which type of cat to choose, go through some of the good books written especially for this purpose. Although you cannot always rely on what breeders or pet-shop owners tell you—they are, after all, trying to sell cats—do visit reputable breeders to discuss the nature and temperament of the breed you are thinking of choosing. Try to determine which breed is most suitable for your household. Whether your family would live more easily with a docile pet or a boisterous and playful one is an important consideration. Nervous pets make nervous people more nervous, and such people should have calm, easygoing cats.

Domestic cats are classified as either short-haired or long-haired. Short-haired types were developed in Egypt, Europe, and the Far East; long-haired types in Persia (Iran) and Afghanistan. Generally, short-haired cats are active and playful, and easier to care for than long-haired ones. Longhairs tend to be quiet, stay-at-home pets, and their fur sometimes needs extra grooming. (Although the short-haired breeds shed as much as the long-haired ones, the latter's hairs are more noticeable. Shorthairs shed a little all year round; the longhairs shed mostly in the spring and fall.) Long-haired cats generally have soft, beautiful voices; shorthairs usually have loud, raucous calls.

Short-haired

The basic breed of shorthair is the AMERICAN SHORTHAIR, the most common domestic cat around today. They come in a variety of both colors (thirty are recognized by the various cat associations) and patterns, including tabby. Physically and emotionally strong, they are affectionate when they want to be, intelligent when they care to be, great hunters when they are hungry, and obedient only when it suits them.

Also included in the shorthair category is the very agile and muscular ABYSSINIAN, which comes in two basic colors—warm red (banded with chocolate brown) and ruddy brown (banded with black or darker brown). Abyssinians make excellent pets as well as show animals. They are affectionate and quiet, hardy and healthy. They are not fussy eaters and their fur is easy to care for.

The BRITISH SHORTHAIR tends to moderate Persian type with short, plushy fur. It comes in almost all Persian and American Shorthair colors, including British Blue. The body is sturdy and strong and the disposition delightful.

The BURMESE is muscular in appearance and has a short, sable-brown coat. These cats are gentle, quiet, and friendly; seldom shy or timid. They are rugged and easy to care for. Their short, silky coats require a minimum of brushing.

The EXOTIC SHORTHAIR is the result of Persian-American cross-breeding and the cats reflect the personalities of both breeds. They are Persian in type and come in most Persian colors, but the coat is medium in length, dense, and soft.

The HAVANA BROWN has a short coat that is the rich tobacco brown which gives it its name. Cats of this breed are very playful and mischievous. They make especially good pets for people who like to be challenged; it is not easy to outwit these extroverts.

The KORAT is an especially loved cat of the Thai people and is considered a symbol of good fortune because of its coloring—silver (it is silver blue all over, tipped with silver). Inquisitive and alert, it is noted for its fine disposition and loving companionship.

The MANX has a short but thick coat, and not all members of this breed are tailless. Those with no tail are called "rumpies"; with a short tail, "stumpies"; and with a full tail, "longies." These cats are stockily built, short and compact, with strong hindquarters for jumping. They are devoted one-family cats.

18

They are best with adults; young children tend to frighten and confuse them. They shed quite profusely when frightened or emotionally disturbed.

The ORIENTAL SHORTHAIR has the type and personality of the Siamese but its color is not confined to its points. It comes in almost all colors and patterns.

The REX has a short, curly coat which is soft, silky, and wavy, and the hairs are not over half an inch in length. These cats are dainty in appearance but actually quite muscular. They are affectionate and love human handling. Usually healthy animals with exceptionally good appetites, they need little grooming because of the curl and texture of their hair.

The RUSSIAN BLUE has short, grayish-blue fur. It is a graceful and proud animal. Hardy and not fussy, it will eat most types of food presented to it.

And then there is the SIAMESE with its four different color points—blue, lilac, chocolate, or seal. In addition, there are red, cream, tortie, and lynx points: these are regarded as Siamese except by certain U.S. registering bodies which classify them as COLORPOINT SHORTHAIR. They occasionally come with kinks in their tails and crossed eyes. There is nothing wrong with this unless you intend to show them. Alert, affectionate, and endearingly sociable, they demand a lot of attention, and although they are more emotional than most breeds, they are not mean or vicious. They get along well with other cats, dogs, and children. In an apartment with thin walls, a drawback could be their tendency to be extremely vocal, for their voices sound much like the crying of a human baby.

Long-haired

The most common longhair is the PERSIAN. They come in a variety of colors—white, silver, chinchilla, black, blue, cameo, smoke, and tabby (which includes thirteen color varieties). (More than forty colors are recognized by the Cat Fanciers Association.) Many people make the mistake of calling any long-haired cat an angora when it should properly be called a Persian. There is no such breed as angora (although there is a TURKISH ANGORA); "angora" is simply a commonly used descriptive term. Persians are quiet and gentle. Generally they are peace-loving and calm-natured and they make devoted pets. They have beautiful fur which requires a lot of brushing; they tend to have problems with hair balls because of their meticulous grooming habits.

The BALINESE is a long-haired Siamese, but gentler and more even-tempered. They are delicate, exotic-looking cats with sweet temperaments. They are easy to handle and care for; their fur does not tangle as badly as the Persians', so they require less combing and brushing.

The BIRMAN resembles the Himalayan, but with shorter, less flowing hair. It has the points of the Balinese, but broken by white paws and by white "laces" up the backs of the rear paws. It resembles both in personality.

The HIMALAYAN looks like a combination of Siamese and long-haired Persian. These cats have the coloring of the Siamese and the body and fur of the Persian, but breeding a Siamese and a Persian will not produce a Himalayan; they are a specific breed that has been developed through years of careful and selective breeding. They make excellent companions and are affectionate and easy to care for.

The MAINE COON cat is charming and friendly—and beautiful. Colors are those of the Persian plus. Big cats, they generally weigh over fifteen pounds.

Other new and rare, exotic, and experimental breeds include the American Wirehair, Bombay, Chartreux, Cymric (Longhair Manx), Egyptian Mau, Japanese Bobtail,

Longhair Burmese, Luchsie, Ocicat, Ragdoll, Scottish Fold, Somali, Sphynx, and Tonkinese.

Selection Considerations

Sex

There is no evidence that one sex is more loving or companionable than the other. Whether to choose a female cat (known as a *queen)* or a male (known as a *tom)* is strictly a matter of preference.

Altering the queen or the tom, which you might do unless you intend to breed or show, will produce a more attentive and loving pet. Altered cats have less to distract them and less reason to roam, and are much more content with their human companions.

It is not easy to determine if your new kitten is a male or a female. It takes an experienced person to tell. Standing behind the cat, lift its tail and look beneath the tail. In a female, you will notice a slitlike opening very close below the anal opening. This is the vulva. In the male, the second opening is much farther away from the anal opening, and this is the round opening of the penis sheath. In the unaltered male, you will be able to feel the two testicles.

Age

There is a widely held belief that if one wants a friendly and satisfactory kitten it should be taken directly from the mother's breast into the home. This is not necessarily so, as many mature cats adjust beautifully to a new environment, and many stray cats adopt a household and become devoted family members. In fact, there are many who prefer to buy older cats because they feel that bad dispositions and serious faults are often hidden by kitten charm, or they simply do not wish to go through the trials and tribulations of breaking in a new kitten. One good alternative is to buy a retired brood queen or a stud

female

male

who is no longer in demand. A cat who has been retired from the show-ring can also adjust to a new owner. Grown and older cats can make splendid pets and deserve a chance at human companionship.

However, if you do want a kitten, cat psychologists say that the ideal time for getting one is when it is about eight weeks old. But if there are young children in the house, an older kitten, three months and up, would be better. Younger kittens are not strong enough to repel rough handling. If there is someone in the family who has a fear of cats, then it is best to get a kitten as young as possible. As the cat grows, the fearful person will more easily adjust to it.

Choosing the Right Cat for Your Particular Household

Children and cats naturally go together. However, a very young child will tend to maul a kitten—with loving hands—and a very young kitten could be badly injured. Most cats, though, will put up with a lot of rough handling from a child. Somehow they seem tolerant of a child's antics while they would object strenuously to similar treatment from an adult. But children should be taught to respect the rights of the cat.

The Apartment Dweller. Cats are esteemed as apartment pets because they are usually quiet, clean, and self-reliant. Their wants are simple: bed and board, a kind word. Whether exotic purebreds or homegrown mixed breeds, cats are small, graceful, odorless, quiet, housebroken practically from birth, and do not require walking. They can live happily inside your apartment all their lives.

As a Companion for Another Cat or Dog

Because jealousy is one of the strongest of all feline emotions, if you are planning to get a second cat you can expect some animosity in the beginning. The older cat will likely hiss and slap at the new kitten, but given a little time they will work out their relationship and live very happily together.

If the older cat is an unaltered tom, I would not advise getting a second tom unless you have both of them altered.

Popular belief has it that cats and dogs are natural enemies. This is definitely not so. Not only is it possible to keep a cat and dog together, but it is sometimes the perfect answer to prevent one pet from being lonely. Ideally, it is best to start the cat and dog relationship when they are still kitten and puppy, however, many close relationships between cats and dogs have resulted regardless of age.

Getting a Cat from a Cattery or a Pet Shop

When you enter the cattery or pet shop, be especially observant of the sanitation and the way the cats are kept. If there are any cats with diarrhea, coughing, or eye or nose discharge—stay away! If you are interested in buying one of the cats, ask the shop owner if you can first take it to a veterinarian to be examined. Be suspicious if this request is refused.

The cat buyer should be wary of "cut-rate" or "bargain" kittens. Most breeders and pet-shop owners are honest, but unfortunately there are some who buy and sell kittens unscrupulously. Most breeders, however, go by the rule book and do their best to maintain and sell healthy kittens.

When you are buying from a cattery, it is a good idea, if possible, to look at the queen and the stud. This way you can often get a good idea of the ultimate conformation and temperament of the kitten.

The object of most breeders is to develop a friendly, intelligent, mild-tempered pet rather than a high-strung, nervous animal that is detrimental to his breeding program.

Most conscientious breeders will guarantee

the health of their cats, and if a kitten shows any signs of sickness within two weeks after purchase, the breeder will usually assume the medical expenses or replace the kitten with a healthy one, or else refund the purchase price.

The Actual Selection

A Show Cat or a Pet Cat?

Cats may be characterized as being of show quality or pet quality. The price of a show-quality cat depends on breed, sex, age, and how close it is to the standards of perfection of its breed. A pet-quality kitten may have a minor flaw that would keep it out of the show-ring, but as long as its personality is suited to living with a family, it will make an excellent pet and companion.

If you are interested in having a show-quality cat, it is best to choose a good specimen with a good pedigree. By good specimen, I mean a cat that looks like the standard of the breed—the better the conformation, the better it is. In other words, I would always pick the good specimen with a fairly good ancestry over one with a champion-studded pedigree but not necessarily a perfect specimen itself. The novice buyer cannot expect to go into a cattery or pet shop and buy a champion; development of champions takes generations of selective breeding.

Choosing the Best of the Litter for Show

It is always difficult, even for an expert, to choose the best in a litter. For although many qualities show up clearly even at a tender age, there are points that cannot be determined in the very young kitten. For example, color can be very deceptive, as kittens in a nest are usually darker than they will ultimately be. Also, some kittens that are born small may soon catch up with their littermates and by the time they are adults surpass them in weight and bone structure.

A kitten excellent at eight weeks can develop faults by the time it is a year to eighteen months old. However, this is not common.

Choosing a Healthy Kitten

In choosing your kitten, be wary of one that shies away from you or is not responsive to your overtures; it could be overly nervous the rest of its life or it could be physically ill. Good personality and temperament, and good health too, will be indicated in a lively, friendly kitten who approaches you playfully and purrs at being petted. But you must also be alert to the kitten's physical well-being.

The basic characteristics of a healthy kitten are as follows:

□ The eyes should be clear, bright, and free from watery discharge and matter. There should be no scars or light spots on the cornea.

□ The nose and ears should be clean and with no signs of discharge. Check the ears for ear mites or any other infestation (see page 207).

□ The small baby teeth should be clean and bright. The mouth should have a pleasant odor and the color of the gums should be a light pink. A pale color is a sign of anemia, which is usually caused by a heavy infestation of parasites. Heavy hookworm infestation can be fatal to a young kitten.

□ The skin should be clean and with no rough spots. Constant scratching is a sign of parasites.

□ The fur should be fluffy, glossy, and slightly oily. A kitten with any fur loss, either generalized or in spots, should be avoided, as it may have mange, fungus, or ringworm, or be heavily infected with lice. (Ringworm is highly contagious to human beings.)

□ The bone structure should be solid and without curvature or bumps in the legs, which could indicate rickets. Beware of a kitten that is stiff-legged or lame.

□ Avoid the extra-plump kitten or the extra-large one. Pay more attention to the kitten who is neither fat nor thin and has a well-proportioned body. Extra plumpness in a kitten may indicate bloat or parasites, and if you are headed for the show-ring, an unusually large cat may be disqualified.

Check for diarrhea or stools that contain mucus or blood. These conditions usually indicate a heavy parasite population or the common and dangerous disease coccidiosis (see pages 174, 202–203).

2 · Kitten Care and Training

Introduction to the New Home · Holding a Kitten · Feeding a Kitten · Housebreaking · Grooming · Toys · Health Problems

The first six months of a cat's life are a most important and formative period, psychologically and physiologically, and a time when the kitten is most susceptible to diseases and parasites. Before taking a kitten home, you should find out if it has been vaccinated or wormed. Obtain any available information about the serum or vaccine that the kitten has been given and the dates administered. Many kittens have become victims of enteritis (see pages 174 and 175) because their owners were not aware that an animal is not immunized for life by a single vaccination (three or four shots spaced a couple of weeks apart are necessary). Similarly, it is incorrect to assume that if a kitten is wormed at the age of six to eight weeks, another checkup will not be necessary for a year or two.

It is wise to take your new kitten to a veterinarian within twenty-four hours for a thorough examination. If there is anything wrong—for example, a congenital defect or disease—the veterinarian will discover it and advise you. He will also give advice on immunization and set up a schedule for future vaccinations and wormings. (See the schedule of vaccinations on page 143.)

It is important to realize that you are taking on at least a ten- to fifteen-year project of providing your cat with proper care day after day. In return for good care, you can expect to have an affectionate relationship and the pleasure of a cat's companionship.

Introduction to the New Home

When the kitten is brought into a new home, it is only natural for everyone in the family to want to hold and fondle it. However, the kitten should be held only when necessary at first; strange hands and smells can be traumatic for a kitten who is used to the familiar companionship of its littermates and its mother.

If possible, bring the kitten home early in the day so that by nighttime it will be somewhat familiar with its new surroundings. Allow the kitten the privacy and peace of that part of the house where it will eat, sleep, and be housebroken. Shut the door and allow it to investigate its new environment—fortified with a few tasty morsels and some milk and water.

The Family

Once the kitten seems quiet and settled in, you may introduce the new family. One family member should take on the role of foster parent in the introduction process and in the care and training. It is less confusing for a kitten to be able to relate to one person, and there is more consistency to its training.

Parents should teach children how to handle the new kitten. Roughness and mauling should not be allowed and the basic privacies should be respected. A child should not be allowed to interrupt the kitten while it is eating, sleeping, or relieving itself.

New kittens in the household should be handled gently. They are much more highly strung than dogs. They hate loud noises and sudden motions. They startle easily, so speak softly to them. Don't rush a kitten. Let it examine and explore the house undisturbed. It will usually wander throughout the house deciding whether it wants to remain with its new family.

If You Have Another Pet

If there is another cat or dog in the household, the pets will work out a relationship in a few days. In the beginning do not throw them together or leave them alone unwatched—give them time. Generally, an older cat or dog adopts the new kitten and mothers or fathers it as its own. A pecking order is soon established: if there are several pets, one will be the protector, another will be the coddler of the smaller pets, another will be the provider, another will be the entertainer. Whatever is needed in the group, there will be a cat to satisfy it.

The Feeding Area

The feeding area should be in an accessible but quiet spot away from the family thoroughfares. If there is a dog in the house, the kitten's eating area should be elevated and secure from interruption and stealing of food by the dog. The new kitten should be introduced with a tempting but light meal to provide adequate nourishment but not upset an unnerved digestive system.

The Bed

Most cats prefer to sleep with people, but even if you intend to allow your new kitten to share your bed, it is a good idea to set up a "kitten bed" for catnaps and daytime security.

The cat's instinctual fear of enemies dictates that it have a bed in a fairly inaccessible spot, for peace of mind. And most cats like a soft pillow or wool blanket to snuggle into. To avoid confusing a new kitten, do not use newspaper for bedding if you intend to use papers in the litter box.

A heating pad turned to "low" might help simulate the warmth of the missed mother cat for a very lonely and unhappy kitten, and a ticking clock hidden in the bedding might make the kitten think a littermate is close by.

Holding a Kitten

By their very nature, cats present handling problems. Knowing the best and easiest methods of holding them can be very helpful when trying to groom, cut nails, or administer medicine. The most important element in holding a cat is gentleness—applying a minimum of physical restraint while stroking and petting the animal and speaking in a soft voice.

There are two emphatic "don'ts." Never, never pick up a cat by the scruff of its neck, and never allow it to dangle. The kitten must be comfortable and fully supported. The easiest and most comfortable way to hold and carry a kitten is to have it sit on one hand and support and steady it with the other hand against its chest and under its front legs. For extra, but still gentle, restraint, it can be held against your chest or shoulder. The wrong approach, either physically or psychologically, can result in a frightened, wild, screaming, snarling, and scratching cat.

Dr. Barrett, a veterinarian in Castro Valley, California, has found that a calming or gentling response can be elicited by gently covering the cat's head (eyes and ears included) with the palms of the hands, similar to the way one would hold an orange in the palms of both hands. The response appears within a few seconds, and persists as long as the cat is held in this manner. The calming response may be due to a combination of the cat's smelling the warm hands of its owner and the partial sensory deprivation, both visual and auditory, that it experiences. It will also work with a stranger holding the cat, although the cat responds best when the owner is doing the holding. It is less effective in young kittens.

Feeding a Kitten

In this terribly important part of the life of your kitten, care and training play a major role. Variety and regular (by the clock) feedings at this stage can prevent a finicky, difficult adolescence and maturity.

It is best to start kittens on a variety of foods so that they will accept more variety as adults. Weaning kittens may be started on solid food at three weeks—baby food, or high-protein cereal products such as Pablum mixed with warm water or milk. Let the kitten lick the food from your finger until it learns how to lap it from a dish. When a kitten is completely weaned from the mother at about eight weeks, it should have four or five meals a day at two-hour intervals. Gradually cut down to three meals a day at about three months of age, while increasing the size of the meal proportionately. As its teeth develop after six to eight weeks, other foods can be added: commercial cat foods, raw ground beef, cooked and boned fish and poultry, small pieces of heart, kidney, or liver, and egg yolk. One to three ounces of food at each feeding is sufficient for a growing kitten; it might beg for more, but don't give it all it wants.

At six months two meals is enough, and after one year one meal is usually enough, although many cats enjoy two meals a day their entire lives. (See the general discussion of nutrition in Chapter 12.)

A Beginning Diet for a Young Kitten

MORNING:
1 tsp. ground beef (warm)
1 tsp. canned liver, soup, or baby food

NOON:
1–1½ tsp. prepared baby cereal with
1 tsp. canned milk and water to make a thin gruel
Add nutritional supplements such as Vionate, Pet-tabs, Unipets, etc. Growing kittens need vitamins and minerals which can be given as drops, powder, or tablets.

NIGHT:
The meal should consist of any one of the following items:
1 tsp. cooked or canned fish (be sure to crush or remove all bones)

1 tsp. cottage cheese
1 tsp. raw liver, finely diced
2-3 tsp. soft-boiled egg yolk

Commercial dry foods, canned foods, and semi-moist pouches will tempt most kittens after two months. However, extra treats are very much appreciated by kittens: cottage cheese; raw organ meats such as kidney, liver, and heart; even table scraps. Kittens need a varied diet as much as you do, and your leftovers are an excellent means of breaking the monotony of your kitten's fare. However, they should be used as a supplement and not as the main part of the diet.

Some kittens get diarrhea from drinking milk or cream; they simply cannot tolerate the lactose contained therein. Canned or powdered milks may not give this reaction to some of these cats, and for the others it is not a problem so long as the cat is provided with plenty of fresh drinking water. (See page 131.)

Most cats are not tempted by foods served directly from the refrigerator. Food is more palatable to them served at room temperature.

Certain foods are taboo: uncooked fish and ham, highly seasoned foods, and the small bones of chicken, pork, veal, lamb, rabbit, or fish. These bones shatter easily and can be injurious to a cat's throat and intestine. Some people put food that contains small bones into the pressure cooker until they are soft. Pressure cooking takes the brittleness out of the bones. Prepared in this way, they will not harm the cat, and the nutritional benefits are excellent.

Loss of Appetite

If a kitten refuses food at more than two or three feedings in a row, it is a reliable sign of an ailment or disease, and a veterinarian should be consulted. A kitten must not go more than twelve hours without food, or it will dehydrate, weaken, and go into shock very quickly. Force-feeding is necessary until you can take the kitten to a doctor. (See the section on Force-feeding in Chapter 14.)

Housebreaking Your Kitten

If this is your first kitten, you may be surprised when you introduce it to the litter box. Usually the mother cat has her kittens so well trained by the time they are weaned that most kittens will find and use the litter box in a new home without a problem. By nature, cats are fastidious animals and instinctively cover their waste with sand or dirt, and the indoor cat finds that the litter box suits this purpose very well. But it is certainly a good idea to give a new kitten a proper introduction: After a feeding, place the kitten down gently in an easily accessible box filled with litter, several times if necessary until it gets the idea. After one or two tries at the litter box, the kitten will usually become housebroken. Although not all kittens will use the litter box readily, I would not give up on your pet if you are having difficulty. Patience and continued loving care should repair the situation shortly.

Housebreaking problems may arise from any one of the following factors:

☐ The kitten may not like the type of litter—either the consistency or the odor may be upsetting. Experiment with various brands.
☐ The box may not be in a private enough spot, or there may be some object near the litter box that is frightening to the kitten.
☐ If there is another cat in the family, it could be a sanitary matter. Cats do not like dirty litter trays.

When a kitten does soil outside the litter tray, the odor will continue to attract it to the same spot. Any such places should be completely cleaned and disinfected to discourage repetition. There is no preparation that will completely remove the urine odor. Materials such as baking soda, vinegar, mouthwash, detergents, and Clorox are partly effective, but nothing has been found yet that is completely so.

When a kitten is sick with diarrhea or some other disease, housebreaking is often impossible. (Indeed, a cat who has been housebroken for years may become unhousebroken temporarily during an illness.) If this is the case with your kitten, concern yourself with its recovery, and resume the housebreaking training when the animal is well.

Very few cats are basically dirty in their habits, but sickness, fright, and loneliness can cause a cat to dirty the house. If the problem is not a physiological one, investigate to see if there is an emotional source. The cat might be rebelling against something that you have done, or it might be frightened of strangers or visitors around the household.

Litter and Litter Boxes

Cats seem to form firm opinions about litter, so stick with whichever type your cat prefers to avoid house-soiling problems. Sawdust, sand, or newspapers can be used as substitutes for commercial litter, but they have their drawbacks. For many people, sawdust and sand are not readily available, and when they are used they quickly become damp and smelly, and sawdust, especially, tends to be tracked around the house. Although newspapers, too, must be done away with almost after each use to avoid dampness and odor, the economic advantage is considerable. (The occasional kitten might nibble and swallow a small bit of paper, but this should not prove harmful.) The money spent for a commercial litter is somewhat compensated for in time saved in keeping the box fresh and the odor at a minimum or completely eliminated. Some cats prefer the scented ones, others, the coarse-grained types. Give your cat a choice and go along with the selection.

If your cat will be spending most of the time outdoors, a litter box is not entirely necessary, but is a thoughtful amenity for when the weather is inclement or the cat is not feeling up to par.

Cats stop using litter pans because:

1) Litter pan is too small.

2) Litter pan is not in a quiet, private spot.

3) Litter pan is dirty. Keep litter clean, pan clean, free of disinfectant or scented odors. Never wash with Lysol—it can be poisonous to cats.

Grooming Your Kitten

Short-haired cats need to be brushed only every so often, but long-haired cats need combing almost every day to keep their coats from becoming matted. If you have neglected to comb out the tangles, the only way to remove matted fur is to cut it with scissors. Routine brushing and combing help prevent hair balls and cut down on cat hair in rugs and furniture.

A kitten's eyes require attention to keep them clean. A mild salt solution (a pinch to half a cup) applied with cotton or soft tissue is excellent. You should also check the kitten's mouth regularly. Clean the teeth with a damp cloth dipped in salt and baking soda.

Routine nail clipping is another consideration in grooming. This will protect the drapes and furniture too. A scratching post also helps keep a cat's nails short and reduces the need for nail clipping, which cats hate anyway. (A more detailed discussion of nail clipping is found in Chapter 13.)

Grooming is an important part of the well-being, health, and training of your cat throughout its entire life, and the earlier it is started, the less difficult and more satisfactory it will be. Early grooming will condition a kitten to this part of domestic living. If you don't groom a cat until it is an adult, you may end up with scratched and bitten hands and find that your cat cannot be groomed without tranquilizers and sedatives. Chapter 13 provides a more detailed discussion of your cat's year-round care.

Toys

Kittens love to play, and the simplest objects can give them hours of pleasure and healthful exercise. Especially if they are left alone much of the time, toys can relieve their boredom. Little things commonly found around the house are often as diverting as and safer than some of the commercial toys. There is nothing a cat loves better than to hide in an old paper bag and spring out at you. A frayed rope or string tied to dangle a few inches from the floor, an old spool, a Ping-Pong ball, can provide as much entertainment as some of the rubber toys that are fragile enough to be chewed and swallowed and are therefore dangerous. Rubber, when ingested, can cause serious intestinal problems, as can cellophane and aluminum foil (and this includes Christmas-tree tinsel). To be on the safe side, consult the list of potential household hazards and the list of poisons on pages 210–219.

If your cat is an indoor cat, until you get to know its habits don't panic when you can't find it anywhere and are afraid that it has somehow gotten outside and is lost forever. When you realize that you have not seen it for hours and there is no answer to your calling, above all remain calm and conduct a thorough search. Don't overlook cupboard drawers, back corners of upper shelves in closets, closed empty boxes, hats, even the washing machine or dryer. If the cat does not appear, go about your business and chances are at the cat's mealtime it will appear from

behind the refrigerator or stove, or leap out of a deep, warm coat pocket.

Health Problems in Kittens

Signs of a healthy kitten:
- ☐ Bright eyes
- ☐ Shiny fur
- ☐ Good appetite
- ☐ Normal weight
- ☐ Well-formed stools
- ☐ Purring
- ☐ Alertness, playfulness, energy

Signs of a sick kitten:
- ☐ Vomiting
- ☐ Diarrhea
- ☐ Loss of appetite
- ☐ Lackluster fur
- ☐ Dull eyes
- ☐ Eyes obstructed or semi-closed
- ☐ Running eyes and nose
- ☐ Dry, hot nose
- ☐ Coughing, sneezing
- ☐ Pitiful crying
- ☐ Lethargy, listlessness
- ☐ Restlessness
- ☐ Scratching
- ☐ Headshaking

Teething

Beginning at the age of four months, the baby teeth (or milk teeth) fall out, allowing the adult teeth to push through the gums. By seven to eight months, if the baby teeth have not fallen out, it is wise to have a veterinarian pull them. If they are left in, they may impede the permanent teeth and the kitten will have a double row of teeth or crooked teeth.

Teething can cause loss of appetite and there may be a slight diarrhea. The gums will be sore, and at such times you should feed the kitten a soft and bland diet for a few days.

Ailments and Diseases

The most common ailments of young kittens are vomiting and diarrhea. If a kitten vomits more than two or three times, one may well suspect that it has swallowed a foreign object. The kitten is curious by nature and will pick up and chew almost anything. I have had to remove surgically from kittens' stomachs or intestines such indigestible objects as pins and needles, razor blades, and on one occasion a diamond ring. If you are ever missing a small article and your kitten is vomiting, have its stomach X-rayed.

If your kitten is vomiting, examine the vomit, and if the vomiting persists, describe it to your veterinarian, especially if there is blood present.

If your kitten has simple diarrhea caused by overfeeding or teething, Kaopectate, Pepto-Bismol, or bismuth is soothing to the stomach and to the sensitive lining of the intestinal tract. Feed the kitten ¼ teaspoon per 2½ pounds of kitten, three to five times a day.

Intestinal parasites (worms) and coccidiosis can be the cause of intestinal upset, and if not treated in time can result in death. Heavy infestation by fleas, lice, or ticks can produce anemia. Hookworms are especially serious; they suck the blood and lower resistance to ailments and diseases. There are efficient drugs for destroying worms in even very young kittens. (Chapter 16 deals with parasites.)

Coccidiosis (see page 174) causes a chronic, insidious type of diarrhea; severe cases show mucus and blood in the stools. The disease is increasing in frequency and is very serious. Pet shops and catteries that do not practice proper sanitation procedures quite often spread it, as it is transmitted from one kitten to another through contamination of the feces.

Infectious enteritis (distemper) also causes intestinal upset. It is most prevalent among young cats and without proper attention is almost always fatal. Prevention is by far the best way of coping with this disease. At eight weeks of age, kittens should be given the first of a series of shots that will immunize them against distemper, pneumonitis, rhino-tracheitis, and rabies. Consult the vaccination chart on page 143 for the schedule to follow.

3 · Adolescence and Puberty

Human–Cat Age Equivalents • Mental Maturation • Sexual Maturation • Birth Control

Human-Cat Age Equivalents

It was once generally thought that one year in the life of the cat was equivalent to seven years of a human life. A new scale of equivalents is now recognized: after the first two years, the cat's life proceeds more slowly in relation to human life, and each feline year is approximately four human years.

The Human	The Cat
10 years	6 months
13 years	8 months
14 years	10 months
15 years	12 months
20 years	18 months
24 years	2 years
32 years	4 years
40 years	6 years
48 years	8 years
56 years	10 years
64 years	12 years
72 years	14 years
80 years	16 years
88 years	18 years
96 years	20 years
100 years	21 years

Mental Maturation

It is useless to be impatient with the mental development of your kitten—to expect so much that you become upset when it is not winning in the show-ring or performing spectacular tricks at the age of six months. As noted above, a six- to twelve-month-old kitten is actually comparable to a ten- to fifteen-year-old child, and kittens are every bit as inconsistent as teen-agers. If you intend to train your kitten for showing, you should not expect much until it is at least a year old, although training should be started at about four months. Some breeds mature faster than others, and some are not completely mature until they are a year old.

As with children, there are precocious cats that mature sooner and learn to perform tricks and do amazing things at quite an early age.

Sexual Maturation

Puberty in the female occurs the first time she comes into heat. For the average queen, this happens between the ages of six to eight months, ten months at the latest. You will know that your cat is in heat about the same time she does: she will cry incessantly, rub against you, and roll around on her back. She will also lie with her front quarters flat on the floor and her rear quarters raised with her tail aside.

Sexual maturity in the tom may occur anywhere between six and twelve months, with the average age being between ten and twelve months. Some males under six months show sexual interest by wrestling with and trying to mount both males and females.

As he matures, he will become interested in the genitals of females. If there is a female cat in heat in the neighborhood, he will cry and try to get out. This sexual stimulation will cause him to spray urine in various spots around the house. The tom defines the boundaries of his sexual territory by spraying, a carryover from the wild state. The odor, strong and unmistakable, is believed to be linked to the male hormone testosterone.

Spraying usually indicates sexual maturity. If the tom is not going to be trained for the show-ring or to be used for breeding, you may decide to have him neutered. The sooner this is done, preferably at six or seven months, the smaller the chances that he will continue spraying after surgery.

Another indication of sexual maturity in the tom is cheek enlargement—the first step in the development of large, handsome jowls.

Birth Control

There are approximately 40 million cats in the United States, with 1,000 to 2,500 cats born each hour. Even though many are stillborn and/or live only a few hours or days, the cat population is increasing by 40 percent each decade and at the present rate of increase, the United States will have nearly 100 million cats by the middle of the next decade.

Stray cats pollute the streets, damage property, hurt other animals, and spread disease. And the strays themselves are usually destined to suffer cruelty, disease, and starvation. Approximately 7.3 million cats (representing 12 percent of the total population) are killed each year at private and public shelters, at an annual cost approaching sixty million dollars. The American Humane Society also estimates that 25 million kittens and cats will die this year because they are unwanted.

In the future there will be a chemical means of animal birth control that will ease the plight of stray cats and end the problems they create. Today there is only a short-term answer: wider encouragement of surgical sterilization—spaying and neutering.

Spaying and neutering are simple and relatively inexpensive operations. Neither operation adversely affects the cat, either physically or emotionally. Neither operation makes the cat fat or lazy or anything other than more lovable, affectionate, and happy. The people who feel that spaying and neutering are against nature fail to realize that starvation and suffering among domestic animals are also unnatural and unnecessary.

Spaying

Reasons for spaying:

□ Heat periods are upsetting to a cat as well as to her owner. There are emotional changes at this time, and the cat may become nervous, fretful, and high-strung.

□ Spaying prevents cats with congenital defects from propagating those defects.

□ Nervous or aggressive queens should be neutered to keep them from perpetuating their bad temperaments.

□ Cats should be spayed to prevent a foreseeable difficult birth. An undersized cat with a small pelvis will most likely be unable to bear her kittens without a great deal of help.

□ Spaying will avoid most types of female

34

problems, such as cystic ovaries, metritis, and pyrometra, especially if done at an early age, preferably before the queen reaches one year of age. Spaying will end the problem of irregular heat cycles and false pregnancies and, more seriously, vaginal tumors and vaginal prolapse.

When not to spay:

□ I do not advocate the spaying of all queens of course. There are many potential brood matrons who have such good temperament and fine conformation that they should be mated to perpetuate their desirable qualities.

□ Spaying will make a queen ineligible for the show-ring Championship Division since it is for the entire cat, male or female. However, they will be eligible for the Premiership Division, which is for the altered cat.

□ Unless absolutely necessary, a queen should not be spayed while she is in her heat cycle. It is more dangerous because all the blood vessels in the uterus are in a state of dilation.

□ A nursing queen should never be spayed. It is best to wait until the kittens are eight weeks old—until she has weaned them and her mammary glands and uterus have returned to normal size and condition. (I should point out that a nursing queen can be fertile during the first eight weeks after delivery of her kittens. Thus, if surgery is performed just after this period, the complete hysterectomy will remove not only all of her female organs but also any unborn fetuses should she have been impregnated.)

Age to Spay

There are many opinions about the proper age to spay a queen. I advise spaying just before the age of sexual maturity (between six and seven months). By this time, the cat has enough of her female characteristics to be properly endowed. And I definitely advise spaying before one year of age because cats spayed before they are a year old rarely develop mammary tumors in later life.

Some people insist on waiting until the first heat period, or until the cat has had one litter of kittens, because they believe this will help her later in life by making her less susceptible to certain female disorders. This belief is totally unfounded; in fact, the opposite is true. If the cat is to be spayed after her first heat period, it is best to schedule the surgery between her periods, that is, two or three months after the cycle.

There is a common belief that the queen should have two heat periods before being spayed. This belief is based on the false premise that the ovaries mature one at a time—one during each heat period. There is no truth to this; both ovaries enlarge, mature, and secrete their hormones at each heat period.

Cats can be spayed up to a fairly old age— up to thirteen years, if necessary. In the aged cat, the veterinarian will base his judgment on the physical well-being of the cat and the emergency conditions involved.

Effects of Spaying

Personality changes. With proper handling, there should be no changes in disposition caused by the hormonal changes which come about with spaying. If a spayed cat is mean, she would have taken on such a disposition whether she'd been spayed or not. If intelligence, devotion, and performance are affected by the spaying process, it is only to heighten these qualities because of the elimination of the instinct to procreate. Spayed female cats appear to have no further interest in sex.

Physical changes. Many people believe that spaying a cat will increase her body weight. This is not necessarily so, although there may be a tendency to put on more weight. Obesity is related to food intake, exercise, and hormonal control. If you are careful with diet and exercise (see Chapters 12 and 13) and are still worried about your cat's weight, see your veterinarian. Under supervision, you can administer estrogen hormone in pill form to counteract the tendency to gain weight. Estrogen dosage should always be determined by your veterinarian because too large a dosage may bring on a false heat period.

Spaying Techniques

Normal spaying. The normal spaying process entails complete removal of the ovaries, after which there will be cessation of the estrus cycles. However, if even the slightest part of an ovary is allowed to remain, the queen will continue to come into heat at varying intervals.

Complete spaying. I do a complete hysterectomy routinely in every spaying operation, removing the uterus as well as both ovaries, and I believe that most veterinary surgeons agree it is the proper procedure. This makes the queen immune from metritis (a uterine infection) and other female infections as she gets older.

Medicinal spaying. Several years ago an injectable anti-heat drug was introduced to veterinary medicine. One injection was sufficient to keep a cat from coming into heat for a period of six months, and it was thought to be the answer to spaying. It was widely accepted and thousands upon thousands of cats were injected. However, many cats developed a female infection called endometritis, and some cats never came into heat after their original injection. Much valuable breeding stock was involved, and many hysterectomies were necessary because of the female infection which resulted. The FDA has proved that the drug produces sterility and undesirable effects in the female cat. Although it had some beneficial qualities, the detrimental effects far outweighed them and the government removed the drug from the market for general use.

Neutering: Castration of the Male Cat

There are many people who do not approve of neutering; they feel that the castrated male is not a "whole" cat. Actually, he is very similar to the spayed female, in that he will stay at home, devoting himself to the pleasure and love of his human family. The loss of his sexual instinct changes his personality only in making him sweeter and more lovable.

I do not advocate castrating all toms, but if a cat is not to be trained for the show-ring (neutered cats are ineligible) or used in breeding, castration slows him down, and his life henceforth revolves around his human family.

Reasons for Castration

There are many more benefits for both you and your cat to be derived from castration than there are disadvantages. A neutered tom will be less likely to come home with a mangled ear, missing tooth, abscessed leg, torn mouth, or broken tail. These, and many other battle scars, are usually the result of a fight to win the affection of some queen in heat.

But *spraying* is by far the most compelling reason for having the male pet castrated. This simple operation completely eliminates spraying in at least 96 percent of neutered males. When spraying continues, it is generally due to emotional problems. (See Chapter 11.) After castration, the unmistakably strong odor of male urine disappears.

Age to Castrate

It has been thought that early castration may contribute to failure of normal urethral development and thus increase the probability of bladder-stone obstruction. However, recent studies have found that early castration does not influence urethral size, that it is uniform in noncastrated and castrated cats.

The researchers did find, however, that too early castration can result in adhesions in the sheath of the penis. This can cause urinary problems due to the collection of urine and subsequent infection in these pockets.

I allow cats to mature sexually before castration. In my opinion, between six and seven months is the most desirable age for the operation. However, a cat of any age can be castrated safely.

Effects of Castration

Personality changes. Most toms become more affectionate and docile after being castrated. Following castration, the hormone levels drop off gradually over a period of six weeks. Fighting and spraying decline within two to four weeks. The roaming instinct gradually diminishes as the desire for sexual gratification ceases. However, it should be pointed out that some cats will roam and fight for other than sexual reasons. Their hunting instincts are not marred by castration and they may continue to bring home rabbits, birds, and squirrels. Nonsexual aggression is not affected by castration: if your castrated cat has an enemy male in the neighborhood, there will be some fights, although not nearly so many as before. In some stubborn toms, the decline in fighting, roaming, and urine spraying is more gradual. But once gone, there is no appreciable return to these objectionable behavior patterns at a later date.

The castrated male has been known to remain fertile for as long as three days following surgery. He could possibly impregnate a queen during this period. Experienced toms occasionally continue to mate following castration for many months, and even for life. Although unable to produce kittens, they still enjoy the sex act.

Physical changes. As with the spaying of female cats, the castration of male cats does not necessarily mean that they will get unsightly and overweight. The addition of male hormones to the diet, in pill form (and only under the supervision of a veterinarian), will replace any male hormones needed to maintain a normal, healthy metabolism. Cats need not get fat; any obesity is the fault of the owners. With adequate exercise and proper diet, these cats can maintain their sleek and muscular appearance.

The neutering operation of a male is a relatively simple procedure, usually without any postsurgical complications. Most veterinarians operate in the morning and the cat, after it awakens from the anesthesia, can be taken home that night or the next day. Usually there is complete recovery in two to three days.

The hormonal changes in the neutered tom take about one month to affect his behavior. He usually will be seen more frequently around the house, either inside or outside. He calms down, becomes more affectionate, wants to have human companionship more often.

Alternative Birth-Control Measures

Tubal ligation and vasectomy. There are some cat owners who do not wish to have their cats produce kittens but also do not wish to interfere with the normal sexual appetites of their cats. Tubal ligation in the female and vasectomy in the male are alternative feline birth-control methods which meet this requirement. Tubal ligation consists of tying off the Fallopian tubes, which connect the ovaries to the uterus; in a vasectomy, a portion of the vas deferens is removed, thus preventing sperm from traveling from the testicles to the urethra.

It is important to understand that these methods do not offer the advantages of spaying and castration. Following a tubal ligation, a female will remain sexually active, continuing to come into heat and to attract males. Also, this procedure does not eliminate the dangers of malignancies developing in the uterus and the breasts. After a vasectomy, the tom will continue to roam, to spray strong-smelling urine, and to fight with other male cats.

Vasectomy in the male can serve a useful purpose in a cattery where there are a lot of frustrated queens who wish to be bred every time they come into heat. Being serviced by a sterile stud satisfies their desires and yet does not contribute to the overpopulation problem.

Although the vasectomy operation is a simple and relatively nontraumatic procedure, it is more complicated and more expensive than the castration operation.

Pills. The birth-control pills that are used in human medicine do not work on cats. However, there is an effective pill now available for cats (Ovaban) which not only pre-vents unwanted pregnancies but also, when properly administered, prevents heat periods if given at least twenty-four hours before the onset of the heat period. (See page 48 for signs of an approaching heat period.) If the cat is already in heat, the pill will shorten the period. The drug is safe and will not interfere with future heat periods if the queen is to be bred at a later date. These pills are also used in the treatment of false pregnancies.

Birth-control food. A canned food containing mibolerone, a nonhormonal steroid which inhibits female cats from coming into heat, is being tested under the name of Lady Friskie by Friskies Pet Food Division.

A new feline birth-control device. If you have ever watched two cats mating, you may have noticed the standard procedure: the female presses her belly into the floor or the ground, her tail cocked off to one side, her hind legs vigorously treading, and her head stretched forward. During her plaintive howling, the tom seizes her by the back of the neck

and proceeds to copulate. For most cats, this neck grab is an essential part of the act: the tom is impotent without that patch of fur between his teeth and the female cat cannot position herself correctly to receive his penetration. The entire act of copulation can be stymied if the tom is prevented from biting his mate. A new birth-control device has been developed that prevents the tom from grasping the female cat by the neck. It is a cardboard or leather shield that covers the female's neck and shoulders. The shield extends over the back of the head and down the sides of the neck and shoulders and is strapped to the body above and below the front legs. Since the normal mounting procedure for the tom involves holding his front paws around the queen's neck, this device frustrates his efforts. I should also add that, although this device works, it is not 100 percent foolproof and I would advise birth-control pills or, better still, spaying.

4 · Prebreeding: Selective Breeding

Types of Breeding · Selection of Parents · Breeding Physical Characteristics · Inherited Abnormalities and Hereditary Diseases

The breeding of cats is a fascinating challenge, and an art and a gamble as well. The challenge to the breeder is to help bring into being a perfectly balanced cat with a good temperament and personality and with all the style, spirit, and grace desirable in the particular breed. And he hopes and gambles that no hidden defects in the ancestry will crop up in a subsequent litter of kittens.

The professional breeder must have a thorough understanding of dominant, recessive, and mixed characteristics. The same applies to the novice who wishes to breed "champions," and I seriously recommend intensive study of the available literature before embarking on a breeding program. Many a fine family strain has been ruined by indiscriminate breeding.

Unfortunately, when a breed becomes popular, there is an influx of "amateurs" who haphazardly breed any two cats so long as they have pedigree papers and possibly a few champions in their background. This can spell disaster for the breed. Beginners must get to know the standards of perfection of the breed—attend cat shows and talk with knowledgeable breeders—before starting a breeding program.

A good breeder has a complete knowledge of the virtues and faults of all the ancestors of his cats through at least three generations. He knows the desirable and the undesirable structural, temperamental, and intelligence characteristics of the various strains he is breeding. Good cats are not produced by hit-and-miss breedings. They are carefully scrutinized and the faults eliminated.

A queen and stud do not always pass on to their kittens the qualities they themselves show. They may carry recessive characteristics which will appear in later generations.

Before setting up a breeding program, the

breeder's purposes must be clear. I believe the three most important characteristics to be bred for (in descending order of importance) are: (1) temperament, (2) mentality, and (3) conformation.

A cat show is primarily a beauty contest in which the entrants are judged solely on their appearance and ring behavior. Although I am in full accord with the standards of perfection for each breed, I also believe that temperament should not be sacrificed to intelligence or beauty. A shy or nervous cat, even though it might have a magnificent body, cannot belong in my household. Temperament should be the breeder's prime concern.

Although temperament is mostly determined by genetic factors, not all problems of temperament are inherited. Environment must also be considered, since experiences after birth affect the cat's personality. It is often difficult to decide which traits are inherited and which are acquired.

Traits such as shyness and bad temper can be due to either heredity or environment. Controlling temperament through breeding depends on a knowledge of ancestral genes. Good temperament is dominant and will pass on to the kittens. Two cats of good temperament may have a kitten which may not have a good temperament, but if a kitten has a good temperament it will not have been bred of parents with bad temperaments.

Nonhereditary influences on temperament include a shy mother, littermate interaction, and isolation. The mother's attitude toward humans can affect each kitten's temperament, as can being bullied by larger and stronger littermates. A kitten reared without human contact and affection is bound to be shy and nervous.

Even though this chapter is mainly devoted to the purebred cat, I know that many cats of mixed ancestry produce highly desirable kittens. I endorse the further breeding of any good mongrel cat if it has the personality,

intelligence, and body conformation that a particular owner likes.

Types of Breeding

Because breeding is complex and requires a great deal of study, I will discuss only a few of the main types: (1) inbreeding, (2) linebreeding, (3) outcrossing (outbreeding), (4) crossbreeding, and (5) gradebreeding.

There is a belief among the misinformed that inbreeding and linebreeding cause mental deterioration, loss of vigor, structural malformation, impotence, sterility, and other weaknesses and abnormalities. This is absolutely not so. Inbreeding and linebreeding cannot create either good or bad qualities— mental or physical—they just bring out the qualities that are already in the stock.

There is also the misconception that kittens bred from father and daughter, or mother and son, or brother and sister, are not eligible for registration. All purebred kittens are eligible for registration whether inbred, linebred, or crossbred.

In the proper hands, inbreeding and linebreeding are excellent ways of helping a breed. The purpose of both is to bring about breed improvement and to upgrade the stock. In the wrong hands they can cause deterioration in a breed. If properly done, they help eliminate recessive faults and help purify a strain.

Inbreeding

This is first-generation breeding, that is, breeding father to daughter, mother to son, brother to sister, half brother to half sister. It is frowned upon by many who do not understand the principles of genetics and by those who may find the moral implications shocking. The truth of the matter is that the best specimens—the most beautiful, the truest in type—are gained through inbreeding.

If the breeder wants to retain as much of the blood of the sire as possible, he will often breed a daughter back to her father. If it is the blood of the queen that is desired, the son is bred back to his mother. This also applies to granddaughters and grandsons. A big danger in inbreeding exists in full brother to full sister matings, especially if repeated for several generations. Half brothers to half sisters seem perfectly safe in your breeding program. By always culling poor breeders of either sex, inbreeding won't hurt your program. However, do not breed for show points by giving it priority over fertility and health.

Inbreeding doubles and intensifies all characteristics, *good and bad,* so the resulting kittens can have either very desirable traits or some terrible tendencies. For instance, a deaf tomcat bred to his own mother would probably produce slightly deaf daughters. Only fault-free cats should be mated (completely faultless back at least three generations). Both the male and female should be uniform in type, size, and general appearance. Close inbreeding tends to make the offspring smaller, so eventually they have to be outbred to make them larger and more vigorous.

I advise inbreeding only by those who are fully aware of the principles involved.

Linebreeding

This is the mating of animals who are related to a common ancestor but are not related to each other.

The danger in linebreeding occurs when selection of parents is made on the basis of pedigree alone, without considering the physical or mental traits of the mating pair. Cats with notable faults often result.

Outcrossing (Outbreeding)

The queen is bred to a male not related in any way to the many generations represented by her. In other words, new bloodlines are brought into combination. Care must be taken that bad qualities are not introduced along with good ones. Kittens of varied appearance and personality can be expected by this method, and on occasion there will be an outstanding specimen of the breed.

Crossbreeding

This is simply the mating of two purebred cats of different breeds.

Gradebreeding

When a purebred cat is mated to a mongrel cat, the union is called gradebreeding and the mongrel kittens are classified as "grades." (This is not acceptable to cat breeders.)

Selection of Parents

The message of this entire chapter can be simply stated: *CAREFUL selection of parents.* When prospective mates are being chosen, be certain that each is as free as possible from inherited faults. As I noted earlier, the breeder must have a complete knowledge of the faults and virtues of the ancestors for at least three generations in order to avoid latent physical and temperamental abnormalities and to discover points of merit in the respective family trees. And he should never mate two cats with similar faults; the faults can be magnified many, many times in the kittens.

Unfortunately, some breeders breed only to sell to the highest bidder, with little interest in improving the breed; others, hungry for stud fees, breed indiscriminately. These practices cause rapid deterioration in breeds.

When a queen and a stud are being chosen, it is important to remember that, even though like produces like, characteristics don't always blend to give the desired results. For example, a female with an especially pointed nose bred to a male with a shortish nose will not necessarily produce kittens with medium noses. The noses of the kittens are likely to be too long or too short.

The Queen

If one is intent on breeding "champions" one must look for a queen of superior ancestry. The overall quality type of the queen is also important.

A breeding queen should be free of any inherited shyness or savageness, both of which would produce undesirable kittens. Careful selection of mates with proper temperament through several generations is the only way to eliminate these faults.

The breeder must be able to recognize a structural defect as far as the standards of the breed are concerned. If a queen tends to be too long of body she should not be bred to a male also too long of body. Mating her with a short-bodied stud sometimes breeds out the defect.

Size. It has not been conclusively proven that the size of the queen determines the birth size of the kittens. Hereditary factors controlling size may be passed on by either parent, and so people breeding a small queen to a larger male can run into trouble during the whelping process. In other words, before mating a very small queen it is well to bear in mind that the size of the kittens at birth will be governed not so much by the size of the parents as by the genetic characteristics of the ancestors.

There is a common misconception that mating a small queen with a large male will produce a litter of small female kittens and males as big as, if not bigger than, their father. Usually a small kitten born to such parents owes its smallness to unfavorable fetal conditions—undernutrition or disease.

This brings up another belief which goes against all the principles of genetics. Some people think they can produce small kittens by withholding adequate supplies of food from the pregnant queen. Undernourishment of the queen to reduce the size of kittens is not consonant with a sound breeding program. Malnutrition may stunt growth, but it will also produce unhealthy kittens.

Telegony (the supposed influence of a previous tom). Years ago it was generally believed that if a pedigreed queen was mated with a cat of another breed, or a mongrel, she would thereafter be useless for breeding pure stock—that all her subsequent litters would be mongrel or otherwise impure. This has been completely disproven.

It is believed by some that if a queen has three or four litters sired by the same stud, each successive litter will look more like the father and less like the mother. This belief has no scientific basis.

The Stud

The stud should be the best male available regardless of related bloodlines, and he should be strong in characteristics which, according to the background of the queen, need improvement.

Sometimes a breeder, trying to obtain a desirable characteristic not present in his strain, or to correct a fault he has not been able to eliminate, will use a stud with the desired trait but also with some fault. This brings out undesirable characteristics and is more likely to destroy the good traits already possessed than to add desired traits.

Breeding Physical Characteristics

The Fur

Condition. Although normal and healthy in all other respects, some queens seem to remain in a state of slight molt or shedding the year round. Scabby skin and brittle or falling-out fur may be attributed to genetic factors that are handed down from generation to generation; to a thyroid problem; or possibly to environmental factors such as year-round indoor living.

If a queen has a poor coat, try to mate her to a stud who has particularly fine fur and is known to have had ancestors who were similarly endowed.

Color. Color breeding in cats is complicated and there is no definite genetic rule. The inheritance varies in each breed, with some colors dominant and others recessive. There is no blending of colors. For example, a black cat bred to a white one will usually produce about half black and half white, but never a blend of two colors such as gray or blue.

Otherwise, black is dominant over every color except tabby and red. A Siamese mated to a black produces black kittens with a grayish undercoat. A Siamese that breeds with a mongrel usually produces black kittens. Burmese is dominant over Siamese. A silver cat is dominant over Burmese and Siamese. Albinism (white with pink eyes) is recessive to all colors.

White is dominant over red if the white cat is not an albino; therefore, a white bred with a red will produce white kittens. But if the white cat is carrying some recessive red genes, there is also a chance of some red kittens.

Black and tabby are not dominant over each other; therefore, breeding a black to a tabby will produce both types of kittens, some black and some tabby.

Length. Short hair is dominant over long hair, which is why two long-haired cats never produce short-haired cats, although two shorthairs occasionally produce a long-haired kitten.

Other Characteristics

Eye color. The inheritance of eye color is not fully understood and is difficult to predict even though the eye color of the parents and ancestors is known.

Deafness. It is known that deafness tends to occur in white cats, particularly those with blue eyes. Of course, not all blue-eyed, white cats are deaf.

Tails. In the Siamese, kinky tails are a recessive characteristic. Since it could be somewhere in the family tree of the queen or stud, a kinky-tailed kitten can appear anytime two Siamese are mated. Breeding two kinky-tailed cats usually results in an all kinky-tailed litter. The Manx cat has a dominant gene for taillessness. When a purebred Manx is bred to a cat of another breed (or mongrel) with a normal tail, the kittens are usually all tailless but they have a short stub where the tail should be.

Extra toes. This is a dominant, inherited condition. A cat with extra toes mated to a normal cat will produce some normal and some extra-toed kittens, usually half and half.

Jaws. Among characteristics which do not blend is the undershot and the overshot jaw. It is a mistake to breed a queen with an undershot jaw to a stud with an overshot jaw and expect the kittens to have normal mouths. The result will be some kittens with undershot jaws and some kittens with overshot jaws.

Inherited Abnormalities and Hereditary Diseases

The veterinary profession has been becoming increasingly concerned with some of the abnormalities that pedigreed cats have been developing through generations of breeding. At a recent veterinary world congress in Paris, a resolution regarding inherited diseases was unanimously adopted. The resolution concerned the health and welfare of cats whose breed standards hinder the physiological functioning of organs and other parts of the body. Large skulls, protruding eyes, and shortened heads are among the examples cited as often being responsible for the increasing incidence of eye injury, difficult whelping, and dysfunction of the nervous, respiratory, and cardiovascular systems.

Monorchidism and cryptorchidism. These are hereditary defects in which one or both testes don't descend to the normal position in the scrotum. When both testicles are involved, the cat is usually sterile. Although a cat with one testicle can be a successful sire, because of the hereditary nature of the defect breeding is not recommended. The cat may have an unreliable disposition; also the testicles are prone to tumors. The CFA disqualifies any animal with monorchidism or cryptorchidism; and the only way the defects can be controlled is by elimination of such cats from any breeding program. In treatment some veterinarians administer hormones to help the testes descend to their normal position. The value of this therapy is questionable.

Some abnormalities are difficult to pinpoint as inherited—ulcerative colitis, hemophilia, deafness, eye diseases.

It is a scientifically established fact that the incidence of hereditary disease is significantly reduced when kittens are bred from parents who show no evidence of defects. Control of hereditary diseases should be possible, therefore, by careful selection of breeding stock. Defective animals should be automatically disqualified from breeding, as should any cat *in any way* associated with a litter of defective animals. These cats should be castrated or spayed. It is up to the breeder, the veterinarian, and the researcher to try to control hereditary diseases.

5 · Breeding

Sexual Maturity of the Stud and the Queen • Heat Cycle of the Queen • Mating and Mismating • Fertility and Sterility in the Queen and the Stud • Breeding Chart • Sex of Kittens and Size of the Litter

I am convinced that the sexual habits of the cat are the most misunderstood of any animals, human included. Whether or not you want to breed your cats, it is important to know all about their reproductive processes.

The most common mistake of novice breeders is to leave a queen and a stud alone together for a certain length of time and then expect a litter of kittens in about sixty days. Breeding is strictly a gamble if you follow this procedure. Although normal healthy animals would be expected to be able to mate with alacrity under these conditions, our "civilized" cats are prone to problems, and there are many factors to be considered before conception can take place and before a successful program can be begun.

Sexual Maturity of the Stud

The male cat reaches sexual maturity between six and twelve months of age. He is then usually sexually active all year round, or whenever a female will accept him.

Toms under six months of age may show sexual interest but this is usually instinctual behavior. It is not a good idea to use a stud until he has reached his full maturity, and I would not advise using a stud—except under unusual circumstances—until he is at least nine months old.

A tom will exhibit sexual maturity by examining females. He will sniff at a queen's vaginal fluids and attempt to mount her back and go through the sexual act even though she is not in heat.

If the tom is confined and there is a female in heat nearby, he will cry—mournfully—to get out. If the owner does not respond to the pathetic cries, the cat will likely spray urine around the house until the owner relents and allows him out to meet his lady love.

Before he is bred a stud should have a physical examination, including a check for intestinal parasites. For the older tom who is not producing kittens as he should, male hormone injections a day or two before he is scheduled to mate will increase his libido.

Sexual Maturity of the Queen

Heat, or estrus, is nature's signal that the queen is ready to mate. It is commonly described as being "in season." When the queen begins licking her vulva, the season is probably not far off.

Most queens reach sexual maturity at six to eight months of age. They have several heat periods in succession during summer and fall, at about three-week intervals.

The cat has attained maturity when, after constant licking of her vulva, she begins to roll about, usually in front of her owner, "calling" in a strange voice. Her calling sounds attract toms from near and far. These aggressive males will try to get to the queen by any route possible—windows, doors, fireplaces. The flattered female will also try her hardest to get outside to the waiting throng.

It is not advisable to breed a queen earlier than one year of age because she should mature both physically and emotionally before she becomes a mother.

Before being allowed to breed, the queen should have a complete physical examination to make sure she is in perfect health. The checkup should include booster shots against distemper, pneumonitis, and rhino-tracheitis, and an analysis of a stool sample to be certain that she is free of worms. It is also extremely important to have her nails clipped so she will not injure the tom during the mating.

Heat Cycle of the Queen

During the breeding season—spring and early fall—the ovulation period is from three to seven days, and up to two weeks if the queen is not satisfied. She can go through several heat cycles during the mating season.

Signs of Heat

Outwardly, the first signs of heat are a slight swelling of the vulva, greater than usual appetite, and affectionate behavior. These signs increase in intensity for the next couple of days until the queen is ready to receive a tom. The stages of the heat cycle are as follows:

1. *Proestrus.* The cat becomes affectionate, restless, her appetite increases, and her body undergoes changes in preparation for ovulation and pregnancy. The vulva begins to swell.

2. *Estrus.* The cat becomes almost unbearably affectionate. She moves her hind feet as if "paddling" and she cocks her tail to one side. Her vulva is swollen and the slight discharge is a pinkish to bloody color. Her appetite diminishes and she cries a lot. If she does not mate during this cycle, she goes into a maneuver in which she looks like she is swimming on her back.

3. *Mediestrus.* This is a period of quiescence until the next heat cycle.

Toward the end of her heat period, her behavior changes quite suddenly. She seems to fight off eligible toms and is quite disinterested in mating. Then, just when the owner thinks she is out of heat, she suddenly accepts some roaming male.

Frustrated queens keep coming back into heat until they are bred. This occurs every few days, every few weeks, during the mating season. Since it is painful and frustrating for her, it is much wiser and more humane to have her spayed if you do not intend to breed her.

Irregular Heat Periods

If a queen remains a maiden for a long time after full maturity, she may have irregular seasons. However, after she is mated and has proven fertile, she may have normal intervals between her heat periods.

As the queen grows older her heat cycles become less regular, and this is one of the first signs of old age. Some older cats come into heat only every year or two, much to the delight of their owners. Also, as they get older they may show signs of heat but may not be capable of conceiving because they do not ovulate. This is also true in "false" heat periods, during which a cat goes through the full symptoms of estrus, such as enlarged vulva and attraction to males. But conception is impossible because it is not a complete period and the cat is not ovulating. I have seen queens fifteen to eighteen years old with false heat periods attract males as if they were still young and fertile.

Silent Heat Periods

This is a very abnormal type of heat period in which the queen does not show any of the usual signs of estrus. Although she will be quite willing to accept a male, she will be in and out of season before she can be bred.

I would be very cautious about using such an animal in a breeding program because there is a possibility that this condition is hereditary.

Prolonged and Abnormal Heat Periods

Some queens stay in heat longer than the normal period. This is usually abnormal, al-though some maiden queens in heat for the first time will stay in estrus for four to five weeks without any abnormal body changes.

When there is a prolonged heat period, the queen should be examined by a veterinarian, as it is important to find out what is causing the condition.

Infection of the uterus can produce all the external signs of a heat period, including attraction of males. A bladder infection which causes irritation and bleeding of the vaginal tract can also be misinterpreted as a heat period.

I would definitely advise against attempting to breed any female with a prolonged or abnormal heat period; the life of the queen should not be endangered by forcing her to breed while she is suffering from some female irregularity.

Mating and Mismating

Mating

Most tomcats are of the "caveman" type and will force their attentions on any queens presented to them. Of course, most average breeding takes place outdoors in places unobservable by human eyes (but upsetting, if overheard, to human ears). However, in the case of the purebred cat it is the usual custom for the queen to be taken to the home of the stud because most toms are more relaxed in their own surroundings. If the female is high-strung and nervous and will not breed in a strange environment, the tom should be allowed to visit her.

A secluded part of the house, away from all distractions, should be provided for the mating, with a high place for the stud to escape to during foreplay and afterwards. When copulation has taken place and the male withdraws his penis, the female is in great pain and will often attack him, quite viciously.

Not only is it very important to have appropriate surroundings for the mating, but the two cats should not be simply put in a room and be expected to breed immediately. Their introduction should be correct and proper, and they should be allowed to have some sexual foreplay so that they can become accustomed to each other and increase their sexual excitement.

Unlike the human male, cats require a long period of adaptation to the environment before they will breed. That is why females should be brought to the homes of males for breeding. Many male cats require as long as a month or more before they will readily mate.

Male cats also have seasons of increased or decreased sexual behavior, usually parallel to that of the heat periods of the female cat. Sexual aggressiveness in the breeding male will fluctuate at different times of the year. It is during these seasonal variations that the tomcat wanders, fights, and sprays half the surrounding neighborhood.

Most breeders and veterinarians involved with cat breeding are aware of the many difficulties connected with mating. Most cats will not mate if there is someone in the room with them. "Virgins" sometimes have no idea what the whole thing is all about, and it is important for one of the cats to have had some experience. Shy and timid females may be helped by tranquilizers. Hormone shots are of some help for the male who is timid or does not show any desire.

The two vital requisites for a successful union are a stud who is keen and persistent, and a queen at the correct stage of her estrus and therefore willing. If the breeder attempts mating too early in the heat cycle, the queen will usually be too aggressive toward the male and will growl at him and bite him. This will decrease his desire, and a young inexperienced male could be ruined for life as a stud.

In the actual coital position the female crouches with her pelvis raised and her tail to one side, while the male mounts her, kneads her sides with his front paws, seizes the back of her neck with his teeth, and treads with his back feet. After several thrusts, he ejaculates and then remains quiet for a few moments before withdrawing his penis. It is the withdrawal of the penis, with its barbs, that causes ovulation and also great pain in the queen.

The male ejaculates during a relatively brief period of five to fifteen seconds. During this time he utters a low growl or cry which is usually not heard because the female is yelling much louder.

The actual act of copulation lasts about four minutes. It may last until the tom is exhausted and it is the queen that wants more sex. She is usually surrounded by a ring of tomcats that take turns servicing her.

Number of matings per litter. Most breeders agree that two or three matings are desirable. In the first place, it is sometimes difficult to ascertain if the queen has actually ovulated. Also, it gives her the opportunity to bear the largest number of kittens possible, and it gives the stud a chance to produce good sperm if he has not been mated for some time.

Artificial insemination. This is a relatively new procedure, being done only experimentally. When it becomes more practical it will certainly be more widely used.

It is a fine solution for breeding a problem queen and for breeding a queen with a desirable stud who is geographically far removed.

The technique involves depositing the semen, by means of a syringe, into and through the cervix of the queen. Conditions must be absolutely perfect: correct temperature of the syringe and the absence of any sperm-killing chemicals are among the primary requisites for successful results.

After mating. The queen should be kept as quiet as possible, because disturbing environmental conditions can cause abortion in some queens, especially highly excitable and nervous ones. She should be kept in confinement for, allowed outside, she could mate with any number of males and have kittens by all of them in the same litter, all colors and types.

Mismating of a Queen

If a queen escapes confinement and is inseminated by some neighborhood toms, the mismating can be aborted.

There is a method (and it must be done by a professional) that is almost 100 percent effective if done within a week of breeding. It is a female hormone injection, and the sooner it is given, the more successful it is. The only disadvantage is that it prolongs the heat cycle a week to ten days.

Fertility and Sterility in the Queen

Any breeding program suffers a serious setback when kittens are not produced. The most common cause of sterility in the female is failure of the owner to present her for service at the right time of her estrus cycle. Other factors which affect her fertility are improper diet, environmental conditions, and her emotional and physical well-being.

A well-balanced diet is essential for the proper functioning of the queen's body. Often an adjustment in diet will enable a sterile cat to produce kittens.

Sterility is often due to emotional or psychological factors. A queen may have her likes and dislikes. One male may be repugnant to her while another will be highly acceptable.

Environmental conditions can affect the queen's fertility. Often a queen shipped to a faraway place will not breed, whereas in her own neighborhood she will breed with the first male to approach her. Before being bred, cats should be allowed time to adjust to new environments and climates.

Physical causes of barrenness in queens include poor hormonal production, blockage of the Fallopian tubes, a thick and tough hymen, and an underdeveloped vagina which is small and constricted.

Poor hormonal production generally responds well to hormone therapy. Conditions such as failure to come into normal heat, frigidity, or abnormally long heat periods can often be corrected by hormones. However, the careless use of hormones can do more harm than good, and this kind of treatment should be left to a veterinarian. The most effective hormones are those which are used to enhance ovulation in humans—that is, fertility drugs. Other drugs such as cortisones and thyroids should be used only on the advice of a veterinarian.

Bacterial infections, tumors, or any other serious illness usually will result in temporary or permanent sterility. Disorders that may lead to sterility are metritis, vaginitis, and ovarian cysts. Tumors in the vaginal passageway can be corrected by surgery and the queen will then conceive.

Cystic ovaries cause nymphomania by keeping the queen in constant heat. Most of the time she is nervous, high-strung, ill-tempered, and inclined to fight both males and other queens. This condition usually requires excision of one or both ovaries. If only one ovary is affected, its removal would result in normal heat cycles and the queen would be able to conceive and produce normal litters. If both ovaries are affected, complete hysterectomy is the only answer.

There is a bacterial infection (metritis) that causes sterility in queens. A queen may appear to be in excellent health and may even have a normal heat period (or a short period, or none at all). There may be a normal mating, but the queen will fail to conceive or will abort before term or the kittens will die shortly after birth. A veterinarian can detect the infection with a vaginal smear and treat it with antibiotics. If medication results in complete recovery, it might be possible to breed the animal in the future.

After a serious illness, such as distemper, a young queen may be temporarily sterile for up to two years. However, if she recovers completely she will have normal reproductive cycles.

Poor health due to heavy worm infestation can hinder pregnancy.

A very fat queen will often fail to conceive, and if she does she will be subject to uterine inertia or a difficult whelping. It is obvious that proper diet and exercise can correct this type of infertility. It is a bad policy to breed a fat queen.

Frequency of Mating

I would advise that the average cat have no more than one litter a year, so that her health and well-being may be properly maintained. But if she is a healthy, fairly young queen, she can have two litters in one year and then skip the next couple of heat cycles to allow her to build up her body and get back her figure.

It is wise to be extremely watchful of visiting toms while the queen is nursing a litter. Queens can actually come into heat while they are still nursing and it is bad for them to be bred too soon after having a litter, as they are likely to be quite run-down.

Age and Breeding Span

Because the number of eggs released by the ovaries during the heat period affects the efficiency of the queen's reproductive organs, as she gets older her ability to produce eggs decreases and she continues to decline to complete sterility. Usually the first sign of approaching sterility is the commencement of irregular heat cycles. Also, as she gets older she is more prone to female disorders due to hormonal dysfunction.

Some people believe that if a queen is bred

at least once in her young life she will become immune to female disorders such as infections and tumors in her old age. This is not true. It has been proven that cats that are not bred are usually less likely to develop growths, cysts, and tumors than are breeding queens.

Aging queens may suffer from several disorders that cause sterility. One of these is pyometra, which is pus formation in the uterine tract. Another is metritis—a very dangerous condition. It is usually seen in middle-aged and older cats following a heat period. This is a time for the owner to be especially alert to any fever or general lethargy in a female cat; immediate professional help is needed to save her. In severe cases the only cure is surgery to remove the infected uterus before general blood poisoning sets in.

Many factors enter into the breeding span of queens. A queen may have a short span due to ill health, bad rearing, emotional changes in environment, arrested growth, or poor nutrition. Sexual puberty is delayed in some females due to the same factors.

I generally recommend a complete hysterectomy after a queen has completed her reproductive years, so that she will not suffer from female disorders later on, when surgery would be more dangerous.

Summary

1. Do not breed a queen under nine months of age; it is best to wait until she is twelve months old, when she is physically and emotionally mature.

2. Do not breed a queen with physical defects or one who is shy or has a bad disposition.

3. Do not breed a queen who has serious faults according to the standards of the breed.

4. Do not breed a queen who is in poor condition, whether nutritionally deficient or

recuperating from a serious illness or heavy infestation of worms.

Fertility and Sterility in the Stud

There are many reasons why a tom may be sterile. Some cases of sterility can be helped by veterinary intervention, while others are impossible to cure. Degrees of infertility may be inherited; potency seems to run in certain families. There are some studs who, for generations, have been known to sire large and healthy litters. And this is a good reason for knowing the ancestry of the cats in a breeding program.

The sperm of some males are weak, immobile, or or even absent. A microscopic examination by a veterinarian can easily determine the degree of potency of the sperm and whether a cat is likely to be a good stud.

A serious illness sometimes causes sterility. But after a long period of convalescence, with proper care, a tom is usually restored to full fertility.

Other causes of sterility include too frequent breeding, underfeeding, lack of exercise, and excessive confinement. Any stud used frequently should be kept on a high animal-protein diet and given plenty of exercise. A faulty diet usually deprives the animal of the nutrients that are important for sperm production. Close confinement and environmental conditions affect a cat's temperament, and an extremely nervous stud may not father many good litters. The male may have millions of sperm in his ejaculate, but if they are weak and anatomically deformed, they cannot reach the ova in the uterus. It has been found by researchers that the male is at fault in about half the reproduction failures.

Frequency of Mating

Optimum frequency of use varies according to the health of the stud and the quality and quantity of his sperm. Most normal, virile males can be bred at least twice a week without any harm to health or decline in fertility. Toms with a lower fertility rate can have their reserves of active sperm depleted by ejaculation once in two weeks.

To keep toms active as studs, it is necessary to deprive them of constant human companionship. Most male cats who receive lots of love and attention from their owners tend to lose interest in queens.

It is recommended that a stud be used often at regular intervals; this is more effective than trying to conserve his potency by breeding him only on rare occasions.

Age and Breeding Span

As the stud gets older, his fertility usually diminishes because of interference with and reduction of sperm production. The quality and quantity of sperm cells affect the conception rate because the sperm have a long way to go through the vaginal passage into the uterus to reach the ova.

Most males kept in good health are fertile until they are eight or ten; after that sperm production begins to wane, and although the tom may sire litters, he may need help with extra amounts of food and hormone therapy.

A male in poor health, whatever the cause, may suffer from reduced potency and his value as a stud is thereby threatened.

Although the number of kittens in a litter sired by an old cat may be smaller, it is not true that the quality will be poorer. Once the sperm make contact with the ova, no matter how old the stud, the kittens will be of the same quality and have the same good points (and bad) as if the sire were only a year old. The factors transmitted by him to his offspring are genetic and not affected by age.

Another misconception is that unless a stud is used when he is young he will be impotent in later years. Many males not bred until they were three or four years of age have sired full litters. If a male is in good condition, his potency is available for many years even if he has never been used as a stud.

Penis Hair Ring

Occasionally, a male cat is unable to complete coitus because of a ring of hair at the base of the penis. The tom's penis is covered with little barbs which project backwards, and these papillae collect hair from the fur of the queen during foreplay. Afterwards, most males remove this collected hair by themselves with their abrasive tongues. However, sometimes they need help from a veterinarian.

Frequently used studs should have a penis examination at regular intervals. A painful penis will keep the tom from servicing the queen.

Summary

1. Do not breed a stud on a regular basis until he has reached full sexual maturity.

2. Do not breed a stud who has obvious congenital defects.

3. A stud should be used only if he is in excellent health and is a good example of the standards of perfection of the breed. Although no cat is perfect, we should strive for perfection.

4. Do not breed any male showing emotional instability such as timidity, aggressiveness, or viciousness.

5. Too frequent breeding, or not enough breeding, interferes with fertility.

6. Studs used frequently should be on high-protein diets, such as steak and oysters. Some sex experts question the value of this type of diet. High proteins increase the vitality of the tomcat, indirectly helping his sexual performance.

Breeding Chart

BEFORE MATING (both stud and queen)
a. physical examination
b. laboratory examination of stools, blood, and urine
c. booster vaccinations for distemper, calici, pneumonitis, and rhino-tracheitis
d. general mating information, e.g., signs of heat, time of breeding, etc.

THREE TO FOUR WEEKS AFTER MATING
a. physical examination
b. dietary information, including necessary supplements
c. pregnancy palpations

TWO WEEKS BEFORE WHELPING
a. physical examination
b. whelping information

WITHIN 24 HOURS AFTER WHELPING
a. palpation of queen for retained kittens
b. discharge examination and douching if indicated
c. injections, if needed, to expel afterbirths
d. examination of kittens for congenital defects and pediatric information

Sex of Kittens and Size of the Litter

Although there are many old wives' tales regarding predetermination of sex and size of litter, to my knowledge at the present time there is no possible scientific way to predetermine either.

Actually, the sex of the kittens is fixed the moment a sperm unites with an egg during conception and is solely determined by chance. As for litter size, it is a fact that this seems to run in certain family strains, and so it is advisable to breed cats whose ancestry shows large litters if such is desired. However, too large a litter can affect the size and health of the kittens and often is detrimental to the health of the mother. She may require outside help to feed and rear her kittens.

6 · Prenatal Care

Pregnancy and Gestation · Nutrition · Health Care ·
Getting Ready for Kittening

After the mating, the chief concern of the owner should be to maintain the queen at optimum nutritional and muscular levels. Under these conditions she can be expected to produce healthy offspring. From this point on, the production of healthy kittens depends on the queen's ability to carry her young the full term, a successful kittening, and the normal development of the nursing instinct and the production of sufficient milk to nurse the kittens.

Pregnancy

Signs of Pregnancy

□ A gain in body weight due to an increase in abdominal fat. This generally occurs after the fifth week of pregnancy.

□ Morning sickness, very similar to that in humans, plagues some pregnant queens. This is due to uterine changes and enlargement.

□ Abdominal enlargement. This is usually observed about the fifth week as a slight filling out of the flanks, but if the queen is carrying a small litter, the enlargement may go unobserved. Abdominal enlargement can also be due to an infection of the uterus, or to tumors in the uterus or elsewhere in the abdominal cavity.

□ Changes in the mammary glands. About the thirty-fifth day of pregnancy, the nipples begin to enlarge and pinken. They continue to become larger and softer in texture until about the fiftieth day. Then they begin to fill with milk and get larger each day. A few days before kittening, the breasts secrete a watery solution. The milk usually does not come down until kittening, although some queens express milk several days before parturition. (Incidentally, most queens have an enlargement of the mammary tissues after the heat period. This is normal and there is no need to think that the queen is pregnant.)

□ Temperamental deviation. During pregnancy a queen's behavior may change. Generally she becomes quieter and more affectionate, although a very nervous cat may become aggressive.

□ There is normally an increase in appetite until within a few days of delivery. When she completely refuses food, kittening is imminent. Should she stop eating and then not deliver within twenty-four hours, this is a signal for a veterinarian to take over and find the cause.

□ Abdominal movement. During the last week of pregnancy, when the queen is in a relaxed position, the unborn kittens can usually be seen moving in the uterus, changing positions.

If you suspect pregnancy but none of the above signs is observed, consult a veterinarian; he will be able to determine if the queen is pregnant. In extremely difficult diagnosis, X ray is usually resorted to, but an X ray will not show a kitten until after the forty-ninth day. It is not possible to use biological tests using rabbits or mice, as in humans.

Gestation

It is helpful to know at the earliest possible time that a queen is pregnant so that suitable arrangements can be made for her prenatal care.

The gestation period of a normal queen lasts from 58 to 66 days; the average is 63. It varies in different cats and also fluctuates with the size of the litter, the time of mating, the breeding season, and environmental conditions. Kittens born under 58 days are considered premature.

In determining the kittening date, always count from the first mating period even if there were subsequent matings. The supposi-

tion is that the cat conceived at the first mating.

Number of Kittens

The gain in body weight during pregnancy does not reflect the number of kittens in the litter. Some people are so eager to know how many kittens will be born that they cause the queen undue anxiety by poking at her abdomen, trying to feel the kittens. Patience is recommended.

It is possible after the sixth week of gestation for the veterinarian to determine the number of kittens a queen is carrying. This is done by X ray, but it is not advisable unless it is necessary for the health or safety of the queen.

There are some who contend that they can tell the number of kittens by counting the nipples (one nipple for each kitten), or by how many breasts are filled with milk. This has no scientific basis.

False Pregnancy

This occasionally occurs in cats, although it is not as common as in dogs. The animal "believes" that she is pregnant and shows many of the symptoms of pregnancy, such as enlarged mammary glands (including production of milk), swelling of the abdomen, and appetite change. At delivery time she shows hyperexcitability in the form of panting and trembling. Many of these queens go through labor pains at about the time they normally would be delivering. Often the queen makes a nest and proceeds to protect her "kittens," which might be toys, bones, or other objects, which she carries around in her mouth. She usually curls up with her "kittens" tightly snuggled to her breasts. Queens in false pregnancy have been known to adopt entire litters of real kittens or puppies and have produced enough milk to raise them during their entire eight weeks of suckling.

Various symptoms include restlessness, looking for kittens, whining and crying, scratching at rugs, trying to make a bed for her "litter." But these are extreme symptoms. The cat generally does not go through all these antics but instead may become quiet, go off her feed, and curl up in a corner wanting to be alone. Fortunately, with the cessation of the false pregnancy, she returns to her normal self.

In some queens with a strong maternal instinct, false pregnancy makes them more affectionate with their human companions, or they will mother a young puppy or a young animal of any species. Their maternal frustrations can drive them to extreme behavior, and there are even cases of queens stealing kittens from other queens. Some cats produce so much milk that the milk drips, stimulated by their highly emotional state. I do not advise milking such a queen, as it will stimulate further milk production. However, if her breasts are extremely swollen and feverish, some milk should be expressed to give her relief. I would then gently apply camphorated oil to her breasts to help relieve the inflammation and to dry up the milk. A veterinarian may prescribe hormones to relieve this condition.

The signs of false pregnancy usually last from about the fifth week following the termination of the heat period until the normal delivery date. Milk production can last six to eight weeks after the onset of the false whelping.

False pregnancy has been widely studied. It is caused by the retention of a growth on one or both ovaries. The queen is affected both physically and emotionally, and the abnormal behavior seems to be controlled by the ovaries that have gone astray.

Researchers have reported that an injection of hormones at the end of the normal heat period can prevent this condition in the ovaries. In treatment of false pregnancy the veterinarian usually resorts to a variety of hormones to counteract the ovarian growth.

Often during false pregnancy the animal becomes feverish, either because of the enlarged milk-filled breasts or because of conditions in her uterus (there are definite uterine changes during this period). A veterinarian will usually prescribe tranquilizers and, if fever is present, put the animal on antibiotics. She is definitely in distress both physically and mentally and needs help in both respects.

A maiden queen's symptoms are usually less severe and less prolonged than an older cat's. I advise breeding the queen during the next heat period, as this is one way of satisfying her maternal instincts and returning her body to that of a normally functioning female cat. If the owner does not want to raise kittens, the queen should be spayed. Queens who have repeated false pregnancies are very prone to female disorders such as metritis and mammary tumors. Also, most queens with histories of irregular heat cycles and false pregnancies will not conceive when bred. I would advise hysterectomy for such animals to keep them from undue suffering.

If hysterectomy is resorted to, it is not wise to spay these cats while they are undergoing false pregnancy, as all their female organs are swollen and hemorrhagic and the operation is difficult for them. Also, an operation while they are lactating might prolong milk production from several weeks to several months. It is much wiser to wait until the queen has completely recovered from her false pregnancy.

In the treatment of false pregnancy it is best to reduce the diet and especially the fluid intake. The more fluid the cat drinks, the more milk she will produce. Try to keep her food as dry as possible and allow her enough exercise to keep her bowels moving to excrete excess fluid.

Also try to keep her away from other cats, especially nursing queens and young kittens. It is difficult to predict how she will react to them. She might jump on a nursing mother and attempt to kill her in order to take over the kittens.

False pregnancy is not to be considered a neurotic tendency; it is, rather, a reaction to an abnormality of the ovaries. It is also incorrect to consider a queen sexually abnormal if she undergoes a false pregnancy. Actually her maternal instinct is strong, and she should make a very good mother. Sometimes breeding her will prevent further false pregnancies. However, if she nevertheless continues to have false pregnancies, they are usually less severe and of shorter duration than those of unmated queens.

Phantom Pregnancy

Many fetuses die within a day or two after the eggs have been fertilized, so that there is no indication of conception, or they may die and disappear several weeks after conception. Often the queen will show all the signs of being pregnant up to the end of six weeks and then gradually become slimmer and pass her delivery date without giving birth to kittens.

Phantom pregnancy is entirely different from false pregnancy. Failure to kitten is usually due to the death of the fetuses in the uterus and their absorption during the gestation period. There is no secretion or discharge from the vagina to indicate a miscarriage—all residue is absorbed by the body of the queen. Sometimes a queen will lose part of her litter through this process—some of the fetuses will die—and she will have fewer kittens than were conceived.

Fetal death and absorption is due to a lethal factor not very well understood at this time. It is thought to be either a hormonal imbalance, or a deficiency of vitamin E, or a lack of certain ingredients in the maternal blood.

Having a phantom pregnancy does not mean that the queen is sterile or unable to bear future litters.

Miscarriage

This is fairly common in cats. Around the fourth or fifth week of gestation the mother cat suddenly looks different—her enlarged abdomen is small again. In some cases there will be vaginal bleeding, but because cats are so fastidious some owners are completely unaware that the cat has lost her kittens. The fetuses at this stage are about the size of grapes and the mother tends to eat the fetuses and afterbirth, leaving no signs.

Causes of miscarriage:

☐ Poor health.
☐ Uterine infection.
☐ Any type of disease.
☐ Improper development of the fetuses inside the womb.
☐ An unexplained lethal factor of the male-female combination. Although researchers are still working on this problem, it is suspected that there may be some similarity with the Rh factor in humans. If kittens are lost in this way, sometimes changing the tom makes for perfectly normal kittens.
☐ Excessive jumping and exercise in the early stages of pregnancy.
☐ Injury. A very sharp blow or any type of shock could prove traumatic to a pregnant female.
☐ Rough handling, excitement, traveling, or any emotional disturbance.

If there is any vaginal bleeding during pregnancy, the cat should be rushed to a veterinarian. It is sometimes possible to prevent impending abortion by administering hormonal drugs to stop the contractions.

It is wise to keep a pregnant cat confined to a small room during the last two weeks of pregnancy. This will prevent her from jumping or falling.

Habitual Abortion

Repeated miscarriages indicate a condition known as Habitual Abortion. Since these queens are unsuitable for breeding, I would advise hysterectomy.

There is still much to be learned about the causative agents of this condition. There is some consensus among veterinarians that it is related to the sire, although little is actually known about this baffling syndrome.

Nutrition

Prenatal nutrition should be ample and balanced because obviously nutrition of the queen determines the nutrition obtained by the developing kittens. If certain nutrients are not supplied by the mother, the embryos will not develop normally. She must have optimum nutrition for the production of superior kittens.

A balanced diet should contain high-protein foods rather than dry, bulky, and mushy types. If the cat has been raised on commercial dry foods, I would supplement that food with meat—either raw or canned—and other high-protein foods such as eggs, liver, milk, and cheese.

During the first four weeks of pregnancy her food intake should not be increased. Quality, not quantity, should be the byword.

After four weeks of pregnancy her daily food allowance should be increased about 20 percent, but she should not be given all she asks for. The increase should be in protein rather than starch or carbohydrates. Throughout the gestation period, she should be in good muscular condition with no excess fat.

I advise dividing the daily ration into two

or three feedings, because if the queen eats too much at one meal, she will feel discomfort from pressure in her already overcrowded abdomen.

Vitamin and Mineral Requirements

The formation of the kittens' bones is largely dependent on the mother's mineral consumption. Absorption of minerals, in turn, depends on the vitamin A and vitamin D content of her diet. If her diet is deficient in these vitamins, her body will be the first to suffer from lack of minerals even though the kittens may seem to be normal.

If the diet is deficient in calcium and phosphorus, the bones of the kittens at birth may be soft, brittle, or malformed, and there will be defective teeth later in life. Rickets is a common result of mineral deficiency.

Birth defects often appear when the diet is deficient in copper, niacin, iodine, pantothenic acid, and riboflavin. Such defects include cleft palate, eye problems, skeletal malformation, and other conditions.

If there is a deficiency of vitamin B_2 (riboflavin) in the diet, the kittens could be born with umbilical hernias, cleft palates, or congenital heart defects.

During the last two weeks of gestation, the kittens put on flesh and there is little bone growth, so they are not in need of many nutrients. Keep the queen's weight down during the last two weeks. Rearrange her diet so that she gets more animal protein and less starch and carbohydrates. Continue supplying her with vitamins and minerals.

There is a belief that feeding the queen supplementary vitamins and minerals while she is in labor will produce abnormally large kittens at birth. This is erroneous. Although inadequate nutrition in the queen will produce weak and small kittens, the size of kittens in the prenatal stage is controlled by genetic factors and by the queen's growth hormones.

The Fat Queen

As noted in the previous chapter, fatness in the queen reduces the chances of conception. It also reduces the chances of trouble-free delivery. Fat queens often produce malformed kittens, attributable to the crowded conditions in the uterus. The queen who is overweight usually has prolonged labor, and the kitten mortality is high.

Health Care

Vaccination

All pregnant queens must have immunity against distemper. Although it is a requisite of breeding to give a queen a booster before she is bred, a booster vaccination after breeding will pose no danger to the unborn kittens. The importance of the booster vaccine cannot be emphasized too strongly. The mother's colostrum (first milk) will then contain immune factors against the various diseases kittens are prone to, and the stronger the immunity, the better. Extremely low immunity in unvaccinated queens may seriously affect the kittens' chances of survival should they be exposed to disease.

Parasites

If possible, worming should be done before the queen is bred or very early in pregnancy. *A queen should not be wormed after the first two weeks of pregnancy.* Worming is dangerous and the medicine can be extremely toxic to the developing kittens. If worming is necessary, be sure to see a veterinarian; he has types of worm medicine that can be used safely on pregnant queens. Commercial medicines can cause abortion or interfere with the development of the embryos.

Additional Advice

Bear in mind that a pregnant queen needs extra-special consideration in time, affection, and tender, loving care. She wants to be spoiled a little, so give in to her demands—except for extra amounts of food and between-meal snacks, which might lead to a hazardous overweight problem.

I advise a professional prenatal examination about a month after mating and again two weeks before the kittens are due.

During the last week of gestation the mother-to-be must be watched carefully so that she does not get *too much* exercise or injure herself. A normal amount of exercise, however, is very desirable to help her maintain the tone of her muscles and to keep her bowels functioning normally.

Don't allow her to roam free, as she might not be able to resist a leap or two; this could cause a misplacement of the fetuses or result in a hard fall injurious to the unborn kittens.

If she must be picked up, she should not be picked up by the middle, but by placing one hand between her front legs and one under her hindquarters. And never, never pick up a cat by the scruff of the neck when she is heavy with kittens (I am not in favor of picking her up in this manner even when she is not pregnant).

Car rides should be restricted because a sudden bump in the road could jolt the cat enough to cause premature labor.

Getting Ready for Kittening

Preparing the Kittening Box

Usually a few weeks before the kittens are due, the queen will begin her search for a nest. A favorite spot might be a shelf or drawer with a lot of linen or clothes—or right in the middle of your bed.

Even though her mind is probably made up about where she intends to have her kittens, it is still a good idea to prepare a kittening box for her about ten days or a week before she is due.

Obtain a cardboard box high enough for her to stand in with the lid closed and roomy enough for her to move in a circle. It should be about double the length of the cat so that she can stretch out with her brood. Cut an opening large enough for her to enter near the top.

The box should be placed in a quiet nook, away from noises, strangers, and other cats and dogs in the household. If disturbed, the queen is apt to jump up to protect her kittens and possibly hurt one of them.

The box should be free of any debris and in a sanitary condition. If a wooden box is used, it should be scrubbed with a good disinfectant (but not Lysol).

There is no substitute for shredded newspapers in the whelping box. Many kittens have smothered in blankets or towels. Also, wood shavings and straw are strictly taboo; the kittens might ingest or inhale particles, which could be fatal. Newspapers are abundantly available, and the price is right. The paper is highly absorbent, provides a good footing for young kittens, and gives the queen an opportunity to dig and scratch prior to labor. (Digging and scratching goes back to ancestral days when the mother would dig a hole in the ground for her kittening nest. Domestication has provided newspapers to satisfy the same need.)

Put in the newspaper and close the lid so that it will be dark inside. Periodically place the cat in the box so she can become accustomed to it and hopefully go to it at the proper time.

It has been estimated that 50 percent of early kitten losses are due to chilling; therefore the kittening box should be indoors, at regular room temperature, 70 to 72 degrees, and free from drafts. A heating pad is useful to have around in case the kittens get cold.

Things To Have on Hand for Kittening

There should be a good supply of clean newspapers. You will need towels for drying the kittens and also for grasping them if there is trouble.

Do not start boiling water at the first sign of labor. Even though this is always done in the movies and on television, the queen has no need for boiling water at any time. Warm, soapy water is sufficient for sanitary purposes, along with alcohol for sterilization.

You should also have on hand a pair of sharp scissors and sewing thread or dental floss for cutting and tying off umbilical cords. Boric acid powder, BFI (an antiseptic powder), or alum powder should be used on the cord when it is tied off. However, do not help with the umbilical cord in a normal delivery. Intervene only if the queen is unable or unwilling to perform her motherly duties.

A plastic medicine dropper will come in handy in case it becomes necessary to remove fluid from the nostrils and mouth of a kitten.

7 · Kittening

Kittening Signs · Normal Kittening · Helping in Labor ·
Caesarean Section · Stillborn Kittens · Causes of Kitten
Deaths · Cannibalism

No two queens kitten in the same manner; each has her own idiosyncrasies which have to be dealt with individually. Close association between the owner and the queen is of great help in interpreting the emotional and physical signs as she prepares herself for giving birth. Although watchfulness and understanding are important, however, overprotectiveness is generally worse than neglect. A mother-to-be is upset by constant surveillance—a thermometer in her rectum every half hour or so and the master's hand feeling her abdomen. All she wants is to be left alone. Outdoor cats generally go off and hide. Indoor cats usually seek out the darkest and most isolated nook in the house—a spot as inaccessible to human intervention as possible.

Although kittening is a critical time in a queen's life, it is not an emergency that should make the owner panic. There will always be time to consult a veterinarian and to get the cat to a hospital if it should be required. If the owner panics, it will frighten the cat, possibly resulting in loss of kittens or even the mother herself. Most queens are capable of handling 99 out of 100 situations with their natural instincts, and the owner need not interfere. The purpose of this chapter is to prepare the uninitiated to cope with the normal processes of birth and to alert them to abnormal situations that require consultation with a veterinarian.

Although the "normal" gestation period is 63 days, the exact day for kittening cannot be predicted. If kittens are born prior to 58 days, they usually will not survive, for not all of their organs and bodily functions are fully developed. There are cases of kittens born at 53 days and surviving, but such kittens require a great deal of professional care.

If the mating date is known, there is no cause for anxiety until the queen is four to five days late. Although she can go 65 to 68 days and produce normal kittens, at the sixty-fifth day she should be examined by a veterinarian. If she is eating normally, seems lively, and has no off-color vaginal discharge (black, brown, or green), there is probably nothing to worry about. Any normal delay in delivery does not endanger the kittens because they are enclosed in their sacs, which nourish and maintain them.

Kittening Signs

The three most reliable observable signs of impending kittening in the queen occur about twelve hours before the kittens are born:

□ Loss of appetite (but some queens insist on eating right up to labor).

□ Tearing things (newspapers, pillows, etc.) trying to make a nest.

□ Disappearance into the delivery "nook" of her choice.

From that point on, if she trusts you enough to allow you to watch over her, the most reliable medical signs are:

□ Temperature drop. Her normal temperature is 100 to 102 degrees. As her delivery time approaches, it starts to drop. When it gets down to 99 degrees, the kittens should be born within twenty-four hours.

□ Approximately twelve hours before her kittens are due, she will lie down on her side. During this period her uterus is contracting, getting the kittens into position for birth.

□ At this time there should be a clear-colored discharge from the vagina. If the discharge is black, green, or brown, a veterinarian should be called immediately; something is going wrong with the delivery.

□ Within a few hours of delivery, she will begin to pant. This will be in a steady rhythm, increasing as the first birth approaches. Her body will contract for a minute or so and then relax, with less time between contractions as she reaches delivery. The contractions push the kitten along the uterus toward the outside world. In actual labor, the uterus contracts and expands as the kittens get into position for each stage of delivery.

Normal Kittening

Kittens are born in transparent, fluid-filled sacs which act as cushions to protect them from shock or injury while they are in the uterus. The sac also serves to dilate the vaginal passageway as the kittens move down and out.

Usually the sac surrounding the kitten bursts, or is ruptured by the queen, as the kitten is born. Normally she will instinctively tear it away with her teeth, but if she shows no inclination to do so within thirty seconds after delivery, you should intervene—as described in the next section—because the kitten cannot breathe until the membranes are torn away.

Once she has removed the sac, the queen bites through the umbilical cord and then proceeds to lick the kitten, rolling it around to dry it and to stimulate its respiration. Here, too, you must intervene (see page 68) if the mother fails to act immediately.

The next object to appear should be the afterbirth, which is normally voided by the queen within fifteen minutes after the birth of the kitten. The fact that the owner usually never sees the afterbirth presents a problem. Because most queens are so fastidious about keeping the kittening box clean, they eat the afterbirth. But some do not, and retention of the afterbirth results in uterine infection in the postnatal period which seriously affects both the mother and her kittens. This is one of the reasons a veterinarian should be visited within twenty-four hours of the birthing process.

Afterbirth eating has long been a subject of

controversy. Some breeders believe that the queen needs the afterbirth because the hormones it contains will help her develop a more personal feeling toward her kittens. Others think that the afterbirth is needed for certain nutritional hormones that promote her general well-being and help stimulate milk production. However, most experts agree that it does no harm to allow the queen to eat the afterbirth but that her health and well-being will not suffer should she not eat it.

After the first kitten has been delivered, the rest of the kittens should follow within an hour or two, depending on the number. The fat queen will take somewhat longer; the queen past middle age will usually be tired between kittens, and will wait a long time. If the queen appears to be in labor and it has been more than three hours since the last birth, this is a sign of trouble.

Within twenty-four hours after birth, mother and kittens should be taken to a veterinarian for examination. He will expel any afterbirths that might not have been released and douche the queen if a purulent discharge is present. She might need a pituitary injection to help her empty her uterus; this will also help in "letting down" her milk. The veterinarian will ascertain if there are any unborn kittens. This is very important since it is not uncommon for a queen to tire toward the end of her labor and leave kittens unborn. In these cases she appears to have finished her labor and goes about the business of nursing her kittens as if nothing were wrong; however, within two to three days, if not attended to, she develops infection.

Feeding

During kittening, the queen will likely need some nourishment. I would not give her solid food; it might nauseate her. Milk or water is suitable and should be presented to her *in* her kittening box (she should not be made to get out of her box).

The kittens will normally almost immediately search out their mother's nipples. In an emergency, newborn kittens can go without feeding up to twelve hours after birth, but the mother's colostrum is a vital part of their first few hours. Each kitten should be carefully watched to be sure it is strong enough to grasp a nipple.

Helping in Labor

Although most queens are capable of doing everything themselves, owners should be able to distinguish between a normal and an abnormal delivery so that they can help if they are needed. And here a word of caution: DO NOT INTERFERE with nature unless an emergency presents itself.

The Sac

Once the kitten is expelled, if the queen fails to attempt to remove the sac within thirty seconds, the owner must intervene. The kitten should be held head downward and the sac torn quickly away from the kitten starting with the mouth, over the head, and back over the tail. The head-down position allows any excess fluid to run out of the nose and mouth.

Sometimes a kitten is born encased in a slimy dark-green sac. This is a sign that the kitten has been in the uterus too long or that there has been a uterine infection. Usually such a kitten is in a weakened condition, and I would consult a veterinarian, as he might want to put the kitten on an antibiotic to counteract any possible infection. The green material should be washed off completely, especially from the mouth and nostrils. The kitten may have a greenish tint for several days but will soon look normal.

The Umbilical Cord

The kitten is attached to the mother's placenta by the umbilical cord. The cord varies from six to twelve inches in length and must be severed within a few minutes after birth if the kitten is to survive. If the queen does not chew the cord immediately, then the owner must perform the task. The cord should be cut with scissors (which have been dipped in alcohol), leaving 1 to 1½ inches next to the kitten. The cord should then be tied off with thread or dental floss (this, too, should first be dipped in alcohol) near the base of the cord to prevent bleeding. Boric acid powder, BFI, or alum powder should then be applied to the tip of the cord.

Before you cut the cord and while it is still attached to the afterbirth, you might consider a procedure which will give the kitten a little extra boost. Squeeze the afterbirth with your hand, forcing some of the blood down the umbilical cord and into the kitten's body. In a very weak kitten this little extra blood can be the difference between life and death.

Rough handling of the cord can cause an umbilical hernia, so be careful not to pull on it. A rupture of the blood vessels where the cord meets the navel can be fatal to a kitten. Also, sometimes a queen will try to pick up a kitten by the umbilical cord. If you see this happening, take the kitten from her and cut and tie the cord yourself.

Drying a Kitten

Once the kitten is detached from the umbilical cord, breathing and blood circulation must commence. If the queen does not immediately start to lick the kitten to stimulate its breathing, the owner must act quickly.

Dry the kitten by rubbing it briskly with a flannel cloth or a soft bath towel. This substitute for the mother's tongue is a good stimulant for respiration and circulation. Once the kitten cries, you can breathe a sigh of relief.

When the kitten is breathing normally it should be put with its mother to get some of her milk.

Difficult Delivery Positions

Although a breech presentation—when the hind feet come first—is considered normal, sometimes the queen does not have enough strength to pass the kitten through her pelvis. If the feet appear and the kitten is not expelled within fifteen minutes, the owner should attempt to help.

Grasp the two feet (you might have to use a hand towel to get a hold on the slippery feet) and pull gently, as the queen labors, in a downward rotating motion. If only one foot can be seen, find the other foot inside the vaginal tract before pulling on the kitten. Be very gentle—don't jerk the kitten, as you might damage it.

Other positions which cause delivery difficulties include: an upside-down presentation, in which the kitten comes out on its back instead of its chest; an "L"-shaped presentation, in which the kitten emerges at right angles; or the kitten's head may be turned backwards, or twisted, coming on the side. These difficult delivery positions require professional help as quickly as possible. If professional help is not available, you will have to do what you can. Using a soft towel, gently rotate and pull the kitten out.

Other Delivery Problems

If labor spasms have continued for some time and the queen appears distressed, there could be several causes. It could be a large kitten stuck in the pelvic canal, or it could be that two kittens entered the pelvic canal at the same time. These difficult deliveries require immediate professional help. Getting a kitten out within an hour is vital, both for the kitten and for the rest of the litter. Do not by any means insert an instrument into the queen's vaginal tract; instruments can mutilate the kitten, or tear and puncture the mother's soft internal tissues and cause a fatal infection. A thoroughly washed and scrubbed finger, with or without rubber gloves, is the only thing that should enter the queen's vagina.

Dry birth. Sometimes when a queen has had a difficult and long delivery she will lose all the lubricating fluid in her vaginal tract. If this happens it will prevent a kitten from slipping out during her uterine contractions. A solution for this problem is to insert a lubricating substance such as mineral oil, Vaseline, or olive oil into the vagina. This lubrication will help release the kitten from the vaginal tract.

Caesarean Section

The Caesarean operation has saved many a queen and her kittens. When done in time, it is a fairly safe procedure in the hands of a skilled veterinary surgeon.

It is best not to treat the Caesarean as a last resort—to be performed when the queen is exhausted and just about dead. Blood poisoning is very dangerous and has shortened the life of many a queen because a Caesarean was neglected or delayed. Many breeders, knowing one of their queens is going to need a Caesarean, will have the operation performed as soon as the cervix dilates and she is ready to deliver.

As a rule of thumb, if there is a delay of more than twenty-four hours after labor has begun, a Caesarean section should be the procedure of choice. The quicker the kittens are gotten out of the queen, the better chance she and the kittens have for survival.

There is no need for the owner to fear a Caesarean. Queens are fully awake and able to nurse their kittens within two hours after surgery. They suffer no traumatic effects because of their inability to deliver their kittens normally. There is a common misconception that once a cat has had a Caesarean, she cannot be used again for breeding. I have performed four or five Caesareans on the same queen and she has maintained good health throughout. Also, once having a Caesarean does not necessarily mean that she cannot deliver the next litter by normal birth.

Factors determining the need for a Caesarean section:

□ A queen who has gone to the sixty-fifth day and does not go into active labor, while showing signs of toxicity and not responding to pituitary injections or tranquilizers.

□ A queen exhibiting signs of difficult delivery (such as rupture of the placental membranes and loss of placental fluids, inability to deliver, or exhaustion after a protracted period of labor and no delivery of kittens).

□ A queen with a prolapsed uterus still in labor.

□ An older queen with heart disease.

□ Queens with deformities of the pelvic canal which could impair delivery.

Of course, the final decision will be up to your veterinarian.

Stillborn Kittens

Some kittens are born squirming, while others lie still and appear dead. Don't give up on the still kitten. Using a dry towel, pick up the kitten, and with its head held downward, rip off the sac. Rub the kitten vigorously, swinging it in a downward motion to propel fluid from the lungs, mouth, and nostrils. Do this several times. If the kitten breathes with a gurgling sound, there is fluid in its respiratory passageway and this should be removed. A medicine dropper is useful in drawing fluid from the nostrils and mouth.

If the kitten is cold, immerse it up to the neck in warm water for a minute or two to help stimulate circulation. At the same time rub the chest cavity, giving a heart massage. A stimulant, such as brandy, on the tongue works well in some cases.

Sometimes after a long and hard delivery, the kittens are sluggish and must be revived. If tongues and gums are blue, the kittens need oxygen badly. (Some breeders keep a small tank of oxygen close by. The head cone is left in the box until all the kittens are pink and active.) If the kittens have mucus or fluid in the lungs, oxygen can save them.

In the home, to provide the necessary oxygen, mouth-to-mouth resuscitation with artificial respiration should be administered. Blow hard enough to expand the lungs of the kitten—one breath every two seconds. Usually several breaths are needed before the kitten shows any signs of respiratory commencement, and then it will begin gasping about every minute or half minute. Keep up the mouth-to-mouth resuscitation until the kitten is breathing in a steady rhythm. If fluid appears in its mouth, keep swabbing it or sy-

ringing it. I've worked as long as thirty minutes on a "dead" kitten, so do not give up easily. When the kitten seems to be breathing normally and is squirming about, give it to the mother and let her lick it and dry it with her tongue.

A kitten is usually born still because it lacked oxygen and had too much fluid in the lungs from staying in the pelvic canal too long. The condition also occurs in a dry birth when the afterbirth has been severed.

Causes of Kitten Deaths
Uterine Inertia

The commonest cause of death in kittens, and in queens, is the inability of the queen to expel her kittens due to uterine inertia—an absence of contractions of the uterus. The contractions are reflex actions thought to be

controlled by hormones present in the queen's body.

Uterine inertia is thought to be hereditary, as it seems to run in some family strains. It may occur in queens of any age, but the shy and nervous queen is more susceptible. The nervous or excited animal releases adrenaline into her bloodstream and adrenaline is a known inhibitor of uterine contractions. Such a queen should be in a quiet, dark place so that she feels as relaxed as possible—preferably in her accustomed environment, because anything strange to her can affect her labor pains.

Another cause of uterine inertia is hypocalcium—a lowered calcium level in the blood. A fat or lazy cat has a greater tendency toward uterine inertia. An emaciated or debilitated cat with hormonal deficiencies can also be affected by this condition. Although the causes are not exactly known, it is thought to be due to a deficiency of necessary hormones at the termination of pregnancy.

The best way to prevent uterine inertia is to keep the queen's weight down—but with a well-balanced diet so she remains in good health.

Cats with uterine inertia seem normal in every respect and show all the preliminary signs of kittening—nest making, restlessness, a slight discharge. But instead of the queen's going into labor, the signs disappear and nothing happens.

If the kittens are not expelled after twenty-four hours, there will be problems. If there is no obstruction or abnormality—as determined by a veterinarian—uterine activity can be stimulated with small, repeated doses of pituitary hormone, which may be continued, if necessary, every twenty to thirty minutes to maintain productive labor.

(Unfortunately, there has been widespread misuse of pituitary hormone. It is a dangerous drug if used incorrectly. For instance, if the queen's vagina is not fully dilated and her cervix has not opened sufficiently, an injection of pituitary to stimulate uterine contractions against the closed cervix can result in a ruptured uterus and the death of all the kittens and of the queen unless surgery is performed quickly to correct the rupture.)

At times there is a secondary inertia—exhaustion. When the queen has been in labor a long time, she may become tired and stop contracting. If the contractions are not resumed, the kittens will remain in the uterus, with serious complications, and a veterinarian should be consulted immediately.

Other Causes of Kitten Deaths

A heavy prenatal infestation of hookworms or roundworms can be fatal to kittens. If the kittens are infected in the uterus, the worms can settle in the fetal liver and lungs.

Sometimes kittens are born with abnormalities of the heart, lungs, or other organs.

In a condition known as atresia anus, the kitten is born without an anal orifice. The kitten may seem normal for a few days, and then there will be an enlargement of the abdomen due to the inability to excrete waste products. In some cases surgery is possible.

Kittens are sometimes born with a constricted anal opening, which causes chronic constipation. Enemas are needed. The veterinarian can stretch and dilate the anal muscles.

Sometimes kittens are born with a tendency for telescoping or twisted intestines. This is a common cause of death in kittens between three and four months of age unless it is detected in time and corrective surgery is performed.

Cannibalism

The ancient feline instinct of cannibalism has to be watched out for in some queens during whelping and for several days after. It can be precipitated by intense pain or fright (trying to save her kittens) and is found especially in nervous queens.

During a difficult delivery—trying to deliver a stuck kitten—queens have been known to mutilate and eat the kitten while pulling it from the vagina.

A nervous queen should be closely watched and all fear-provoking factors, such as noise, strangers, too frequent handling of her kittens, should be avoided.

There is a theory that cannibalism is linked to a shortage of certain hormones and that ingestion of the kittens makes up for this deficiency. There is no evidence to support this theory.

Cannibalism is not restricted to queens. If there is a male cat in the house or in the neighborhood, it should be kept away from the kittens until they are well able to fend for themselves, lest he try to harm or destroy them.

8 · Postnatal Care of the Queen and Her Kittens

Lactation • Behavior of the Queen • Postlabor Complications • Nursing and Feeding • The Care of Orphans • Growth Rate • Mortality in Kittens • Kitten Disorders • Behavior and Socialization

THE QUEEN

After the queen has completed her delivery she is exhausted and relieved. Change the bedding in her quarters and give her some milk or water.

If she has had her litter on your favorite bedspread or in some dark, remote recess, mother and babies should be transferred to a box (as described on page 63). The normal mother will then settle down and tend to her kittens. Her maternal instincts will take over; a good brood queen will lick her kittens, clean them and dry them, and proceed to nurse them.

The Milk

Colostrum, the first milk secreted by the mammary glands, which is produced for only the first six to twelve hours after birth, contains antibodies that give the kittens resistance to diseases. The kitten who gets colostrum has excellent early protection for a long time. If for some reason a kitten does not receive colostrum, I advise injections of feline serum to protect against the ravages of kittenhood diseases.

Milk production in the queen is largely controlled by hormones, as is the maternal instinct. An inadequate milk supply or an unwillingness to nurse is usually due to a lack of these hormones. Some queens are stimulated in their milk production by injections of hormones, such as pituitary.

On the other hand, lactation is stimulated by the suckling of the kittens. The flow of milk is usually adjusted to the demands of the kittens, and many a queen has nursed six to eight kittens without any outside help. This is a tremendous drain on her body, and her diet has to be supplemented with all the calories, vitamins, and minerals necessary to feed the extra little creatures.

The Problem Queen in Nursing

Sometimes the maternal instinct fails to take over and the queen is indifferent to her new babies. This indifference could be due to a background involving poor rearing, poor feeding, lack of proper exercise, or debilitation from injury or disease. Some of these queens are products of show breeding, where the sole interest is beauty without regard to fertility, litter size, ability to kitten normally, or maternal instinct. Other queens after kittening are exhausted, hysterical, or in a state of shock from the traumatic experience of a first litter.

A queen who shows outright aggressiveness toward her kittens should be tranquilized, and the kittens removed from her until she becomes calm; otherwise, she might hurt or even kill them. When she has calmed down—and this applies to all indifferent queens—she should be made to lie on her side and should be firmly held while the kittens are put at her nipples and allowed to nurse. This will overcome some queens' fear of the kittens and they will then take over. If the mother persistently refuses to nurse her kittens this procedure may have to be repeated at frequent intervals for the first few days. She will then usually allow them to nurse by themselves.

If kittens do not nurse, the milk decreases and stops altogether within twenty-four hours. When, for any reason, kittens are removed from a nursing queen, or die, she will need some help with her milk-filled breasts. Injections of hormones can help decrease the milk supply, and the breasts can be bathed with camphorated oil to help the flow decrease. The diet should be changed to a light one with little fluid and no red meat. She should be put on laxatives (see page 75) to keep her bowels open and to draw fluid from her body.

Nutrition During Lactation

The first week after the kittens are born the queen's diet should be light, consisting mainly of milk and egg yolks, along with a small amount of her usual daily fare. She should not be overfed the first week, as this may cause an overproduction of milk, which could lead to breast problems.

After she has returned to normal and the kittens are keeping her breasts depleted, her diet should be gradually increased. She should be given foods which stimulate milk production—milk, raw meat, egg yolks, fish, and liver and other organ foods—as well as plenty of fluids. A nursing queen should be fed four to six times a day with the last feeding just before bedtime because the kittens continue to nurse during the night. Calcium is a very necessary part of her diet because of the demands on her blood calcium. Cats who don't normally drink milk will crave it. A deficiency will lead to eclampsia in the queen and bone deformities and faulty teeth formation in the kittens. Supplementary vitamins and minerals are also of the utmost importance.

The vital time for nutrition during lactation is between the second and fifth weeks. During this period the food intake has to be increased to at least three times the queen's normal daily maintenance requirement. But if she seems to be producing too much milk, her diet should be reduced.

After the fifth week, the kittens usually will have supplementary feeding and will demand less and less of their mother's milk.

As the kittens are being weaned the queen's diet should be gradually reduced. By the end of eight weeks she should be receiving her normal (prepregnancy) amounts of food and supplements in order to aid the milk-drying process.

Behavior with Her Kittens

The first couple of days after delivery, most queens are reluctant to budge from their kittens, and during the first two weeks they will not leave their babies for more than a few moments at a time.

For the first five days the mother should be made to leave the box four or five times a day to relieve herself. After the third day her outings should be for longer periods, and by the end of the first week she should be having regular periods of exercise to keep her body functioning normally. Exercise also seems to stimulate lactation.

The queen needs to be assured that her kittens will not be disturbed while she is away from them. The fewer people who see them until after weaning, the more secure she will feel and the less exposure the kittens will have to disease.

When it is necessary to let people see the kittens, always take the mother away from the kittening box. And never allow children to pick up the kittens before they are weaned.

It is quite normal for a queen to vomit her food for her kittens to eat. Although not a pretty sight, it is a maternal instinct. She partially digests her food and then regurgitates it as a step between breast-feeding and teaching her kittens to eat solid food.

Postlabor Complications

Anytime after delivery that the queen refuses food, her temperature should be taken. A reading above 102 degrees indicates a problem. The trouble might be an infection in her uterus or a retained afterbirth. It might also be an inflammation of the breasts (mastitis—see below). Constipation and diarrhea usually cause fever. Constipation is usually relieved by milk of magnesia; in severe cases an enema might be indicated. I advise one teaspoon of milk of magnesia following the birth of the kittens; it helps clean out all the debris the queen has eaten during delivery. Diarrhea is debilitating, and the queen will decline food and even refuse to nurse her kittens. As a preventive, it is advisable to restrict her diet for the first few days.

For about a week after delivery there is a vaginal discharge, usually reddish in color, and varying from a slight drip, which is normal, to a more copious discharge, which signifies some abnormality.

When there is a retained afterbirth, a mummified fetus, or a dead kitten remaining in the uterus, there will be a brownish and sometimes blackish-green discharge and the queen will usually show signs of being feverish and lethargic. She will decline food, and will likely refuse to nurse her kittens. Her temperature might rise to 103 to 105 degrees, and she is obviously a sick cat. A veterinarian should be consulted immediately, to save not only her life but the lives of her kittens, since her milk will be affected.

If the normal red vaginal discharge continues for more than a week, there is some abnormality in the vaginal tract. Upon examination the veterinarian will probably find a tear in the cervix. These tears, caused by a difficulty during delivery, heal slowly and exude a continuous discharge. If they are not

75

treated properly, they can result in scar tissue which may prevent conception in subsequent breeding.

Mastitis

This inflammation of the breasts can set in when the queen's milk is not being suckled by the kittens in large enough quantities to empty the breasts, because of either deformed nipples or an overproduction of milk. Sometimes bite wounds and scratches become infected, or bacteria gain entrance through the nipples.

The breasts are feverish and swollen and the milk is scanty and brownish in color, or even blood-tinged. The skin of the breasts becomes shiny and purplish.

Remove the kittens and feed them a formula until the mother can nurse again. The infected milk is dangerous for the kittens.

The milk should be expressed from the affected glands by hand every few hours to reduce the swelling and remove the toxic milk from the queen's body.

Veterinary consultation is important both for the life of the mother and for her kittens.

Eclampsia (Milk Fever)

This is a condition caused by a lowering of the blood calcium after delivery. Occasionally it occurs prior to delivery if the queen is so deficient in calcium that there is not enough for the developing fetuses. To save the queen's life, immediate treatment by a veterinarian is necessary. He will give her intravenous injections of calcium.

One of the first signs is restlessness. The queen's eyes are anxious. Respiration is short and rapid. The mucous membrances are pale. She has spasms during which her legs jerk and her body shakes. She may lie on one side, kicking all four feet and salivating profusely. Her temperature can rise above 103 degrees

and she is subject to paralysis and collapse. If there is no treatment within twelve hours she will die.

Most queens, if treated in time, recover without complications. The mother's nursing duties should be suspended (the kittens will have to be nursed by hand). After she is fully recovered, the kittens can be allowed to nurse gradually—for half an hour or so, two or three times a day. A cautious return to nursing duty is very important because the attacks can recur. The queen should be taking large doses of calcium, phosphorus, and vitamins.

Agalactia (Inadequate Milk Supply)

This condition reveals itself in the behavior of the kittens. They are hungry, noisy and unkempt. The queen's milk can be helped to flow by injections of pituitary and other hormones. Increasing the high-protein foods in her diet and giving her plenty of fluids will also raise her milk production.

Caked Mammary Glands

The breasts become filled with milk and are hard, sore, and quite feverish. This condition occurs in heavily milking queens if the kittens have not suckled enough milk to empty the glands regularly.

Kittens should be weaned from such queens, but gradually—one kitten each day. Your veterinarian can give hormones and antibiotics to ease soreness of the breasts. He will advise gentle massage with camphorated oil, expressing some of the milk from the breasts as you massage. Reduce fluid intake to help lower her milk production.

Metritis (Infection of the Uterus)

This may occur after an extremely difficult labor and is indicated by a rapid pulse, high temperature, drooping head, and refusal to lie down because of severe abdominal pains. Professional help is needed immediately to save the cat.

Hair Loss in Lactating Queens

Many queens, particularly the long-haired breeds, lose much of their hair following delivery or after nursing a litter of kittens. This hair loss is usually related to nutrition: a low-energy diet that may be adequate for the normal adult cat is inadequate for the lactating queen. A diet ample in protein and fat will alleviate hair loss.

With a proper diet and worming (after her kittens have been weaned) a balding cat should regain her normal healthy coat within three or four weeks.

THE KITTENS

Nursing

In my opinion, there is no substitute for natural nursing, even though many good artificial methods have been devised. I do not believe we can improve on nature in this respect. It has been proved time and again that kittens fed at the breast are usually stronger, more resistant to disease and parasites, and easier to rear than those fed artificially.

However, there are cases in which artificial nursing is necessary, and countless thousands of kittens have been reared on artificial milk with good results. And in a large litter it is often necessary to supplement feeding if the queen does not have enough milk for all the kittens—although they should be allowed to have as much natural milk as possible.

Although the suckling instinct is strong in kittens, sometimes the queen with a first pregnancy does not know how to help her kittens. When they try to grasp her nipples, she pushes them away, and she might even leave the delivery box as they persist in their search for milk. A kitten should be put at a breast; if the queen protests, she should be scolded, and the kitten's mouth put directly on the nipple. Usually she will then allow the kittens to proceed without incident.

Sometimes the queen does not have enough milk to feed her brood. The veterinarian can give her certain drugs, such as pituitary injections, to stimulate the formation of milk. To produce a plentiful supply, the queen should be in good health and have adequate nutrition. Also, nursing kittens seem to stimulate milk production.

A queen may have nipples that are not fully formed. Instead of being erect and conical-shaped, they resemble unripe raspberries, and it is difficult for a kitten to extract milk. Or the nipples may be too large for the kittens and it will be necessary to massage the nipples and milk them by hand. The nipples should be examined carefully to be sure they are open and expelling milk properly.

Often after a difficult delivery the queen may be so exhausted that she displays no interest in her kittens. The kittens should be put to her nipples.

There are some kittens, such as those with cleft palate, who cannot suckle milk from the breast. Watch the litter carefully and make sure that the small kittens are not being pushed away by the larger kittens. Often a small kitten is pushed off into a corner, and the mother may leave it alone to perish. A mother cat instinctively knows when a kitten is sick or weak or dying.

Occasionally a kitten is too small or weak to grasp a nipple and must be held to the mother's breast for the first day or two until it gains the strength to keep up with the rest of the litter. If it is too weak to suckle, hold it to the nipple and with the other hand massage the queen's breast, squirting the milk directly into the kitten's mouth. This life-giving milk is very much needed by newborn kittens. Of course, if the queen does not have enough milk or if the kitten cannot get milk on its own, it will be necessary to resort to a simulated formula, using a baby bottle or medicine dropper.

On rare occasions, queens are not reliable and could even kill their kittens if left alone with them. In these cases, we have found foster mothers or have immediately started artificial feeding. We've saved many kittens by using foster mothers with kittens born at about the same time—not more than a week earlier or later.

The old wives' tale that each kitten has its own nipple and will not nurse on any other is entirely untrue. A hungry kitten will nurse on the first nipple that it finds, and instinctively grasps the teat in its mouth.

A healthy and well-fed kitten is quiet. It usually spends most of the time eating and sleeping. If a kitten is restless and cries a lot, it is hungry or sick; in either case, it needs attention.

Lactation of the Queen: A Summary

The lactation period, in which the queen produces milk for her kittens, lasts about eight weeks.

The first three days following the birth of the kittens are the most important because that is when the colostrum is present in the milk. The colostrum gives the kittens their much-needed protection against "baby" diseases.

"Mature" milk is formed during the second and third weeks following birth.

During the fourth and fifth weeks, the milk becomes more concentrated.

During the sixth, seventh, and eighth weeks, the quantity of milk decreases, and it stops soon after the kittens are weaned.

Not all kittens should be weaned abruptly. If the mother cat is still producing milk, wean gradually. It is not uncommon to see half-grown kittens, three to six months old, still nursing. The breasts provide no nourishment, but they serve as a pacifier for the "hooked" kitten. Some kittens as large as their mothers still enjoy the suckling experience. And the mothers probably enjoy it as much as their offspring.

The size of the queen and the number of kittens influence the amount of milk produced. The breed itself has no effect on the composition of the milk; the milk of all breeds is the same. Milk varies in quality with the diet and habits of the queen, and the milk flow can be affected by emotional factors. Whereas a happy, contented queen produces a lot of milk, a nervous and panicky queen will temporarily dry up when she is frightened, as when strangers come by to admire her newborn babies.

Feeding Orphaned Kittens

A recent study determined that one tenth of breast-fed kittens were dissatisfied with their mother's milk. They were unduly restless and did not thrive and grow as they should have. Many queens produce low-quality milk, and others cannot produce enough. The kittens of such mothers need individual hand feeding. The owner must also intervene if the queen dies or develops a postdelivery disease or infection of the mammary glands. In many cases involving Caesarean section, the mother is unable to nurse her babies. Sick kittens and kittens too weak and tiny to nurse should be fed by hand.

If the queen is alive and does not have a contagious ailment, the kittens should be with her except when they are taken away to be fed. She can provide them with warmth and take care of their eliminations and other needs.

The Feeding Formula

In order to produce healthy and vigorous kittens it is necessary to use a formula that simulates the quality of the mother's milk. There is an excellent commercial formula—Borden's KMR—which meets all the nutritional requirements of young kittens. It is a carefully balanced blend of proteins, fats, carbohydrates, vitamins, and minerals—an almost perfect alternative or supplement to the queen's milk.

There is also an excellent "home" formula. This consists of a can of condensed milk and an equivalent amount of boiling water, the yolk of one egg, and one tablespoon of Karo syrup (light or dark). This can be kept refrigerated for several days and the necessary amount warmed to the correct temperature for each feeding. It should be served tepid.

Feeding Techniques

Bottle feeding. You can use a baby-doll bottle or a premature-infant nipple (which is anti-colic); or you may find a medicine dropper (but it must be plastic) easier to manipulate into the little mouth. To bottle-feed a kitten, hold it with your left hand and place it on its stomach. It should never be fed while on its back because the formula is more likely to run into the lungs and cause a foreign-body pneumonia. Put a towel in front of the kitten to give it something to cling to. Gently open the kitten's mouth with a finger of your right hand and edge the nipple (or dropper) into its mouth as you gradually withdraw your finger. The bottle or dropper should be held at about a 45-degree angle, and no air should be allowed to enter the kitten's mouth. Let the milk flow slowly, and be patient. The kitten may fight the nipple or dropper in the beginning, but hunger will help with this new trick. Encourage vigorous sucking by keeping a slight pull on the bottle during feeding. But do not let the kitten nurse too fast. After each feeding the kitten should be burped, to prevent digestive disturbances: hold it upright against your shoulder and rub and pat its back.

Immersion feeding. This method consists of placing the kittens in a shallow dish or pan containing the feeding formula. Some kittens begin lapping immediately while others take several days to get the idea. The dish—with sides high enough to keep them from crawling out—must not be filled to a point where they would drown. In their first three weeks they have to be watched carefully to be sure they are not getting milk in their noses. Only healthy kittens should be fed with this method; it would be fatal to a kitten with a cleft palate or an opening in the soft palate, and so a veterinarian should be consulted before immersion feeding is instituted.

The tube method. This is a particularly good way of feeding weak or sick kittens, and a lifesaving method for kittens with cleft palate. The milk and food (diluted strained baby foods) go directly to the stomach and so the dangers of choking and foreign-body pneumonia are eliminated. Small rubber tubes are attached to a large syringe which holds between ten and twenty centimeters of formula (adequate for one feeding of several kittens). The feeding ends of the tubes are inserted into the kittens' mouths and swallowed to the stomach. This method takes skill, patience, and dexterity, but is well worth learning. An owner can manage it, but he must be instructed by a veterinarian.

Amount to Feed. A good rule of thumb is to feed enough so that the abdomen is slightly enlarged after the feeding. It is best to underfeed the first two to three days so that the kitten can become accustomed to the formula. Most researchers agree that demand feeding is the best. When the kitten is sleeping, it should not be disturbed; when it is stirring about and restless, feed it. Four feedings a day should be enough for normal kittens. Weak or sick kittens may have to be fed every half hour or so, a few drops at a time.

The Care of Orphaned Kittens

Proper Environment

The most serious danger to a newborn kitten is chilling. The owner must assist kittens who do not have a warm mother to snuggle up to. An incubator-type box can be rigged with an electric heating pad or an overhead infrared bulb. The temperature should be kept between 85 and 90 degrees for the first five days, at about 80 degrees for the next two weeks and gradually decreased to between 70 and 75 degrees by the end of the fourth week. Overheating is almost as bad as chilling, and the heat in the incubator box must be well regulated. If the kittens are panting, there is too much heat.

It is also advisable to separate the kittens into individual compartments because when deprived of their mother's breasts they tend to suck each other's tails and genitals. Also, if they are kept apart it is possible for the owner to keep track of stools and watch for diarrhea or constipation. Each compartment should be lined with a clean soft diaper or folded newspaper. This lining should be pinned smoothly to the box so that the kittens cannot crawl under it and smother.

Proper Management

Proper management of the orphaned kitten is guided by weight and the feel of the body. A kitten should be round and fat and there should be a steady increase in weight. If it is not receiving enough nutrition, it will tend to become tight-skinned or dehydrated.

The condition of the stool is a very impor-tant guide. Consistency and regularity indicate health; any change in consistency or color of bowel movements indicates some abnormality. A normal stool should be firm and yellowish in color. A normal kitten fed three to four times a day should have three to five movements, or at least one after each meal.

During the first week of its life, the kitten relies on instinct for urination and defecation. These functions may have to be aided by the owner. If artificial stimulatation is necessary, after each feeding the anal and abdominal regions should be gently rubbed with a cotton swab slightly warmed wih warm water or baby oil.

Daily grooming is necessary and should consist of wiping the kitten's eyes with a boric acid solution and gently massaging the skin (this stimulates circulation and thoroughly awakens the kitten). The best time for massage is just before feeding, while the formula is being warmed. Stroke the kitten's sides and back with a soft folded diaper. It is also good to rub the kitten's skin with baby oil occasionally because of the drying effect of the incubator heat. If the kitten gets dirty, it can be sponged with warm water and rubbed dry with a soft towel or diaper.

Constipation. Constipation usually causes swelling of the abdomen and colicky pains. A further addition of Karo syrup or honey to the formula will have a mild laxative effect. If the bowels continue sluggish, a drop or two of mineral oil on the kitten's tongue should clear up the condition. Unless regular defecation after each meal is maintained, bowel disorders may develop that will jeopardize the kitten's chances for survival. In severe cases, a warm-water soapy enema is indicated. (See page 152.)

Diarrhea. A loose stool could mean that the kitten is ill, is being overfed, or that the formula is too rich. At the first sign of diarrhea, the formula should be diluted by half by adding more water and leaving out the Karo syrup. A few drops of Kaopectate is excellent for diarrhea. If the condition persists, a veterinarian should be consulted.

Growth Rate

Kittens gain very little the first week, but add weight rapidly during the second week and thereafter. During this period kittens from small litters uniformly gain more weight than kittens from large litters—four or more times as much. However, the rate of gain at this stage does not affect adult size. After the kittens are weaned, if they are given the proper foods they will usually attain a weight that is normal for their breed. Kittens getting too little protein, or protein of a poor quality, may grow normally but will be more susceptible to ailments and diseases.

Mortality in Newborn Kittens

The most critical time in the life of a kitten is the first week. During this period deaths can be caused by various congenital and environmental defects or by injuries resulting from difficult deliveries; the greatest number, however, are attributable to chilling and to an infectious disease known as feline herpes virus.

Chilling

When the kitten leaves the warmth of the mother's womb its body temperature drops sharply.

During the first few days of life kittens have no shivering mechanism to compensate for heat loss when the room temperature is lower than the temperature of the nest. Consequently their body temperatures can drop quickly, and they develop cooling of all body functions.

When a kitten remains cold its condition quickly becomes critical. The first signs of chilling are restlessness and crying. As the kitten becomes colder, the crying is high-pitched and occurs with almost every breath. The respiratory rate increases and the temperature of the kitten continues to go down. The kitten becomes cold to the touch, limp, pale-gummed, and appears dead. It can sometimes be revived by quickly immersing it up to the neck in hot (but not scalding) water, then gently rubbing and stimulating its body over a long period, and giving it warm milk.

Feline Herpes Virus (Fading Kitten Syndrome)

This is a very insidious disease because the queen appears healthy, the milk production seems adequate, and all the kittens nurse in a normal manner until just a few hours prior to their deaths.

The early signs are cessation of nursing, chilling, and painful crying. Abdominal pain is a diagnostic feature and it is generally associated with a yellow-green diarrhea. The bright-colored stool usually appears three to four hours before death, and then acute abdominal pains begin. There is sometimes retching and vomiting. The cry of the kitten is pitiful. The breathing becomes labored and gasping.

The disease usually affects kittens about one week after birth, and the kittens continue to die over a two-week period until all are dead.

I would attempt to have the kittens treated even though the chances of success are low. Vitamin K injections are given to help prevent internal hemorrhaging. Blood transfusions are used to try to build up resistance to the infection; there are blood-building vitamins that can be given; and the kittens must be force-fed.

It is believed that kittens acquire this infection while passing through the vagina at birth. The herpes virus is not in any way related to feline distemper. Usually kittens older than three weeks will not die from it but will go through mild symptoms of the infection. Most deaths occur up to fourteen days after birth. Postmortem examination shows areas of hemorrhage in the liver, lungs, and kidneys. At present there is no vaccine for the prevention of the virus.

Some breeders advise the use of normal feline serum to help suppress the herpes virus in suspected cases—given to queens a week before they kitten and to the kittens soon after birth. This serum will not affect an already established infection but might prevent one from getting started. Antibiotics, such as Terramycin and Chloromycetin, can be used. They are not especially beneficial in fighting the virus but they do help against secondary infections.

Blood Infection

This bacterial infection in the bloodstream can occur when the kitten is between four and forty days old. It is usually contracted from the queen or the environment. The symptoms are crying and bloating. Uusually the kitten is dead within eighteen hours.

The kitten should be taken from the queen and given medical help, but if it lives it is likely to have kidney damage.

The only cure is preventive medicine. Always examine the queen's vagina and the stud before breeding. A blister that resembles a cold sore may be carrying the germs which will affect the vaginal tract at the time of delivery. In suspected cases, a human douche solution at half strength may be used on the queen just prior to breeding.

Other Causes of Death in Kittens

There are congenital defects in kittens related to the digestive, respiratory, and circulatory systems. Heart defects show up much as in human babies. If a kitten dies from a congenital defect it must be recognized, and the queen or stud responsible should be eliminated from further breeding. At the next breeding substitute another stud.

Signs of a Sick Kitten

It is of the utmost importance to spot a kitten in the very early stages of sickness because an hour, even minutes, can mean the difference between life and death. Some signs of sickness are:

1. Rejection by the mother. Instinct seems to tell the queen when a kitten is sick and she usually pushes it aside. If such a kitten is discovered in time it might be saved.

2. Cessation of nursing. When a kitten does not nurse, something is wrong. If it is merely that the kitten needs to be taught how, this should be done, or the kitten should be nursed by hand.

3. Crying. Crying means help is needed; the kitten is either hungry or sick. A quiet, sleeping kitten is usually a healthy one.

4. Weakness or limpness. It is easy to spot vigorous, healthy kittens by their quick movements from the moment they start to wriggle about. A sickly kitten moves slowly and with great effort.

5. Dehydration. Normally the skin of a kitten is resilient. When the skin is pulled and does not bounce back into place, you can be sure that the body is being depleted of fluids. This could indicate lack of nourishment, diarrhea, or a disease.

6. Pale gums. A kitten's gums should be pink or reddish pink. Pale gums indicate mal-

nutrition—insufficient food or parasites—or a disease.

7. Dark-tinted skin. A dark red or bluish tint to the skin indicates disease. The skin of a kitten's abdomen should be pink; reddish blue means trouble.

8. Bloat. A bloated kitten—one with a pot-belly—may mean constipation, parasites, or inadequate milk intake. The constipation could be a congenital deformity at the anus (atresia). A surgical procedure can be performed by your veterinarian to save the kitten. If the bloated condition is caused by parasites, your veterinarian will worm the kitten and the condition will disappear. If the kitten is not getting adequate nourishment it should be fed by hand.

9. Diarrhea. I would estimate that intestinal disturbances are the greatest cause of fatalities in kittens. Unless the diarrhea is checked immediately, dehydration and death follow quickly. Mucus in the stools, with blood, could indicate roundworms or hookworms.

Kitten Disorders

Digestive Troubles

One of the most common digestive problems seen in young kittens is colic-like pains after feeding. These can be caused by the milk itself, eating too fast, or irregular bowel movements due to constipation or diarrhea.

Colic is usually caused by an infection of the bowels, such as enteritis; the symptoms are acute intestinal spasms which cause the kitten to cry pitifully, and usually vomiting and loose and fetid stools.

Mild enemas and milk of magnesia are sometimes beneficial. When there is severe pain, a drop of paregoric every half hour will give relief until the spasms stop. If a kitten has diarrhea, a drop of bismuth or Kaopectate is helpful.

Sometimes constipation results from having an absentminded mother. It is her duty to lick the anuses of her kittens to stimulate elimination.

Nutritional Anemia

This causes death in 40 to 100 percent of some litters, usually when the kittens are ten to thirteen days old. The most obvious symptom is pale mucous membranes.

The best treatment is to prevent the ailment. This is done by keeping the queen in good health during gestation, usually with adequate quantities of liver and iron. If the mother tends to be anemic, her kittens will suffer from a similar affliction. This disease can be spotted by the veterinarian in his prenatal examination of the queen, and he will advise proper supplements before the kittens are born.

Impetigo

This skin infection develops in kittens at least a week old and reveals itself as puffy blisters on the body. The condition is caused by staphylococcus bacteria which have infected the mammary glands of the queen or her vagina. The kittens subsequently become infected when nursing or coming in contact with their mother's vaginal discharge.

Since the lesions are very infectious, the infected kittens should be washed thoroughly with an antiseptic soap and the sores treated with an antibiotic ointment. In severe cases the kittens should be put on oral antibiotics to prevent a generalized blood infection.

At the same time, the queen should be treated to prevent reinfection of the kittens.

Eye Trouble

The kittens' eyes should begin to open when they are seven to ten days old. The lids part first at the inner corner and gradually slit open to the outside. If they don't open, there may be a pus formation.

The best treatment for an eye infection is an antibiotic ointment, such as neomycin or bacitracin. A layer of ointment should be gently worked in across the lids two or three times a day. This will soften the lids so that they can be parted at the inner corner and drained.

If the eyes are neglected, the kitten's sight could be lost or impaired for life.

However, do not attempt to force the eyelids open too soon. The mother often stimulates the eyelids to part by licking her kittens' faces.

There is an eye infection which is now thought to be contracted from a queen with infectious vaginitis. The eyes redden and become swollen; in severe cases the eyeball is completely covered with pus.

If the kittens are not treated quickly, the eyes can become permanently damaged. Even death can result. Your veterinarian has antibiotics and medication for quick alleviation of the infection.

Prolapse of the Rectum

This is seen in kittens with severe diarrhea and is due to strain. The first step in treatment is stopping the diarrhea—getting to the cause. See Chapter 15 for a further discussion.

Declawing Young Kittens

Much public sentiment is against declawing cats. However, in some households it is a necessity to avoid destruction to curtains, furniture, and other expensive household objects.

There are some breeders and veterinarians who advise declawing kittens from three to fourteen days of age. They claim it is less painful at such a young age, very similar to tail docking and declawing young puppies.

Usually only the front feet are operated on. The surgery is performed under a gas anesthetic by the veterinarian. The kittens are again nursing their mother in ten to fifteen minutes. Within a few days the paws are completely healed.

There is an occasional case of a cannibalistic queen who would eat her kittens if they were operated on under three days of age. Therefore three- to ten-day-old kittens are the best subjects for this surgery.

Instincts and Behavior of Kittens: Week by Week

The *first week* is completely devoted to sleeping and eating.

At *two weeks* the kittens are roaming around the box, snuggling up to one another, and having friendly little fights. Still half blind, they're exploring their new world.

By *three weeks* their senses are obviously beginning to function, and they start to perceive the existence of humans. It would be a poor beginning for them if they were handled roughly or subjected to frightening or loud noises at this point.

Between the *third and fourth weeks* the kittens start manipulating their wobbly legs, and this is when they begin to learn the difference between the nest and the papers. They dislike being in their own excrement and will use another part of the box for urination and defecation.

After *four weeks* they are able to learn and feel happy or unhappy about their environment.

After *six weeks* there should be gradual weaning and the kittens should learn to eat from a dish. If they are being well fed and the queen has lots of milk (as is often the case in small litters), they will probably be reluctant to cooperate. A formula such as that for orphaned kittens should be enough to tempt them away from their mother.

By *eight weeks* they should be on a full outside diet without help from their mother. To teach a kitten to lap milk, dip a finger into the milk bowl and give it to the kitten to suck. The close proximity of your finger to the milk bowl will lead the kitten to drink. It may walk into the bowl, but it will manage to clean itself, possibly with the help of its mother. (See weaning chart, page 27.)

Socialization and Transition

The critical period in any kitten's life, according to most breeders, occurs between the ages of twenty-one days and four months. This is the time the "socialization" temperament develops.

Kittens raised under cattery conditions with little human contact will tend to show fear reactions in later life. However, if they are handled by humans around the time they are six weeks of age, this tendency to shyness can be averted. If they are not handled until they are twelve weeks old, it will be quite difficult to socialize them.

At six weeks, when the kitten has entered its learning age, it needs daily periods of socialization with humans. It should be handled, played with, and treated as an individual.

With daily attention, when the kitten finally leaves the litter for good to go to a new home it will know how to be responsive to its owner. This is a traumatic change and it should be made as gentle a transition as possible.

New kittens in the household should be handled gently. They are much more highly strung than dogs and hate loud noises and sudden motions. They startle easily, so speak softly to them. Don't rush them. Let them examine and explore the house undisturbed. They will usually wander throughout the house deciding whether they want to remain with their new family.

9 · The Old Cat: Geriatrics

General Care · Nutrition · Effects of Aging · Ailments and Diseases · Euthanasia · Getting Another Cat

Today, cats, like people, are living longer. Veterinary medicine and nutrition research have progressed to the point where cats, once considered old at eight to ten years, are now living eighteen to twenty years. A cat's average life span is twelve years, but cats sixteen to twenty are seen daily in veterinary clinics. The oldest cat I have treated was twenty-five years old. The most durable cat on record lived to the amazing age of thirty-four.

Environment is another important factor in longevity; the more sheltered the cat, the greater the possibility of a long life. The completely outdoor cat has to forage for food and combat natural enemies, infections, poisons, and other adverse factors. Its life span averages about six years. Obviously, the outdoor-indoor cat has a better chance for survival; its average span is eight to ten years.

The cat who never leaves the house has the best chance to reach old age; its average life span is fifteen years—provided that it gets adequate exercise. This cat's greatest threat is the overzealous owner who overfeeds to the point of obesity. This can lower the life expectancy. A lean cat generally lives longer than a fat one.

And one of the most important ingredients for long feline life expectancy is human relations. A happy home, companionship, and security can add years to the life of a cat.

What You Can Do for Your Older Cat

As old age creeps up on your cat, you will notice diminishing vigor in every activity. And there may be some inconveniences to you and your family, such as a wet spot on the rug once in a while and having to prepare special diets, but such things are a small price to pay for all the years of love and loyalty. As a senior citizen, the cat is entitled to special considerations.

It is important to be aware that older cats should be kept in a warm place, free from drafts, because with advancing age they are more susceptible to diseases and colds. Also, they are more sensitive to hot weather and should be kept comfortable, in a shaded area, or better still, in an air-conditioned house, to keep the respiratory system and the heart from being overtaxed by heat and humidity.

Rest, quiet, and privacy are what an old cat wants most. However, if you move an outside cat inside in old age, be sure to provide some safe indoor recreational facilities such as a scratching post, a stepladder to run up and down, or a "perching tree," and toys to provide diversion in the transition period.

It is normal for the aging cat to take longer rests after play exercise. If your cat is not overweight, it is probably exercising as much as it needs to. Exercise is good for an older cat, but in moderation.

Nutrition for the Aging Cat

As the cat advances in age, feed it smaller and more frequent meals, but less in total daily intake. A certain amount of finickiness may develop. But go ahead—spoil your aging cat.

As a cat gets older, its ability to assimilate food diminishes. Fried, greasy, spicy, and salty foods should be avoided. Any sudden change in diet will upset its digestion. Chicken, lamb, and beef seem to be the foods most easily digested by the aging cat. Introduce some greenery such as leafy vegetables into the diet if possible. It aids digestion and bowel elimination. Raw red meat and crunchy hard foods are also good. (See also Chapter 12.)

Obesity

Sometimes obesity is due to heredity, but cats who love to eat are the ones who are most prone to overweight in old age. It is during middle age that they begin to show signs of an overfat condition.

Watch the weight of the cat after middle age. Each cat requires a different amount of food to maintain weight and health, and its diet should be adjusted to its general activity and emotional condition (for example, high-strung cats usually require more food than passive, lethargic ones).

Once a cat is overweight, reducing is difficult. It is much easier and healthier to prevent this condition. Overweight predisposes the older cat to heart trouble, constipation, skin infection, and general lethargy. Overeating is one of the greatest causes of shortened life.

Vitamins

If an old cat seems thin or its fur dry and brittle, you should change its diet. Milk and eggs may be added to help maintain weight. Vitamins are beneficial to the aging cat, though they may not live up to such claims as "youth pills" and "cell rejuvenation" vitamins. There are special pet vitamins, and your veterinarian will be able to advise you on types and dosage. Vitamin E, vitamin C, vitamin B_{12}, and hormones have been proven beneficial to the geriatric cat. Vitamin E has generally been credited with increasing life span, improving skin and fur, and prolonging fertility and sexual stamina. It can be found in wheat-germ cereal and wheat-germ oil, or in capsule form.

Hormones

With age, the muscles weaken. Artificial hormones can help muscle tone and general metabolism and contribute to overall well-being.

Vitamin-hormone preparations are available in wafer, liquid, or powder form. Added to the cat's food, they indeed help maintain and prolong all the vital bodily functions. I endorse the normal use of hormones in an old cat, but only on the advice of a veterinarian, as misuse will upset the balance of nature and can cause uterine infections in the female, prostate infection in the male cat.

Effects of Aging

Cats quickly become fixed in their habits and are easily upset by change. In their old age especially, they are geared to daily routine, and any deviation may annoy them. They might become irritable and hiss occasionally. Be patient with these old folks and remember the days when they did everything to please.

Physical Changes

With age, the hair around the muzzle begins to whiten. The nerves and muscles of the hind legs are the first to show signs of deterioration. Sometimes there is partial paralysis of the rear legs due to arthritis of the spine, or generalized arthritis or rheumatism. The vital organs—heart, liver, kidneys—begin to show less efficient functioning. General stress and the wear and tear of living cause this deterioration. If any vital organ has been damaged or diseased, there will be a general deterioration in the functioning and structure of the organ, and the life of the animal will be shortened.

I advise that you arrange a checkup for your cat every six months once it has begun to show signs of age. The veterinarian can then discover in time what may be necessary to keep the animal healthy and alive.

Loss of Hearing

One of the first senile changes is loss of hearing—usually before sight and smell. The cat will have difficulty detecting the source of sounds and will hear higher-pitched sounds, such as whistles, more clearly than voice commands.

A veterinarian should be consulted because, sometimes, with proper treatment and care, hearing can be prolonged. There may be a heavy coating of wax plugging the ear canal, or ear mites or an infection may be causing loss of hearing.

As the cat becomes deaf there will be more reliance on sight and smell—and on the whiskers, which act as another vital aid to a cat's sensory perception.

Loss of Sight

Quite often a cat's eyesight begins to fail soon after the onset of deafness. The cat will come to rely more and more on its ability to find its way around familiar surroundings and will not want to be disturbed.

With the dimming of vision, there will be a bluish-gray color in the eyes, usually caused by cataracts. In a dimly lighted room, the cat may bump into objects. Cataract eye surgery is often practical and many a blind cat has had its eyesight thus restored.

Actually, a totally blind cat can get along surprisingly well as long as it is with its family in a familiar environment.

Loss of Hair (Alopecia)

Sometimes as cats get older they lose their hair on their undersides and the upper parts of the legs. The hair disappears and only a fuzz remains. There is no skin infection or irritation. This condition is due to a glandular or hormonal loss. With an injection of geriatric hormones there will be a gradual restoration of hair growth and glossiness.

Teeth

The teeth of old cats need regular attention. Tartar should be removed, as well as loose and defective teeth; they can lead to serious infections of the teeth and gums. Close observation and regular checkups will reveal any conditions that should be treated.

There is an old saying that when the teeth go, the rest will soon follow. Good oral hygiene is necessary to maintain and preserve the teeth and gums throughout the cat's life, and especially in old age.

Ailments and Diseases

Because the old cat has less resistance to ailments and diseases, and recovery time is slower, prevention is essential. Periodic examination by a veterinarian will detect many ailments and diseases in the earliest stages, and proper treatment can be instituted.

Signs in an old cat which warrant veterinary consultation are:

□ Increased respiration (rapid breathing) with shortness of breath (heart trouble)
□ Coughing (congestive heart failure)
□ Fainting spells, collapse, or paralysis (heart attack, cerebral stroke)
□ Increased thirst and urination (nephritis)
□ Halitosis (bad breath and poor gums)
□ Urine odor from the mouth (possibly uremia)

Old cats have many of the sicknesses that plague their owners. Cancer is common in the older cat, and the tumors enlarge with advancing age. Kidney and heart diseases, liver and pancreatic ailments are also widespread.

According to a recent survey of veterinary clinics, cancer was the leading cause of death in cats. Surprisingly, there was not one case of lung cancer. Kidney ailments and diseases came next—17 percent of the total.

There is no reason why an older cat cannot be operated on, especially with the latest techniques in anesthesia. Of course, surgery in an old cat does entail certain risks, but you can rely on the judgment of your veterinarian, who will guide you through these trying years. The cat need not suffer undue pain because of your apprehension about surgery.

Constipation

Constipation is a fairly common ailment in older cats. It is caused by lack of exercise and changes in metabolism. It is a simple condition to prevent and can lead to many problems if not cleared up.

Such foods as bran, liver, and cooked vegetables have a laxative effect and should be added to an older cat's diet. Too many bones and too much dry food impede elimination.

If a laxative is needed, milk of magnesia (one teaspoon) is both gentle and effective. I do not advise mineral oil; it retards the absorption of food from the digestive tract. When necessary, a mild enema (see page 152) may be given to an older cat. The bowels should move daily for complete freedom from complications.

The Kidneys

As the cat ages, there is a gradual degeneration of the kidney tissue along with a lessening of the kidney functioning which is so vital for life. Although this is a normal process, it is aggravated by specific diseases such as nephritis, cystitis, prostatitis, or possibly stones in the bladder or kidney. Kidney diseases occur in about 76 percent of cats over ten to twelve years of age.

In an old spayed female, dribbling of the urine can be controlled fairly easily with female hormones. With an altered male, male hormones are helpful.

Kidney disease is kept under control by adjusting the diet to cut down on certain proteins and by providing more water. An older cat should be expected to consume two or three times more water than a younger cat.

The diet in an old cat with diseased kidneys is very important. High-protein animal meats seem to be detrimental to diseased kidneys. Foods with salt and spices should be avoided, as should ham and bacon. The kidney patient needs a low-quantity but high-quality protein diet, and suitable scientifically prepared prescription diets can be obtained from your veterinarian. However, some cats do not find these prepared diets palatable, so the owner must look for an alternative. Cottage cheese and eggs are good sources of high-quality protein, as are lamb and chicken. Cooked oatmeal or rice, flavored to taste, provides extra nourishment.

Although the cat loves the high-protein foods and has been eating them all its life, a change has to be made because of their deteriorating effect on the kidney tissue.

Heart Disease

Clinical heart disease is found in about 10 percent of the older feline population. Many of these animals develop congestive heart failure. With the advances in veterinary medicine and the advent of adequate heart therapy, and with the help of a controlled diet, the effects of heart failure in many cats have been reduced and their lives have been prolonged.

Exercise and excitement should be kept to a minimum. When excitement is anticipated, such as friends coming to visit, either put the cat in a quiet place or administer a tranquilizer. Tranquilizers for your cat must be prescribed by your veterinarian.

The heart patient suffers greatly in hot weather or high humidity. When the days are hot, let a cat with a heart condition outside only early in the morning and late at night. Getting such a cat through a hot summer is difficult; complete rest in an air-conditioned room is helpful.

Weight and diet control are extremely important, and low-sodium diets are essential for preventing hypertension in heart patients. Prepared prescription diets can be purchased from your veterinarian, but there are also many foods that the owner can prepare (see page 173).

Tumors

Constantly observe the older cat for small tumors. Any lump or growth should be examined by a veterinarian; early detection and surgery can often save your cat's life.

Mammary tumors grow markedly after the heat period because of the excessive female hormones in the bloodstream. Many veterinarians treat the tumors with male hormones. At best, the hormones merely slow the growth of the tumors and do not cure them. A mammary tumor should be removed as soon as it is discovered; any delay will let it continue to grow and spread to the point where other organs are affected and surgical intervention may be impossible.

Other Ailments and Diseases
Female Irregularities

As the unspayed female approaches old age, she should be checked frequently. If there is any abnormality in her heat cycle, take her to a veterinarian.

Prostatitis

Prostatitis is an infection and enlargement of the prostate gland in older male cats. It gives rise to painful symptoms—the cat might appear stiff-legged and show fever and pain. There will be frequent trips to the litter box, but merely a dribble of urine will appear. It should be dealt with quickly by a veterinarian, who will decide whether the condition can be controlled with hormones or whether castration is necessary.

Arthritis

Stiffness in the hindquarters is an early sign of approaching old age and usually indicates arthritis. This painful chronic ailment of the bones and joints is still without a cure, but drugs containing cortisone can reduce the pain to a minimum. A warm bed close to food and a litter box can make life quite comfortable for such afflicted cats.

Rheumatism or Rheumatoid Arthritis

Since rheumatism is usually aggravated by cold, damp living quarters, a soft bed in a warm area free from drafts is the best medicine. Vitamin C and steroids can reduce the pain.

Distemper

For many years it was erroneously thought that older cats were not susceptible to the virus of distemper. It has been found that booster shots are necessary because old cats can contract a mild form of the disease. The symptoms of distemper are: loss of hair, apathy, weight loss, poor appetite, and complications in the brain, with neurological damage. Your veterinarian can confirm any suspicion of distemper with certain laboratory tests.

Parasites

An old cat is susceptible to worms, which can be very debilitating, so this should be part of the six-month checkup. The most common parasite in the older cat is the tapeworm. (See Chapter 16.)

Shock

Any stress condition, traumatic event, or even surgery or anesthesia can produce shock in an old animal. This is why the veterinarian is cautious about advising surgery. However, with the improvement in anesthetics and with blood transfusions and oxygen infusions, many older cats can be prevented from going into shock during surgery.

Euthanasia: A Quiet and Painless Death

The right to end the suffering of a loved one, human or otherwise, has long been argued. I am constantly asked, "What would you do if it were your cat?" It is a difficult and haunting question. If my cat faced a life of unrelieved and inevitable suffering, I must say that I would choose for it a quiet and painless death.

Unfortunately, some people make the decision hastily or cold-bloodedly. It is heartbreaking when these people—and there are many more of them than you might suppose—thrust a sick animal at me and say, "Put it out of its misery." It is *their* misery—and inconvenience—that they are so anxious to be rid of. Their first concern is not for the cat. Many of these cats, with proper care and treatment, could have many more happy years of life.

There are those people for whom a cat is a beloved friend and companion, who suffer dreadfully when confronted with such a decision. These people, who have a special kinship with their cats, will do everything in their power to save the life of their pet. After all, a cat can lead a good life with one leg amputated, with the sight gone from an eye or the hearing from an ear, with a cranky heart or even a toothless jaw. What such a cat requires is just a little more love and care. So long as the cat is near its loved ones and is not suffering, I do not advise euthanasia.

However, I firmly believe that any animal that is diseased beyond hope and with no prospect of relief from suffering should be allowed out of its misery. There are many cases that cannot be benefited; in the case of advanced cancer or some other incurable disease, the decision should definitely be to put the animal to sleep.

I put several cats a week to sleep in my clinic. These animals are suffering, with no hope of cure, and so I help the owners make the decision. It is the decision I least enjoy in my practice; however, there are some people who cannot make the decision themselves, and so they seek my guidance.

The two questions I ask myself are: Is the cat undergoing undue suffering that cannot be relieved? Is the cat no longer enjoying life? If the answers are obviously unfavorable, then I wholeheartedly advise euthanasia, which is literally going to sleep while the lethal dose is injected into a vein. There is no pain, no struggle, and the cat has no knowledge of what is happening.

For those of you who are faced with this decision, it is very important to be objective—to overcome feelings of self-pity and self-reproach—and put the cat first. Even though you and your veterinarian may be able to keep the pet alive a few days, or weeks, or even months longer with life-sustaining drugs and force-feeding, the animal must not be kept alive to pamper selfish human emotions. It should be allowed to go—with dignity.

Getting Another Cat

Sometimes grieving owners claim that they will not replace their cats. I know that it hurts to bring a new kitten into the house while still mourning for another, but I try to reason that the loss of a cat should not prevent getting another—in fact, the sooner, the better.

One can soon learn to love another animal, maybe not in the same way, but all animals are individuals and they all have their own wonderful ways and quickly become an integral part of the family.

Part 2
Personality, Intelligence, and Behavior

10 · Instinct and Intelligence in the Normal Cat

Personality · Instincts · The Senses · Intelligence · Behavioral Influences · Principles of Training Your Cat

Just as with people, no two cats are exactly alike (even identical-twin littermates); there are always differences in features, traits, temperament, personality, intelligence, and certainly in behavior. This chapter will tell you what is known about what goes on in those splendid heads, beyond those inscrutable eyes.

Though you may have heard from numerous "authorities" such generalizations as "Mixed breeds are smarter than pedigreed cats" or "One breed is smarter than others," none of them is true. Every degree of intelligence and every personality type can be found in every breed and mixture. Your cat's intelligence and personality depend in part on heredity and in part on the treatment it receives from you.

Personality

In a group of cats we usually see almost every personality type and temperament: the leader, the follower, the brave cat, the coward, the sly, the dumb, the friendly, the timid, and, of course, the bully.

The cat's personality and temperament are the sum total of physical, mental, emotional, and social characteristics as modified by instinct, experience, and training in early kittenhood. Proper training and a favorable environment usually produce a cat with a pleasant personality and an even temperament.

Cats are not cold and disdainful. They thoroughly appreciate companionship with humans and other animals. When human love is not available they become wild. Also, contrary to popular belief, they are more attached to a person than to a place. They know when they are really loved and understood and have many ways of communicating their desires and feelings. Cats do not show affection like dogs. They are more subtle about being demonstrative. They show affection by rubbing against your ankle or hand. They love to have their ears or chin scratched. They also show affection by purring.

True, they are intensely self-centered. This makes them independent, self-reliant, dignified, and resourceful. People not kindly disposed to them call them disobedient, arrogant, fickle, unpredictable, and ungrateful. But they walk tall—they are proud. They will not allow themselves to be abused or mistreated in exchange for a favor. Probably no other animal, in its association with man, has so completely maintained its indomitable freedom and independence as the domestic cat. Its devotion is voluntary and cannot be commanded.

The Language of Cats

A cat emits an astonishing jumble of purrs, mews, growls, chirrups, wails, squawks, howls, spits, and gurgles. They all signify something—anger, affection, discomfort, contentment, desire, or hunger.

Cats can communicate with their eyes, their ears, their tail, their fur, and with their whole body.

The cat's tail is a barometer of its emotional ups and downs. A contented cat carries its tail high and lets it droop when feeling dissatisfied. A twitching tail is ambiguous; it may indicate either satisfaction or annoyance. When the cat wags its tail, beware. It is getting angry. Crouched low with the tail straight behind, the cat is stalking.

When a cat flattens its ears against its head, it is angry. When it pricks its ears forward, it is alert and expectant.

Rubbing its whiskers against your leg shows affection. Arching its back with fur raised means hostility.

98

Purring, is still a mystery. Cats purr when they are contented but occasionally when they are in pain. Once thought to come from the larynx, purring is now believed to come from vibrations in the chest cavity.

It is important for us to understand the moods and gestures of our cats so that we can respond to them properly.

Instincts

Your cat has many curious and unique instincts which are a legacy from its wild ancestry. In reality you have a breath of the wild in your home, still retaining traces of the days when its ancestors roamed the woods, matching wits with prey and predators.

One of the basic instincts and the most important for the well-being of kittens is the maternal instinct, which I have discussed in the chapter on whelping. One aspect of this is the care-giving and grooming instinct. Cats, especially mother cats, will sometimes engage in an advanced type of social behavior, combing for fleas or foxtails either in the young or in their human family. Some cats show affection by nibbling on their owner's arm or leg. Males exhibit this more often; the tom also nibbles the queen's neck during the mating ritual.

The Suckling Instinct

This, of course, is a strong instinct. If the kittens are not suckled by their mother, a substitute must be provided. It is best to use a bottle with a small hole in the nipple so the kittens will have to work to get the milk. If a kitten is not allowed to suck, a non-nutritional suckling habit will often develop and persist in later life.

The Kneading Instinct

The kneading instinct, or "making bread," is familiar to all cat owners. Kneading usually signifies excitement when emotionally aroused by a favorite person, another cat, a stimulating smell, or an interesting fabric texture. This instinct is first seen in newborn kittens, who knead their mother's breast to stimulate the flow of milk while sucking.

The Sexual Instinct

Originally, in the wild state, cats usually were monogamous and stayed with their own mates. Today, however, not unlike their human counterparts, male cats play the gallant to every queen in heat, even complete strangers.

The Hunting Instinct

Do not scold your cat when it brings you a dead bird or a baby rabbit. It is actually showing you what a fine hunter it is and is giving you a present. The cat has always been a highly specialized predator and no amount of domestication will change this instinct. Its hearing, sight, retractile claws, strength, speed, sense of balance, and homing abilities are the factors which make it such a great hunter.

Killing birds. This may be a serious concern for some cat owners. However, punishment is not effective, since the desire to hunt is instinctive. Throwing things or hitting a cat does not deter it from hunting. The best way of dealing with the problem is prevention.

A mother cat teaches her young kittens to hunt by bringing small prey to the litter, and as they get older she will take them on hunting expeditions. It is known that kittens born from queens who are not hunters are less likely to become hunters themselves. So if the mother cat is a hunter, you might try remov-

ing the kittens from the litter before the hunting age arrives, which is about eight weeks.

The most commonly used preventive devices are bells attached to the cat's collar. However, there are some ingenious cats who can still catch birds even with their bells on.

The Homing Instinct

The outdoor cat, when hunting for food for her young, must be able to find her way back to her kittens. Her homing instinct is thus a vital part of her equipment.

The Territorial Instinct

A house cat usually has a favorite spot in the house. This is its particular territory although it roams the entire house.

Outdoor cats have a home-territorial range which they cover daily. Clawing or scraping bark off trees is one way these cats show the neighborhood felines that this is their territory. Odors from the paws are transferred to the trees so that curious marauding cats know whose domain they are invading. The tree bark is further "personalized" by urination or spraying.

The Perching Instinct

Cats usually like to lie in high places where they can relax and sleep in comfort without having to worry about enemies.

The Senses

Smell

The sense of smell plays an important role in the social life of a cat as well as in its survival. Odor perception is a natural survival mechanism which helps cats avoid larger predatory animals, find their own food, and communicate with other cats. Scent glands are present on the side of the cat's head, and when it rubs its head against objects and people, it leaves a scent as a mark of possession—or love and affection. The cat's nose is a very sensitive organ—even the slightest amount of strange odor will bring an immediate reaction from the cat. Newborn kittens have many inherited sensory instincts but they are born without knowledge of all the complex odors around them. Throughout its life the cat continues to learn new odors through contact and association. If a cat has a bad experience with an odor, it will respond by avoidance.

The nose is the smallest part of the cat's sensory system. The internal part of the organs of scent are much more important and are located inside the nasal sinuses and on the palate behind the upper incisor teeth. This is why a cat will open its mouth to enhance its sense of smell.

Hearing

The fact that the cat's ears are relatively large, erect, and highly sensitive is a tremendous asset for survival. Research indicates that cats may be able to hear sounds beyond the acute range of dogs. They certainly hear far more than humans do. The cat turns its head toward the source of the sound and either cocks its head from side to side or tips its ears forward or backward to pinpoint the angle and direction of the sound.

Sight

The cat is blessed with extremely keen eyesight. As in the case of hearing, the cat's eyesight greatly exceeds that of humans. It has been proven that cats see ultraviolet rays and other kinds of light which humans are unable to see. It is not true that cats can see in total darkness, but their pupils dilate so widely in darkness that they can see fairly well in light so dim that a human would be helpless in it. The highly sensitive eyesight of the cat is also affected by very bright light and the pupils narrow to a very thin slit to protect the eyes. Bright lights are not favored by cats; they prefer shade and semi-darkness.

When a cat turns its head for best sound reception, the eyes also focus in the same direction; both hearing and eyesight are very well coordinated.

Cats are color blind; they can see only shades of black and white and distinguish degrees of brightness. They can see small forms and usually can differentiate between triangles, squares, and circles.

Taste

Cats have a keen sense of taste. The cat's tongue can distinguish four basic qualities of taste—sweet, sour, salt, and bitter. They are not as fond of sweet-tasting foods as most other pets are.

Balance

The cat has a remarkable sense of balance and equilibrium. It is commonly known that a falling cat has the ability to turn right side up in midair. It rotates its hindquarters ahead of its forequarters, and with a twist of its strong tail, drops lightly on all four paws with grace and ease. However, I must stress that a cat cannot usually survive a four- or five-story fall, and no one should ever experiment with a cat's sense of balance.

Other Physical Equipment

Whiskers. The long whiskers of the cat are sensitive tactile feelers which supplement its nocturnal vision and keen sense of smell, enabling it to prowl about in complete darkness. Of course, cutting or trimming the whiskers is both cruel and injurious to the cat.

Claws. The cat is provided with strong, needle-sharp claws for climbing and for hooking and holding. When not in use, the claws are retracted into protective sheaths. However, they can be released instantaneously when needed. (Some declawed cats continue to go through the motions of claw extension and retracting exercises. They are attempting to keep their hunting and climbing muscles in good trim even though they have no nails.) When dirt or other foreign matter gets embedded in a nail, the cat dislodges it by drawing its claws across a tree trunk, a chair, or any other handy object. Scratching removes the frayed and worn nails, leaving a sharp new claw underneath. Cats may also remove the worn outer claws with their teeth. Scratching is a natural, healthy instinct—the cat does not do it to displease its owner. For suggested remedies for the problems of scratching in indoor cats, see pages 103–105.

Muscles. The cat's muscles are remarkably strong and the leg muscles are especially powerful. It is not considered extraordinary for a ten-pound cat to leap over a six-foot fence to escape a pursuer. And the muscular movements of the cat are lightning fast. When chased by a dog, the cat can sprint at an incredible speed in quest of safety.

Intelligence

There is growing controversy between psychologists and cat owners over whether performances of cats are the result of training or indicate intelligence, reasoning power, and judgment. I am not a psychologist, but there is much evidence that convinces me that many cats have a high degree of intelligence. Psychologists contend that as cat training mostly involves repetition, cats learn only by conditioned reflexes. But I have seen many cats show judgment in thoughtfully appraising certain situations and then carefully taking the correct course of action.

It is not fair to compare the intelligence of various species of animals. Some animals are better adapted than others to a particular terrain, climate, way of life, or role. For instance, cats are better adapted to tree climbing, but this cannot be considered a measure of intelligence.

In comparative tests with other animals, the cat does not rate very high because it simply will not cooperate in this type of research. The conventional intelligence test consistently underrates the cat because the cat considers it just plain nonsense.

The cat's ability to survive under stress shows a high degree of intelligence, more than purely instinctive reaction. Even an apartment cat thrown out into the wilderness can somehow survive the elements and predators.

There are some who maintain that cats never consciously think about their actions, but rather are motivated purely by instinct. I do not agree. Cats demonstrate their intelligence in a number of ways. They are ingenious and inventive in the use of their paws—rapping on doors, opening doors, operating gadgets, knocking telephone receivers off the hook. Learning to cooperate with other cats in joint ventures such as hunting is a sure sign of intelligence.

Although cats cannot read clocks, there is no doubt that they possess the ability to know what time of day it is. At one time I lived in the top floor of a high-rise apartment building in New York City. My wife could tell the time I was to return in the evening by our cat, Hosea. Every day, five minutes before I was to arrive, Hosea yawned, stretched, and sauntered over to the door.

Behavioral Influences

Behavior is never wholly inherited or totally acquired but always developed under the combined influences of heredity and environment. The goal in socializing a cat is to produce a well-balanced and well-adjusted animal.

The ideal cat, according to breeders, is self-assured, friendly with people and other cats, with a strong pride in its own intelligence. It is neither overfriendly nor shy.

Each cat is very much an individual and should be regarded and treated as such. If you study your cat's individual traits and reactions, you will be able to train and manage it more effectively. And when you are familiar with your cat's personality and normal behavior patterns, you will be quick to notice the slightest deviations. The normal-behaving cat is usually the happy cat, and the happy cat is the product of your mutual association.

It is difficult to establish a fine line between normal and abnormal behavior in either cats or humans. A docile pet might turn into a ferocious tiger when being combed or having its nails clipped. It would not be considered abnormal behavior if the cat were to bite the owner in these circumstances. This is a normal reaction to grooming. Usually the pet wins the battle, and the fur does not get combed, nor the nails cut.

Prenatal Influences

Research has shown that prenatal environmental influences can affect the behavior of kittens. When the mother is handled gently during pregnancy, the offspring are likely to be more docile and less easily upset by sudden disturbances in the environment. On the other hand, certain drugs given to the pregnant cat can alter the behavior of the offspring, and it has been demonstrated experimentally that administering electric shock to pregnant queens results in the birth of overexcitable kittens.

The Effect of Normal Handling on Kittens

A kitten should be handled as early as possible. During the first six weeks the mother usually provides all the food, warmth, and love that a kitten needs. The pattern of kitten behavior is sleeping, eating, and playing. At the end of that time the kitten becomes receptive to the outside world, and begins to learn. The treatment that the kitten receives from humans between six and eight weeks is likely to influence its temperament as an adult. Emotional stress at this time—such as long separations from the mother, being roughly handled or frightened by strangers, loud noises, or being left in a strange location—might have a detrimental effect on the kitten's personality.

From the sixth to the eighth week the kitten begins to investigate the outside world. It learns to recognize the scents and the voices of the human beings with whom it comes into daily contact and also learns to recognize other animals. Most kittens raised under cattery conditions, with little human contact, will show fear reactions to people at six weeks. However, if the kittens are handled within the next two weeks this fear will disappear. Kittens who are not handled until after twelve weeks become increasingly timid and may be extremely difficult to teach. They can be trained but will always be more timid and less responsive than those socialized with humans at an earlier age.

The period of investigation usually ends at weaning time, when the kitten is confronted with new problems. It is during this period that the intelligence develops quickly in favorable surroundings. By the time it is four months old a kitten can learn almost anything that is properly taught. Even though its body may be too weak and immature to execute correctly some of the exercises learned at this age, later in life it will show the results of proper early education.

A properly reared kitten is naturally sociable and eager to make friends. It desires gentle handling and will respond favorably by growing up without fear. After weaning, a kitten should be handled by strangers—gently—so that it may learn that there are other gentle human beings. An animal learns by association and repetition. The more often it is exposed to tenderness and love, the more favorable will be its impression of humans. A kitten's basic instinct is to love and be loved. However, if it suffers an unhappy kittenhood its confidence in people could turn to anxiety and distrust. We then have a problem cat.

Principles for Training Your Cat

It must be evident by now that it is impossible to have a thoroughly happy, well-behaved cat without a lot of love, understanding, and a certain amount of discipline.

Patience, kindness, words of praise, and a tidbit will work wonders in discipline and training. It is futile to expect instant obedience from any cat. Cats generally respond to a command only when it is convenient, fun, or profitable.

In reality, your cat will train you to suit its convenience—how it likes its food and what kinds, when it likes to be served and where, and in what part of the house it wishes to sleep, including with you. Cats can train humans amazingly well, and some humans are quick to learn.

Although it can be too early to start training (except for housebreaking and scratching), it is never too late. It *is* possible to teach an old cat new tricks.

In disciplining, a simple "no" with facial expressions of disapproval is generally sufficient. Physical punishment is not only cruel; it will get you nowhere, and you most likely will never be forgiven. Cats do not forgive and forget easily. And since cats have long memories, you must above all be consistent in your requests, responses, and methods so as not to confuse or deceive.

Collars and Leashes

Training a cat to a collar and leash is best started in kittenhood.

A collar can be dangerous to an outdoor cat, as it can get caught on objects. Always be sure the collar is loose enough so that it will slip over the cat's head in an emergency. A collar that stretches is the safest kind.

Since cats fight collars and sometimes get their mouths caught in them, the collar should not be too large.

A bell on a collar is a worthwhile addition for warning birds of the cat's presence. But some cats are so smart that they quickly learn how to move without ringing the bell.

Harnesses are recommended for cats who walk on leashes. They are not as easy to wriggle out of as collars.

Scratching

Since scratching is such a deeply ingrained normal instinct in cats, its distressful consequences in a house full of modern-day furniture, rugs, and draperies are all too familiar to most cat owners. Indeed, scratching is the most common problem faced by cat owners. No amount of scolding or punishment will make this natural tendency go away, but it can be channeled into one source with the proper training. A scratching post is one of the most successful methods of dealing with the problem.

There are many types of posts—from twelve inches high to ones that extend all the way to the ceiling, and many variations with ladders and shelves spaced along the pole. A ball or other toy attached to the post can entertain a cat for hours while allowing it to hit and scratch away all its frustrations.

Drs. Ginger Hamilton and Mollie J. Robbins, consultants in animal psychology, give the following advice on destructive scratching:

WATER DISCIPLINE

There are several techniques which have proven effective in stopping the cat's destruction of furniture and plants, but some of these will not be mentioned since they should not be used in a haphazard manner. For one thing, they could destroy your furniture, and for another, they could destroy your cat. For a grown cat, therefore, attempts to stop this well-ingrained habit should be implemented with caution. The one relatively harmless method we might suggest is the use of a water gun. If your aim is sufficiently good, a squirt of water when the cat is caught in the act could be effective in at least making it think twice before going to that spot again. Cats are not particularly fond of being hit with a stream of water. (*Do not* attempt this same cure with other misbehaviors, such as urinating outside of the litter box. Misapplication of a technique could bring forth other behaviors which are much more difficult to treat. In this case, it could serve to start the cat's eliminating any place in the house, just so long as it is out of your sight—in your shoes or on your bed, for example. Do check your furniture and drapery material for possible resistance to water-spotting prior to initiating even this technique.)

PROPER PROVISIONS FOR SCRATCHING

In whatever manner the animal is discouraged from generalized scratching, it must be provided with a suitable alternative where the behavior is not only permissible but actually promoted. The best way to facilitate the cat's developing the desired association between this or any behavior and the proper object of that behavior is to "catch him in the act" in the wrong place and immediately remove him to the sanctioned area. In this case, the animal is placed on a scratching post. This method is very effective with kittens but it is less effective in changing the behavior of an adult cat who has had years of misdirected experience. Training the kitten to a scratching post is relatively easy, however, and with patient guidance from the owner this will soon become the preferred object.

SCRATCHING POSTS

Good commercial scratching posts are difficult to find. Somehow, they always seem to be built for kittens that are never expected to grow into cats. Many cat owners may purchase scratching posts, and feel that they are well on their way to having a pleasing nondestructive pet, only to find that within a few weeks the kitten has gone elsewhere for stretching exercises, and the scratching post is knocked over in the corner. While outdoor cats find trees quite satisfactory, a scratching post, or something equivalent, is an absolute necessity for proper training of the kitten which is expected to live within the household. If an adequate one cannot be readily purchased, they are relatively easy to build. Some people are skilled in carpentry and build rather elaborate structures. We have found, however, that a quite suitable scratching post can be made by attaching a three-foot length of two-by-four to a base of any flat piece of wood approximately two feet square. Cover both the base and the post with carpet remnants. To place the post on a slant, simply cut the bottom at a 45-degree angle and provide a support at the back between the upper end of the post and the base. The post should rise from a position at one corner, crossing the base diagonally, The completed structure will then fit neatly into a corner.

A scratching post should be available when the kitten is first introduced into the household, and it should immediately become an object of play. The kitten should be taken there several times each day, particularly when there are any indications of scratching. It is also good practice, during the first few weeks, to take the kitten to the scratching post each morning. When cats first awaken, there is usually a period of stretching and other muscle-toning exercises, and a scratching post provides an excellent vehicle for this performance. This procedure serves to exclude the selection of other household objects, which may be expected if the young cat is allowed free choice.

Loving praise and a little tidbit can strengthen the cat's will to please in this aspect of training. Patience, repetition, consistency, and firmness should eventually pay off.

For those owners who end up with a pristine scratching post and frayed household objects and nerves, there are a couple of things to try before resorting to the cure-all—declawing (see page 143).

Some people have had good results with mothballs used as a repellent. These are put into little cloth bags and placed in areas which the cat especially favors for scratching. Mothballs are also spendid flea deterrents, but they should be contained in some way (not available for nibbling on) because they are quite toxic to cats when ingested.

Balloons have also been used with some success. Any piece of furniture especially favored by the cat is adorned with inflated balloons. Curiosity will entice the cat to the balloons; inevitably the cat will stab one with a claw and the resulting explosion usually proves startling enough to get the point across in short order. After such an experience, generally one balloon placed in a strategic spot will indicate to the cat that the area is out of bounds.

Tricks

Cats learn tricks only when they are inclined to do so. Most cats will not bother with tricks unless they are convinced that such goings-on will be worth their while. The cat must be in the mood and the teacher must be loved, loving, interested, interesting, and patient.

Training sessions should be just before mealtime, and should be short and fun—play and rewards should be an integral part.

Any cat who enjoys tricks should be encouraged and trained to its full potential.

In summary:
□ Cats will not be forced, but they will respond to love, persuasion, enticement.
□ Reason with your cat; encourage, do not command or boss.
□ Treat your cat fairly and be liberal with your praise and rewards.
□ Above all, communicate, to your utmost, your love and affection.

11 · Abnormal Behavior

Inherited Nervousness · Physical Disorders · Drugs and Alcohol · Aging · Loneliness · Spraying Behavior · Psychosomatic Ailments · Tranquilizers · Essay

Misbehaviors in Cats, an essay by Ginger Hamilton, Ph.D., and Mollie J. Robbins, Ph.D., Consultants in Animal Psychology

A recent survey indicates behavioral problems in 10 to 20 percent of the cats in our midst. From their primitive ways we have changed their behavior patterns so much that it is small wonder that their difficulties are increasing apace. It appears from the research that a direct relationship exists between the behavior problems of the cats and those of their owners, suggesting that animals may reflect the emotional atmosphere of the household in which they live. There are certain such conditions that can adversely affect a cat's behavior: a tense, stressful family life; owners who are fearful, anxious, extremely noisy, excessively permissive, bored, or overly introverted. If a kitten is reared in an unsuitable environment, in seclusion, or had a bad relationship with its mother, it may be expected to grow up to be unhappy, nervous, and timid. Although there are many cats past the point of remedial help, there are many more with innate or learned objectionable behavior patterns for whom a good deal can be done.

Inherited Nervousness

Although most cases of nervousess are basically due to environmental factors, some cats do inherit the tendency. If a nervous cat was bred from non-nervous parents, then it is fairly certain that the nervousness is environmental. Inherited nervousness should be eliminated from the strain by not allowing such cats to breed; they should be spayed or neutered. Behavioral abnormalities that should be watched for before allowing an animal to breed are: excessive timidity and fear of strangers; refusal to leave a familiar environment; sound, touch, and sight shyness; fear biting; excessive scratching; fear of sudden changes; and excessive activity. Any of these traits would most likely be inherited by the offspring and compounded by exposure to the neurotic queen. The vast majority of offspring of the shy, fear-biting, and scratching queen will be neurotic even though the studs may be normal and friendly creatures. In addition to the direct inheritance of shyness, the behavior of the mother is likely to influence the kittens to react violently to strangers and other disturbing influences. Nor is this shyness overcome by training.

As a general rule, you should not breed nervous cats because that nervousness is transferred through heredity or association. If you must breed a nervous cat, take the kittens away at four weeks of age and hand-feed and hand-raise them (see page 79).

Physical Disorders

When I examine a cat that is brought to me because of abnormal behavior, there are many factors that I consider. We must always investigate the possibility of a physical disorder as a cause of any abnormal behavior before we can say that the cat has a mental problem. I usually give the animal a complete physical checkup, looking for one of the following disorders which can affect behavior: worms, thyroid ailment, spinal disk disorder, poisoning, constipation, diarrhea, urinary ailments, allergic reactions, milk fever in a nursing queen, sex organ malfunction, anal gland infection. Diseases such as rabies, spinal meningitis, distemper, and epilepsy also could be causes. Brain tumors, abscesses, ear mites, and such traumatic events as a blow to the head or an inner-ear infection can cause abnormal behavior and affect a cat's temperament. I have seen cats with head injuries undergo loss of social and sexual drives, complete lethargy, and regress to kitten habits and even further back to the point of primitive, wild feline behavior.

You should be aware that any changes in the normal behavior of your cat could indicate that something is wrong. When a cat is sick it often becomes hostile to the people it loves. It can even become angry and act like a wild animal. However, we have to confess that we ourselves have a tendency to act the same way when we have a headache, a fever, or a gnawing pain.

Cats seem to have a low threshold for pain and high sensitivity to discomfort or illness. This is why your cat will run away from you and hide. The cat is scared and wishes to be left alone. In the wild, cats either get well or die. Fortunately, an alert cat owner can seek professional help, and should do so as quickly as possible. After elimination of the organic problem, the abnormal behavior generally clears up.

The Effect of Drugs and Alcohol on Behavior

An overdose of tranquilizers or sedatives will change behavior. Some drugs accumulate in the bloodstream and gradually, over a period of time, cause dysfunction in mental abilities. If the cat becomes dopey, sleepy, or groggy under a particular medication, have your veterinarian check it out to be sure there are no sedatives in it that are affecting the cat's mental ability. Strange-acting cats have also been found to be under the influence of marijuana.

A cat behaving abnormally can conceivably be under the influence of alcohol, especially around Christmastime, when always at least one pet is brought to us who has consumed too much eggnog. At a recent veterinary convention there was a discussion about the increase in the number of alcoholic cats. You can tell when a cat is hung over; the eyes are bleary, and it is listless with manifestations of a headache. Unfortunately, the drinking generally starts as a gag at a party; the cat acquires a taste for the stuff and becomes a sneaky party drinker.

The Effect of Aging on Behavior

As senility affects the various organs of the body, so will there be a gradual change in some behavioral patterns in the aging cat. As it gets older, the cat seems to change its attitudes toward its human family, perhaps wanting more and more to be left alone in comfort instead of romping and playing. The cat may sometimes seem to be a little irritable and not want to be handled. Accede to these simple demands and try to be even more sympathetic, loving, and patient. I have discussed these physiological and behavioral changes in more detail in Chapter 9.

Loneliness

Most cats adjust magnificently to being alone. However, there are some who would rather have human companionship than be left alone, and the resultant loneliness and boredom can cause some abnormal behavior. Some lonely cats will groom themselves excessively, which can lead to fur pulling and self-mutilation; others will literally chew their tail to shreds.

Some people who leave their cats alone for long periods salve their conscience by leaving the television set running for the entertainment of their pet. However, a group of animal psychologists in West Germany who have studied the effects of television on pets has found that too much TV can make cats neurotic. It appears that if a cat watches TV more than an hour a day, it becomes nervous and suffers acute loss of appetite. However, if a radio is left on quietly, the low voices and music tend to be soothing to a cat. Some people make sound recordings of their voices and play them quietly all day for the lonely cat.

If you cannot get another kitten or puppy to keep the cat company, see to it that your cat has toys and a perch on a window with a view.

Spraying Behavior

Spraying is caused by depression and frustration if you are not using the tom for breeding purposes and letting him lead a normal life of lovemaking and marauding.

Once a whole male starts spraying, he cannot be taught otherwise. Yelling at him or beating him will usually not change this instinctive behavior. There are a very few males who will never spray at all. Then there are others who have weak instincts for spraying. Some of these will stop spraying if caught in the act the first few times and frightened by their owners making noise either by whacking a folded newspaper against the palm of their hand or screaming at them.

For those altered males or tomcats who continually spray, there is an alternate method that might work in a few isolated cases. It is the use of *stud pants,* a diaper-type pants, made out of a drip-dry material, that is worn by the male cat. It is very similar to the doggie britches used by female dogs in heat. When first put on the cat, he may act very strangely, rolling and jumping, being very puzzled and disturbed. However, by distracting him with food or toys or catnip, you can soon overcome his hurt feelings. A cat can run, jump, and perform all his daily chores with these pants on. Washing the pants with a Borax solution is a daily necessity to combat the stench of tomcat urine. Do not allow the tomcat to wear these pants while there is a queen in season. This is too cruel and frustrating to the male (and also the female). These stud pants will allow the tomcat more freedom while in the house and save your home from that telltale male cat odor. See illustration.

Psychosomatic Ailments

Psychosomatic ailments are a form of abnormal cat behavior. They are closely allied to emotional reactions and are resorted to as a

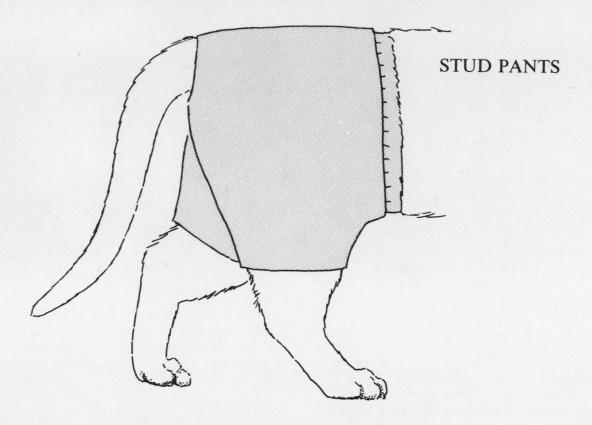

means of gaining attention. These animals are not faking a sickness—they are actually ill. Various emotions are responsible for psychosomatic illnesses, but the principal ones seem to be jealousy, emotional problems brought on by loneliness, and sexual frustration. Psychosomatic ailments are actual organic ailments of which emotional factors are a cause. Although psychosomatic medicine is a fairly new field in veterinary medicine, help is available in many cases of emotionally caused physical disturbances.

Psychosomatic ailments include bronchialasthmatic-type attacks (wheezing and coughing), nausea and vomiting, diarrhea, constipation, loss of hair, and even eye problems. One cat I know had a personality clash with a person who was visiting its human family. This resulted in the third eyelid of one of its eyes closing over the eye. The eye resisted all medical treatment but went back to normal the moment the visitor left.

110

False Pregnancy

This fairly common hormonal dysfunction is discussed on page 58.

Loss of Appetite and Overeating

When a cat is suffering from emotional stress, its eating habits are often affected. Some cats go on hunger strikes, while others eat everything in sight. Of course, you should first make sure that the cause is not physiological before investigating the possibility of emotional distress. The problem might be caused by something as simple as the presence of strangers in the house.

Wool and Material Eating

Some determined wool chewers swallow so much fabric that they develop chronic intestinal problems. Although much research has been done on this subject, it is still baffling as to both causes and cures. Boredom, loneliness, and nutritional deficiencies have all been investigated. You should consider whether your cat gets enough attention and love, whether it needs more and longer play periods, or a playmate. The problem has also been alleviated by feeding the cat a well-balanced, palatable diet with vitamin and mineral supplements, salt or seasoned salt, even some herbs and spices as supplements, large uncooked bones, and by allowing the cat to have large chew toys.

Perverted Appetite

At times you may notice your pet eating dirt, feces, or other unsuitable materials. This perverted craving generally indicates a dietary deficiency of minterals or vitamins, usually caused by worms in the intestinal tract. Stool eating can be caused by an enzyme deficiency or may be only a bad habit. It is not unusual for an extremely nervous or high-strung cat sometimes to display a perverted appetite. Boredom often leads to this condition; it may also be a result of confinement or insufficient exercise.

Tail Biting

Although cats are relatively independent creatures, they do want attention and affection from time to time. Many nervous and high-strung cats will bite and chew on their tails for emotional reasons: loneliness, boredom, or frustration. (Also, if there is anything wrong with a cat's tail—such as an infection—the cat will often turn on it and attack it as if it were not a part of itself. What was a minor abrasion may turn into a festering and bleeding sore. If the original disorder is cured, the tail biting will probably stop.)

This habit is especially seen in kittens and could be related to the sucking instinct, but if the habit is not broken, it can persist into adulthood. For the sake of the cat's health as well as its appearance, you should discourage the habit. Sometimes tranquilizers help; sometimes bitter-tasting preparations such as ipecac, pepper, or anti-thumbsucking preparations are used on the tail. Extract of orange is also very distasteful to most cats.

Alleviating the Problems of Neurotic Cats with Tranquilizers

Tranquilizers play an important role in veterinary medicine and especially in handling and quieting nervous and neurotic cats. But these drugs are potent and should not be used without the advice of a professional.

They are useful in calming cats fearful of storms, too much company, cars, firecrackers, or guns. They are helpful with the queen undergoing false pregnancy, to overcome her anxiety over the "missing" kittens; with the shy queen, to overcome her fears of the male during mating; with the nervous queen, when she is whelping and to circumvent the possibility of her refusal to nurse the kittens; and with the queen who has been known to kill her kittens.

They are useful in the control of itching skin, in some coughs caused by irritation, in asthma, and in vomiting.

BUT tranquilizers are not a permanent cure for any behavior problem. They are just in-between treatment until proper rehabilitation can be initiated. You must concern yourself primarily with discovering the cause of the problem, and in most cases that in itself will bring about the cure.

Help for the Neurotic Cat

With the pet population increasing and with more and more cats living in close confinement, an understanding of their emotional problems is of growing importance to the veterinary practitioner.

111

Cats do respond to proper treatment, and it is up to each of us to find the proper way for our cat. In severe cases in which the owner seems to be unable to help the neurotic cat, I would recommend asking a veterinarian to suggest an animal psychologist who is trained in the correction of abnormal behavior in cats.

In the following essay, Dr. Ginger Hamilton and Dr. Mollie J. Robbins discuss the most common cat behavior problems and the various treatments that have been successfully applied.

MISBEHAVIORS IN CATS
Ginger Hamilton, Ph.D., and
Mollie J. Robbins, Ph.D.

Consultants in Animal Psychology
Wheaton, Maryland

Writing from the vantage point of a practice directed at understanding and dealing with problem behaviors in animals, we will restrict this discussion to those cats, maintained as pets, which may be brought to us as patients. As psychologists, and consequently students of animal behavior, it is our task to diagnose causes and prescribe treatment in cases of misbehavior—after a veterinary examination has determined that the animal in question is in good physical health.

The dictionary defines the term "pet" as "any domesticated or tamed animal that is kept as a favorite and cared for affectionately." It is a reasonable assumption, therefore, that a pet is a source of pleasure to the owner. When the pet's behavior deviates from the owner's expectations, the pleasure is diminished, and the animal's continued tenure as a "favorite" is in jeopardy. At this point, the owner seeks professional help, and we are contacted.

Our first step is to ascertain the degree to which the owner's expectations and demands are realistic in terms of behaviors that are normal for the animal. If the owner's complaint is legitimate—that is, a true misbehavior has developed—we attempt to discover or describe probable reasons and to set forth remedial procedures. We do not retrain an animal for the owners, because we believe that the agent of change must be the owner himself. Since the misbehavior evolved within the context of the pet's environment, it is within that environment that behavioral change should be accomplished.

We could not, in a single essay, discuss all the misbehaviors that occur in cats, but we have attempted to present those most often brought to our attention. Most of our discussion, therefore, deals with the Big Three: *Aggression, Destructiveness,* and *Housebreaking.* It would be impractical, if not impossible, to provide all of the answers for dealing with problem cats. We have attempted to clarify some behaviors which are grossly misunderstood, to provide clues enabling the cat owner to know when professional advice is in order, and above all, to suggest guidelines for shaping a healthy kitten into one of nature's most enjoyable, affectionate companions.

AGGRESSION

Cats constitute almost one third of our patients, and of this group, approximately half exhibit aggressive behaviors. In our practice, we are not concerned with competitive and defensive forms of aggression which accompany hunting and mating activities and which are necessary to species survival. When we refer to aggressive acts as misbehaviors, we mean those behaviors, biting and scratching directed toward other animals and people as habitual responses, which yield gratification in and of themselves. While all behaviors may have some genetic basis, how they develop is a function of environmental opportunity. Habitual aggressiveness in cats can generally be traced to early experience, whether the kitten has been subjected to abuse, indifference, or indulgence. All such experiences constitute improper socialization.

Some owners come to us seeking help with their aggressive cats, but out of every six aggressors, two will have been brought to us for entirely different misbehaviors, and of these two, one owner simply will not have considered the possibility that the cat's behavior is anything out of the ordinary. "After all," say these owners, "isn't it normal for all cats to scratch and bite?" Our answer is a clear and emphatic "No! Not when the scratching and biting are directed at you."

If close to 20 percent of our clients who own aggressive cats accept abuse from their pets as being natural, then it would seem reasonable to assume that a very large number of cat owners are being scratched and bitten daily and little or nothing is being done to prevent this behavior. There are several reasons which might account for this. The most important of these stems from the fallacious idea that it is normal. If owners believe that a cat's natural behavior includes biting and scratching them occasionally, then it would follow that they would also believe that they could do relatively little to prevent it. Consequently, these owners would not seek help for their cat's misbehavior because they would not consider the pet to be misbehaving.

Another important factor in accounting for the indifference toward aggressive behavior in cats is the fact that a bite from a cat is not usually severe, nor does the victim ordinarily have to rush to the hospital emergency room, which is often the case following an equally aggressive act on the part of a dog. In general, pet dogs are bigger than pet cats, their bites inflict larger wounds, and the owners are quite subject to lawsuits. Anyway, who ever heard of a cat biting the mailman or tearing the seat off the pants of the trash collector?

These analogies serve to point out two further reasons why aggressive behaviors in cats are perceived as less noteworthy than similar behavior in dogs. One is the place of occurrence, and the other is the object of aggression. It is rare to hear of cats attacking anyone outside the confines of their own homes. Hostile displays, therefore, are usually against owners, relatives, or friends of the family. Under these circumstances the cat owner maintains a rather comfortable sense of security. The incident has not been observed by outsiders, and therefore no hostile witnesses would be brought into play in a legal action. Besides, what "friend" would initiate a suit? The owners simply treat the injury, apologize, and comment that "cats will be cats."

Some cat owners do attempt to handle aggressive behaviors in their animals while still believing that the behavior is normal and will occur if they do not act in a certain manner. These owners avoid direct physical contact with the animal, either by ignoring it indoors or by relegating it to the outside world, permitting entry only at mealtimes, after dark, or during a storm. In such cases there is no affectionate interaction. This arrangement not only serves as an effective barrier to aggression but also provides further support for the belief that cats are aloof creatures. Indeed, cats will obligingly withdraw under these conditions, living in virtual independence of the humans in the household. Dealing with aggressiveness in this manner renders the term "pet" inappropriate.

Some of our clients, despite being witnesses to and recipients of unprovoked attacks by the family cat, quietly deny that actual aggression is taking place. More often than not, these owners will not even discuss the issue. When a friend is bitten, little acknowledgment of the act is made by the owner, and absolutely no disciplinary measures are taken. Quite often the owner fails to utter even a verbal reprimand.

We see these same personality types in dog owners who seem to take a kind of sadistic delight in the fact that they own an animal who has a dozen or more bites to its credit. Such owners, regardless of whether their ani-

113

mal is a dog or cat, appear to be venting their own hostility or anger through the actions of the animal.

As animal psychology practitioners, we have had little success in encouraging these owners to deal with the aggression. It has also been difficult to predict whether such owners would be conscientious in carrying through our suggestions for modifying the other misbehaviors in their animals for which they came to us. These people need to seek the help of a psychiatrist or clinical psychologist. Dealing with deep-seated emotional problems of the owner is not within the realm of our practice. Our purpose is to assist the owner to bring about the best possible environment for the healthy pet. Fortunately, the majority of people who come to us for help with their problem pets are well-adjusted human beings who simply have little knowledge of animal behavior.

In most cases by the time cat owners come to admit that they have an aggressive pet, and are prepared to treat the behavior as a correctable problem, the situation has reached an intolerable level. At this point, they consult us. Of course, we would much prefer to take a preventive, rather than a reactive, approach to this misbehavior, but seldom do we have kittens as patients; if we did, we could instruct the owners in basic cat-raising procedures. Our patients, as a rule, are older cats who have bitten or scratched once too often. In desperation, and generally as a last resort, the owners decide it is time to seek professional help. In general, we find that these animals have a long combat history. Nothing had been done to prevent the nipping in kittenhood, and the behavior had increased in frequency and intensity. The kitten grew stronger, and the nips became vicious bites. Since the owner had set no limits on the type of play permitted, the cat had established its own rules. Once we guide these cat owners through the procedures, involving protective clothing and gentle interaction with their pet,

for gaining and enforcing control, we end up with happy clients who have found that you *can* teach an old cat new tricks.

NIPPING NIPPING IN THE BUD
The easiest time to deal with cat aggression is before the behavior begins. We find that one method is excellent for use with kittens, while still permitting the owners to enjoy their pet to the fullest extent. Kittens will nip at fingers. At each and every instance of this play behavior, gently flick the kitten's nose with your finger while continuing to hold it. We have also found it useful to pair this finger flick with a firm command of "No!" by the owner. Your kitten will soon get the idea that this behavior is not permitted, while at the same time both cat and owner can engage in affectionate play. There is no reason to ignore your kitten, or turn him outdoors, and there are many benefits to be derived from proper upbringing. Both animals and children need to know what is expected of them.

FIRST OFFENDERS
Very infrequently, cats have been brought to us as a result of a single aggressive act, there having been no previous history of such behavior. Happily, in most of these cases, we find that the isolated incident involved a reflexive bite in response to pain, as when a child had stepped on the cat's tail. The owners became frightened and immediately came to us for aid. The most difficult aspect of working with these clients lies in calming their fears and persuading them that they do not have a monster on their hands. We cannot guarantee the clients that their cat will never bite again, for it most certainly will under similar circumstances, but a fearful owner may do more harm than good. Any act of aggression on the part of a pet should be of concern to the owner; however, if all available evidence seems to support the cat's actions as self-defensive, any change of the

114

owner's attitude and behavior toward the pet could *produce* true misbehaviors.

For some cats which are brought to us following their first attack, the outcome is not a happy one. These cats suddenly, and without apparent provocation, explode into a growling, spitting rage. During the episode, the animal's physical characteristics undergo a drastic change: the pupils are widely dilated, the hair is erect, the ears are back, the back is arched, and the slightest external stimulation elicits a well-directed attack. Verbal and physical attempts to interrupt the behavior are to no avail, and so abrupt and violent is the behavior that observers generally retreat. The brave individual who remains is in extreme danger of being severely injured. The fury stops as suddenly as it began, and the cat reverts to its typical, affectionate behavior.

In these very rare cases, we have suspected brain damage. Subsequent veterinary examination generally yields corroborative physical evidence. The damage may have been caused by the pressure of a slowly growing tumor, the trauma of a blow to the head, or an infection. Regardless of the reason, the lesion is usually in an area of the brain which is not readily accessible through present surgical methods. Ongoing research holds promise for help in the future, but at this time the usual fate of the animal is euthanasia.

AGGRESSIVE BEHAVIOR TOWARD OTHER ANIMALS

Occasionally clients come to us with a cat who acts aggressively, not toward humans, but toward other family pets. Circumstances surrounding this behavior are variable, but the outcomes are usually very successful. In most cases, the fighting is a form of dominance testing, either because a new animal has been brought into the cat's territory or because kittens have grown up and one is going to show the others who's boss. In some ways, animals are more civilized than man. It is seldom in the nonhuman animal that one animal assumes dominance over another through killing. Ritualistic display behaviors have proven successful in establishing one member as leader and the others in a descending order of submission.

CAT VERSUS CAT

When two cats are fighting for leadership, both cats may spit, snarl, assume threatening postures, and perhaps engage in sparring, but eventually, and most often without any fur flying, one of the cats submits and quietly withdraws. This testing may take place many times until leadership is determined, then recur occasionally during succeeding weeks and months whenever the submissive member decides to take another crack at leadership. It is quite normal behavior, and unless the owner sees that the fighting is becoming physically harmful to one of the animals, it is best to let the cats work it out for themselves. They are much better equipped to establish their places in the household in this regard than are the owners.

FIGHTING LIKE CATS AND DOGS!

We never cease to be amazed at the number of people who still believe the myth that cats and dogs are natural enemies, and peaceful coexistence is not possible. Not only is it possible for a cat to tolerate a dog, but it is more the rule than the exception that the two can become marvelous companions. We often have clients who come to us with dogs who are presenting some rather extensive behavior problems. After careful history taking, we may find that the dog's misbehaviors stem from loneliness. In these cases, we suggest that the clients obtain a companion for their pet. Unless circumstances are completely prohibitive, we strongly recommend a kitten as the new addition.

Many clients initially resist our suggestion and tell us that their dog would never get along with a cat. We often discover, however, that the real reason for their resistance is lack of knowledge about cats. When these owners do follow through, the results can appear to be miraculous: not only do the dog's misbehaviors stop, but the two animals become intimate playmates, and the owners discover the full enjoyment of raising their first kitten.

If the reader has a misbehaving dog, please don't rush out into the night to purchase a kitten with the idea that this will be a panacea for your problems. We would particularly caution people who have never owned a cat. Before anyone obtains a kitten, or any animal for that matter, he should obtain explicit instructions on proper rearing. Without thorough investigation, it is impossible to determine the source of any particular pet problem, and introducing a new kitten could present more problems than you had at the start. For one thing, you could end up with a dead kitten. Although it takes a relatively short time for a kitten to learn to defend itself effectively, gradual, protected introduction is the rule.

It is comparatively easy to bring a new kitten into a dog's domain, but it may be quite different with bringing a new puppy into a grown cat's domain. It is, of course, possible to bring about an accommodation, but it will generally take a longer period of time. The young puppy has few defenses that are up to taking on a cat whose home has been invaded.

Lone cats, as well as lone dogs, can engage in any number of rather strange behaviors. If we diagnose loneliness as a cause for certain misbehaviors in a cat, we may again recommend a kitten to the owners. In these cases, we do warn the client that the cats may engage in some "mantel soccer." When a dog and a cat play together, the cat tends to stay grounded. When two cats play together, however, their antics may take place at any accessible level.

The reader should be alerted to the distinct possibility that, should the cat in residence be a male, he may, regardless of castration, begin to spray (this behavior will be discussed in a later section).

The fact that we find a variety of causes for feline fighters serves to emphasize a very important point. There are no general methods for handling aggression. Techniques for inducing or restoring acceptable pet behavior, regardless of the misbehavior, are very much dependent upon the combined factors of inheritance and experiences in the social and physical environments. We have never had two cases matching in these factors, and therefore we will not present a single formula for changing the aggressive pet. Certain principles of animal behavior have emerged from studies conducted by scientists engaged in research into instinct, temperament, and learning, but these principles are still affected by variables unique to individual situtations. There is no universal strategy for dealing with the various forms of a misbehavior. Generalization must be sharply limited outside the laboratory setting, and the indiscriminate application of a behavioral "rule" to all conditions could lead to a dangerous state of affairs. This is particularly true in cases of aggression.

NEIGHBORLY ADVICE
The hazards of the well-meant, but inappropriate, advice offered by friends and neighbors are exemplified by a case in which the owner had observed the beginning of aggressive behavior in her pet. She had been advised to confine the animal to a dark closet when biting or scratching occurred. By the time we saw the animal it was quite different from the friendly pet who had, prior to closet confinement, displayed some relatively minor aggression toward the owner. It was now withdrawn and fearful, urinating at random spots throughout the house, and openly hostile when the owner approached. This advice had been costly to the owner and the pet. The

technique used to stop the initial misbehavior had actually increased the aggression, and other misbehaviors had appeared to greatly complicate the case. Furthermore, and quite understandably, the owner's feelings toward the animal had changed. It is very difficult for an owner to remain affectionate toward an animal no longer bringing pleasure, inflicting wounds if she gets too close, and increasing housecleaning chores. When incorrect techniques are used, negative results are all too often predictable. The original misbehavior remains and often increases, and other misbehaviors unnecessarily develop. We were able, in this case, to help the owner to regain her pet, but it was a lengthy process to restore trust and affection in both the owner and the animal.

DESTRUCTIVENESS

Plants, drapes, sofas, chairs, and clock pendulums are among the common targets of a cat's destruction. It is not unusual, therefore, for cat owners, with reluctant resignation, to forgo certain attractive but purely ornamental additions to standard household furnishings, such as a luxurious philodendron, or to rationalize that shreds and tatters give a home a "lived-in look." So prevalent is the notion that to bring a cat into proximity with furniture and carpets is to invite ruin that many apartment-house owners refuse to rent to families with such creatures of destruction. Unfortunately, there is substantial support for this restriction.

In Chapter 10, the problem of normal (albeit destructive) scratching has been discussed in detail with various suggestions for curbing or redirecting this instinct. Instructions for clipping your cat's nails are found in Chapter 13.

Much confusion surrounds the act of scratching. Cats do not scratch simply to sharpen their claws! While scratching does condition the nails by removing the worn outer shell, it serves also as a muscle-toning exercise. Declawing a cat will not stop the scratching behavior, and we have had clients with such cats who still complained of their furniture being destroyed by scratching. Over a period of time, calluses had developed on the toe pads which then acted almost as effectively in tearing as the claws had originally.

PSYCHIC TRAUMA OF DECLAWING?

Cat owners often question us about the possible psychological effects of declawing their pet. Declawing is not a cure-all, or the absolute preventive measure, for destructive behaviors. If, however, an owner wishes to have a cat declawed, there should be relatively little concern about detrimental psychological side effects. The cat will experience sore paws, but there is little likelihood of a sore ego.

There are precautions that cat owners must take if they have declawed pets. Such animals should not be permitted to roam freely outdoors. While generally only the foreclaws are removed and tree climbing may still be accomplished, these claws constitute the first line of defense for the trapped cat, and without them the animal may become easy prey.

Permanent restriction of a previously free-ranging cat may bring about a dramatic behavioral change not directly related to the surgery, but perceived as such by an owner suffering from feelings of guilt; hence, the idea of "psychic trauma" gains credibility.

Another form of guilt springs from the accurate interpretation of dispositional changes in the newly confined cat, but it is rooted in the misconception that *all* cats need the freedom of outdoor life. This need develops as a result of experience, and whenever a cat's life space is reduced, whether from the outside world to the house, or from the entire house to certain rooms, personality effects must be anticipated. In other words, confinement per se will not generate adverse reactions in cats which have been accustomed to a confined existence since kittenhood, provided, of course, that the confinement area is essentially equivalent to the family living area. Behavioral alterations arising from a shrinking of the cat's world are not irreversible, but the process of converting such an animal into an adjusted house pet will demand a generous amount of patience and understanding on the owner's part. These remarks do not apply to bachelor tomcats. The instinctive sexual drive in these males will compel them to seek the mating opportunities available "on the town." Even males with household mates tend to promiscuity and respond to any females within calling distance.

CHEWING AND THIEVERY

The cat's teeth are designed for flesh eating. They are therefore sharp and are capable of remarkable gripping and tearing. One client, having had her cat declawed because of sofa scratching, found to her dismay that the cat soon began tearing the sofa to shreds with its teeth. One of our suggestions was to spray a repugnant substance on a rag and pin the rag to the sofa. Through this and our other recommendations, the sofa was saved from further abuse, and the cat was saved from losing its teeth. We are appalled by the number of people who resort to exodontia, the surgical removal of teeth, with their pets. We have never condoned this radical measure.

Destructive chewing is a possibility with cats, and the behavior can lead to the death of the animal if certain materials are ingested. Household insulation, Christmas tinsel, and wool are targets for some cats. Insulation, in particular, can be extremely abrasive in passing through the digestive tract. If a cat ingests unusual materials, there may be a nutritional deficiency and a checkup by a veterinarian is in order. The cat, of course, should not be permitted access to these materials, but, as is the case with wool eating, prevention fre-

quently is not possible. In such cases, repellents may prove effective in the conditioning of an avoidance response by making the material unacceptable to the cat.

Similar precaution—not permitting access—should be taken with other articles. Jewelry and cigarettes, for example, are fun to play with. Shiny rings and watches are attractive, and cigarettes easily roll with the push of a paw. If objects such as these are within the cat's reach, the owner may find tobacco strewn around the floor and a favorite ring may not be found for months. It is wise to inform overnight guests of the cat's playful antics in order to circumvent a household search for a cuff link the next morning. Un-emptied ashtrays are also subject to a playful paw. We have not found that cats are necessarily repelled by extinguished or smoldering cigarettes, and the hazard of sparks on flammable surfaces is obvious. The burden of responsibility for preservation of home, pet, and other possessions falls to the owner. Cats can be trained, but they show amazing discrimination of circumstances. Given this training, the kitchen table and sink will not be walked upon, articles will not be chewed or hidden, *in the owner's presence*. When the owner is out of sight, however, his rules may well depart with him, and the cat plays quite a different game.

HOUSEBREAKING

Although cat owners ask for guidance in dealing with many feline misbehaviors, one far outranks all others in serving to prod owners into seeking professional help. When a cat stops using the litter pan, owners are devastated. Few people have ever taught kittens to use litter pans. This routine is part of the mother cat's basic training of her kittens. When a human being obtains a kitten, there is little to be done other than to show the kitten where the pan is located. After the initial introduction, and provided that the distance from the pan to where the kitten is at a given moment does not exceed the ability of the young animal to delay relief, behavior of the pet in this regard generally is not a consideration. If infractions do occur, the owner is totally unprepared to rectify the situation.

There are essentially four types of cats that do not use the litter pan: (1) the "dirty" cat; (2) the senile cat; (3) the post-disease cat; and (4) the environmentally stressed cat. Each category involves a different cause for the same misbehavior, and the animals of each type, with the exception of the "dirty" cat, have histories of adequate housebreaking.

THE "DIRTY" CAT

We have never encountered any of the first group, the "dirty" cat, but cats of this type are documented in literature. These cats apparently have never been trained to a litter pan, and, as reported, it may be impossible to ever bring about this training. Further, the behavior seems to be familial, occurring within and across generations. Although clients have brought in patients that were, on the surface, examples of this class, we have always been able to trace the source of the misbehavior to factors appropriate to the other categories, or we have suggested changes that eventually returned the animal to a proper use of the cat pan. In general, therefore, it would appear that the actual "dirty" cat is rare, and professional help should be sought before automatically casting a cat into that category.

THE SENILE CAT

The senile cat is another matter. These pets have long histories of fastidiousness, but with advanced age physiological changes lead to the loss of bladder and/or bowel control. This is not an inevitable event in all old cats, but if it occurs, little, if anything, can be done. Just as human beings may become enuretic and encopretic in senescence, so may cats.

THE POST-DISEASE CAT

Cats in the third group, which we term the post-disease cat, break down in using litter pans following some physical disorder. During cystitis, for instance, small amounts of urine are excreted at short intervals. If owners rapidly discover their cat's distress and obtain medical help from the veterinarian, there will, as a rule, be no subsequent changes in the cat's litter-pan behavior. If, however, recognition of the ailment is delayed, there will be an almost inevitable breakdown in housebreaking. Urination is painful, frequent, and urgent, and the cat cannot always manage to reach the litter pan in time. If this persists for an extended period, it often develops into a "functionally autonomous habit." This means that urination outside the litter pan will continue after the physical cause has been medically treated and alleviated. Owners of these cats now have a job on their hands.

The first step is a thorough cleaning of the house, so that urine odors will not lure the cat back to certain spots. Many owners have come to us having already accomplished this feat, but they found, to their consternation, that the cat then began urinating in even more areas than previously. The choice of cleaning agent was the fatal flaw in their otherwise commendable approach. They had used an ammonia-based compound. Ammonia is a constituent of urine. Their cleaning, therefore, served to spread the odor over greater areas; hence, to the cat, the house became one huge litter pan.

In some instances, cats have returned to regular litter-pan use following housecleaning. More often, other procedures must be initiated by the owners. These additional remedial techniques are dependent upon numerous other factors, such as the physical plan of the home, the number of people and pets in the household, and the time available for owners to devote to the correctional procedures.

THE ENVIRONMENTALLY STRESSED CAT

The last group of cats exhibiting inappropriate elimination behavior present possibly our most challenging cases, and undoubtedly are the most exasperating for owners. The best descriptive term that can be applied to the cause of the misbehavior is "change." A change that is traumatic to the cat is often not perceived by the owner, and even when recognized, the owner views it as inconsequential, and not a possible cause for the pet's repugnant behavior. These owners often believe that their cat has suddenly become neurotic—a term too easily used as a catchall for undiagnosed misbehaviors.

An illustrative case, in which seemingly routine matters become overwhelming to a cat, was presented to us when a young couple came to the office with a two-year-old cat that had suddenly begun defecating and urinating in one of the rooms. Our initial questioning brought assurance from the owners that *nothing* had happened to bring about the behavior. On the contrary, the animal had quite inexplicably developed a full-blown neurosis! Careful inquiry, however, revealed: (1) the clients had spent two weeks in Europe while boarding the animal for the first time; (2) a new kitten had been introduced; (3) the cat had been declawed; (4) a baby had been born; (5) the family had moved into a new house; (6) the husband's new commuting schedule had allowed him less time to spend with the cat; (7) workmen had been in and out of the house, and there had been general disorder during the first month of the move; and (8) they had moved both the food dish and the litter pan to a frequently trafficked bathroom. The owners had attempted some quite reasonable corrections to no avail, and, in fact, these attempts had compounded the problem. None of the precursive events had appeared to be of sufficient moment to the clients, or even noteworthy. The clients were obviously bright, but working under the assumption that their cat was "neurotic," they believed its behavior could not be readily understood or treated. These events had not occurred simultaneously. They had not even fallen within a short time span, but had begun when the cat was eight months of age. The cumulative effect had eventually broken down the cat's resistance. A less strong cat would have succumbed much earlier in this chain of events. Once we had determined the causes we were able to reinstitute acceptable elimination habits in the animal.

This case does not fit neatly into a typical-atypical dichotomy. Certainly the number of potentially traumatic events the cat encountered is atypical, but it is typical in that changes had occurred in the cat's environment which resulted in its neglect of the litter pan. If a previously well-behaved, physically fit pet starts selecting places other than the litter pan, most assuredly "something," not "nothing," has happened. Ascribing the behavior to neurosis defines neither cause nor solution, and interferes with the search for either.

It would be impossible to present everything that might constitute traumatic change. The previous case presented several examples. We have also found this misbehavior stemming from: the ringing of a nearby telephone while the cat was in the process of elimination; the prolonged absence of a regular family member; marriage or remarriage of an owner; a new animal in the neighborhood within sight, hearing, or smell of the cat; disturbing events in the owner's life which subtly affect changes in the cat-human relationship; and alterations in the composition of litter-pan filler.

THE LITTER PAN

Care of the litter pan is of the utmost importance. Regardless of manufacturers' instructions listed on the bags of some brands of litter, advising the cat owner that best results are obtained if the litter is not disturbed between changes, we have obtained far better results by agitating this filler. Many cats are fastidious animals; they will not eliminate in litter pans with even relatively small amounts of excrement. We have brought about rapid and complete return to proper cat-pan use through instructing the owners to clean the pan twice a day. This involves removal of solid waste, which can be flushed down the toilet, and stirring the litter, which hastens the drying process. If the litter is cared for in this manner, total changing of the litter and washing the pan is not usually required (for a single cat) more often than every two to four days, provided that enough litter is placed initially in the pan. The required height is approximately three to four inches.

The green litter containing chlorophyll has presented problems for many of our clients. This substance is supposed to eliminate odors common to uncared-for litter pans. It may well serve to make the pan more attractive to the owner, but it may also repel the cat. While some owners have had success by adding some of the chlorophyll litter to the plain litter, for the majority of our clients who have attempted even this partial change, the results have been disastrous. If, despite clean maintenance, the owner insists on that extra touch, a drop of liquid deodorant, specifically sold for this purpose, will render the cat pan inoffensive to both owner and animal.

Occasionally, seemingly minor changes in the brand of litter have brought about disuse of the cat pan. Some cats prefer noncommercial substances, such as shredded newspaper. If a cat is properly housebroken, the wise owner will maintain the procedures currently in effect. If the cat pan is not being cleaned as regularly as we suggest, adoption of this practice might prevent the onset of misbehavior in the future. If more than one cat resides in the household, more than one litter pan might be advisable.

OTHER BEHAVIORAL PROBLEMS

SPRAYING

A review of the literature on the topic of spraying reveals certain ambiguities. It is referred to as simple urination outside the cat pan, or urination by brief jets directed at particular objects. The spray is described as consisting solely of urine, urine mixed with anal-gland secretion, or, probably more correctly, urine combined with a highly scented fatty substance. It may serve to mark territorial limits, may be simply social in nature, and may occur under conditions of stress. Spraying tends to increase in the courting male, indicating its sexual role. A protective function is suggested by the report of one cat which faithfully sprayed the legs of the new baby's bassinet each time the infant was tucked in, as though to safeguard the small tenant. The only points of total agreement are that it is a phenomenon primarily occurring in males and that, while normal, it is a perfectly dreadful behavior.

We define spraying as the spurting of a malodorous substance on various household articles such as rugs, sofas, and drapes, while the cat continues to use its litter pan for ordinary elimination. The resultant stain and odor are extremely resistant to cleaning materials. Spraying is very likely to occur in natural males confined to the house, and may even happen with freely roaming toms.

Since spraying is primarily associated with sexual behavior, forming an integral part of the mating sequence, castration is the logical treatment. If a male begins to spray prior to castration, the behavior may continue for an extended period of time. Although neutering a male who has never evidenced spraying is generally an effective means of prevention, it does not guarantee that the behavior will not occur under traumatic circumstances. Environmental events may trigger spraying, even in the castrated male with no prior history of such behavior, when the animal's response is one of stress.

If the odor from spraying has ever been encountered, the decision to prevent a further occurrence of this behavior is readily reached. If a male cat is intended as a house pet, have the animal neutered. If the male is to remain intact, permit free access to the outdoors, but be prepared for indoor infractions. Whenever changes are to take place within the household, introduce the cat to these changes gradually, and provide the pet with an abundance of tender, loving care.

FOOD INTAKE

So well accepted is the notion that all cats have finicky appetites that owners are readily susceptible to advertisements for variety diets which promise to tempt the highly particular feline palate. When, however, an especially preferred food remains untasted, the cat owner is likely to become alarmed. This implies, of course, that the owner is aware of the quantity of food normally consumed by the cat. Unfortunately, this may not be the case in homes occupied by more than one pet. In order to monitor daily food intake, separate dishes should be provided for each animal. Since it is common for dogs to eat a main course of their own dishes and then sample the cat's food for dessert, the cat's dish should be placed in an area not accessible to the dog. This may simply involve setting the dish at a higher level. Separate rooms may be required to prevent scavenging among cats.

As is the case with other behaviors, the eating habits of cats are subject to change under stress-inducing conditions in the environment. The most common response is that a cat stops eating. A short period of appetite suppression of one or two days, in a normally healthy, well-nourished cat, is rather typical following the introduction of a newcomer to the home, boarding, or a family's move into a new house. Under circumstances such as these, the owner should be prepared to offset such a reaction by providing the animal with additional attention—attention that is so easily diverted elsewhere at the birth of a baby or during the upheaval of changing households.

Extended periods of non-eating in a cat should never be ignored. Anorexia nervosa, a neurotic refusal of food over long periods of time with no observable physical cause, has been experimentally induced in cats by placing them in an extreme approach-avoidance conflict. The approach response to food, necessary to survival, is met with such aversive punishment that an avoidance drive effectively counters the instinct for preservation. Cats have been known to starve to death under such conditions. This type of conflict can exist in the home situation, and without professional intervention, the pet may die.

A less common neurotic response to stress is polyphagia, or overeating. Indiscriminate and voracious eating of a compulsive nature far exceeds bodily need. This is a phenomenon not dissimilar to psychogenic overeating in humans. Again, professional intervention is indicated.

WITHDRAWAL

Classifying withdrawal as a feline misbehavior most certainly will surprise many people. As was observed in an earlier section, popular consensus would place withdrawal within the range of *normal* cat characteristics. Admittedly, this essay would have been completed with greater dispatch had "standoffishness" prevailed. As it was, a certain feline played with the typewriter keys, purred thunderously in the authors' ears, and in general made a nuisance of himself in his avid pursuit of human contact.

It commonly happens that people enter the home of cat owners, spend several hours visiting, and take their leave without indisputable proof that a cat is in residence. The cat pan and food bowl are merely circumstantial bits of evidence. In one extreme case, an acquaintance of the authors had five cats in an apartment. Periodic visits were made to the apartment over a three-year period, and not once were the cats visible. These particular cats had been born in a closet and hidden from the landlord, who would have evicted the tenant had he known of the animals' existence. The early experience of these cats had molded a strong pattern of withdrawal. To what extent the behavior might have been subject to change must remain speculative, since the owner was comfortable with the situation and no attempts at socialization to humans were made. The owner was, however, aware of both the origin of the behavior and its peculiar nature.

One case was brought to us in which withdrawal had evolved over a period of time and was not directly connected with the cat's socialization during kittenhood. This cat lived in a home with several other animals, cats and dogs. After a year or so of peaceful cohabitation among all the animals, one female cat, which had been the first pet, began to engage in aggressive displays toward the other female cat, which had entered the household a year after the first cat's arrival. By the time we saw the animals, there had been a time lapse of approximately eleven years. The owner had sought advice periodically during these years, but no solution had been offered other than separation of the two cats, preferably in two different households. When we first saw the intimidated animal we were somewhat shaken. Had the recipient of the alleged aggression been in a laboratory setting, we would have suspected brain damage, due to its marked obesity. It was also one of the most passive cats we had ever encountered. The aggressor at least partially fit the owner's description. She strutted around the office, explored all rooms, and maintained control over the cats' play. We classified her behavior as dominant but not aggressive, and the history related by the owner confirmed our observations. We diag-

nosed the present situation as having arisen primarily from the owner's fear of what *might* happen, rather than having developed from actual life-or-death confrontations between the two cats. As a result of the owner's reaction to what was viewed as potential danger, constant vigilance had been maintained. The passive cat had been kept in a separate room, closed off from all other animals, except when the owner was around to monitor the situation. Human interaction had also been drastically curtailed, out of concern that the dominant cat would become jealous and later "take it out on" the passive animal. Although the owner was acting in a manner intended to protect the passive cat, the protective measures had resulted in two neurotic behaviors: compulsive overeating (discussed in the previous section) and withdrawal. So extreme had the withdrawal become that the cat would not leave the secure confines of its room even given the opportunity. Successful resolution was brought about in amazingly short order, once we had worked through the owner's anxiety and instituted a program of controlled, rather than restricted, interaction between the two cats. In addition, food intake was rationed by the removal of feeders which had previously permitted free access to food.

This case serves to illustrate three important points: (1) behavioral change can be brought about in older animals (these cats were twelve to thirteen years of age); (2) neurosis can assume more than one form in the same animal (in this case, withdrawal and compulsive overeating); (3) owners' fear reactions can intensify and compound behavioral problems in their animals.

OVERSOCIALIZATION
We are advocates of having more than one pet in any household where the owners go out to work every day. As discussed earlier, misbehaviors stemming from loneliness are varied and can assume neurotic proportions. In the American society of today, it is more the

rule than the exception that owners vacate the premises several hours each day, leaving pets to find their own diversions. It is wise to provide such animals with companionship. A dog and a cat are good playmates; however, once this relationship has been established between species, the cat owner should be aware that the cat which has been raised with dogs may not be sufficiently wary of aliens. This cat may, therefore, not react to canine aggression quickly enough to escape injury. Generally, cats are better prepared than are dogs to fend for themselves in the absence of human care, and they ordinarily show discretion in encounters with strangers. Still, owners must exercise caution in permitting sudden freedom to any cat with a history of canine companionship. Although we have personal knowledge of only one case ending in death, there have been others with near-disastrous results. The chances of injury to an overly trusting cat, therefore, are not worth the risk.

SEXUAL BEHAVIOR

Cats intended solely for the purpose of being pets should be neutered. This not only provides some control over the feline population—there are already too many cats subjected to abuse either through excess or through neglect—but it will also save the cat from the undue stress effects of an unfulfilled sexual drive. Moreover, owners will not be confronted with resultant behavioral changes.

When a natural cat is maintained in a setting with enforced non-breeding, the animal is placed in abnormal circumstances; hence, abnormal behavior may very well follow. It would be a rare tomcat that would remain celibate within a home and not exhibit behavioral and possibly physical disturbances. One or a combination of changes may take place, such as spraying, aggression, weight loss, and restlessness. Although rare in the queen, false pregnancy may develop, and she may be subject to other psychosomatic disorders, such as uterine inflammation and diarrhea. Even seizures have been documented in the restricted queen. The same misbehaviors noted for the tomcat may also be seen in the queen's behavior.

Neutering—spaying the queen and castrating the tom—may alleviate the problems. A risk remains, however, that some behaviors will have become autonomous, and professional guidance will be necessary.

OWNER MOTIVATION

Obviously, misbehaviors will undoubtedly persist in any cat despite accurate diagnosis and proper corrective procedures if the owner fails to implement the recommendations. While this failure may be due to any number of factors, not the least of which is a confused interpretation of the instructions, it is most often a function of the owner's inability or refusal to expend the effort required in remediation. This variable, the extent of owner motivation, is the most important factor in the successful resolution of problem behaviors. Unfortunately, some owners are all talk and no action. Any person who acquires a pet automatically acquires responsibilities of care and training. Behavioral disorders in cats place demands on the owners—responsible cat owners meet these demands.

TOWARD HEALTHY CAT BEHAVIOR

Select a healthy kitten from a reputable source, institute the training techniques we have outlined, and the odds are very much in favor of the development of a "pet" in every sense of the term. Potentially traumatic events, however, are inevitable in every household, and misbehaviors can happen. If these occur and the veterinarian gives the animal a clean bill of health, then the owner must engage in some soul searching. What changes have taken place in the cat's environment? Has the cat pan been moved? Has the litter brand been changed? Has a strange ani-

124

mal come into the neighborhood? Is the cat getting into the insulation or the plant that was recently brought into the house? Is the telephone ringing too loudly, or the old furnace finally making too much racket? What about the construction on the house next door?

Questions such as these could fill a volume, but one is important enough for separate discussion. Are expectations of the cat's behavior realistic? The nibble of the young kitten (though it should be dealt with) is more likely a display of affection than of aggression. Furthermore, don't expect the cat to maneuver around the antique glass, gracefully leaving each item untouched. Some cats are exceedingly clumsy, as are most kittens prior to mature muscular development. Although human-type IQ measurements are not in use with cats, behavioral differences exist, and some cats may fondly be labeled "retarded." These cats look handsome, wise, and regal as long as they are stationary, but the image is shattered when they attempt that short jump between couch and coffee table, and miss! Or they never learn that an undisrupted walk on the kitchen sink can occur only during the owner's absence.

Since this essay has been devoted to the recognition, prevention, and treatment of misbehaviors in cats, much of what we have discussed has been presented in a serious tone. The soiling of expensive carpeting, the marring of furniture, and the inflicting of painful bites on humans are not humorous subjects. When we suggest, therefore, that owning a cat can be a delightful experience, the reader may well lift a quizzical eyebrow. The procedures we have prescribed for raising a healthy, trouble-free animal need not mean hours of drudgery. Basically, you need to know your cat. Training practices and enjoyment go hand in hand. In fact, periods of romping provide ideal situations for teaching the limits of scratching, kicking, and nipping, but the lessons are fun. This very personal contact is the key to later adjustment. Misbehaviors do develop under the best of conditions, but most can be successfully resolved with professional guidance, a little common sense, some time, and knowledge of where things went wrong.

125

Part 3
An Ounce of Prevention

12 · Nutrition

The Well-Balanced Diet · Normal Eating · Finickiness · Commercial Foods · Home-Cooked Foods · Basic Dietary Requirements · Some Hazards and Harmful Feeding Practices · Weight Watching · The Sick Cat · At the Kennel or Hospital

The Diet and Eating Habits

Animals living in a natural environment choose their diets with incredible discretion. The cat is primarily carnivorous; in the wild state the cat eats the entire body of its prey—fur, entrails, etc. In this way, the cat is assured a well-balanced diet with muscle and organ foods and roughage. Today's house pet has little need to hunt for its food, and the responsibility for a proper diet must be assumed by the pet owner. Because you have an intimate, day-to-day relationship with your cat, you can, by exercising a little knowledge of nutrition, provide your cat with better and more healthful choices in its diet. And with fewer environmental risks: although housecats who are allowed outdoors sometimes supplement their diets with rodents and birds, there is always the possibility of poisoning from pesticides and herbicides (see Chapter 17) or the even more common possibility of contracting parasites (see Chapter 16). While you cannot (and should not try to) stop your cat from hunting, you should keep a watchful eye out for symptoms of poisoning and parasites.

But whether your cat is an outdoor or indoor pet, or both, it has never before been in such a nutritionally favored position. Today's commercial cat foods are the product of years of research and almost all of them contain the basic ingredients of a well-balanced diet. And they relieve the owner of most of the burden of devising a good nutritional program.

However, regardless of our nutritional sophistication, in my clinic I am increasingly seeing many diseases that are caused by dietary deficiencies and excesses. For even though most commercial foods have been carefully tested by nutritionists, certain precautions should be taken—and some additives are necessary for a *complete* diet.

I also caution those owners who try to improve on commercial cat food without having proper knowledge of nutrition, and those who do not use the commerical products at all, either out of necessity or out of a desire to pamper their pets; it is all too easy to upset the balance of a pet's diet.

The appetite and food requirements of the cat are influenced by a variety of physiological and psychological factors, such as the amount of light and noise in the feeding area or the presence of unfamiliar people or other animals. Even the particular type of food dish used—whether it is flat or deep—and the cleanliness of the dish (and the dishwashing detergent used) have been found to affect the appetite of some cats. And, of course, spoiled cats are more finicky than a cat who is not used to being catered to. Because the cat has an acute sense of smell and taste and bases its food preferences on these senses, it is difficult to change the dietary fare once it has been established, which is a very good reason for starting off your relationship with your pet with some awareness of what constitutes a proper diet. Also, it is important to consider the age and metabolism of your pet—young and active cats need more food than older and less active ones. Pregnant and nursing queens have special nutritional needs (see Chapter 6), as do ailing cats, who have to be pampered and carefully fed (see Chapter 14).

This chapter will introduce you to an appealing and well-balanced nutritional program for your cat. There is, of course, no *perfect* diet. Each cat is a confirmed individual, and diets should reflect that individuality. By intelligent experimenting, you can find out what foods your pet likes and needs, put them into a proper mix, add a heaping portion of tender, loving care, and enjoy the companionship of a sleek, happy, and energetic pet.

The Well-Balanced Diet

Nutritionists have worked out what is called a maintenance diet: the amount of food intake required to keep an animal in good health under normal circumstances, neither gaining nor losing weight and free from deficiency diseases. The well-balanced diet consists of foods which contain the correct proportions of proteins, fats, carbohydrates, vitamins, and minerals. These requirements can be met by a good commercial cat food with the addition of high-quality proteins (such as milk, egg yolk, poultry, fish, cheese). The daily intake for the average adult cat should be between six and eight ounces, plus water or milk and the supplements discussed later in this chapter. Like human beings, many cats become bored with the same food day in and day out. To keep a pet interested in food, I recommend varying the diet a bit. About every fifth day, it can be fed an entirely different food, or the same basic commercial food can be used and another food added.

High-quality proteins are those that are most efficiently assimilated by the body, and thus when they are included in the cat's diet, less protein is required to meet the animal's needs. The less protein eaten, the less waste products formed, and this reduces the stress and strain on kidney functioning. Also, the liver does not have to work so hard to convert protein and fat into glucose. Prescription diets are used in kidney diseases, liver diseases, intestinal disorders, urinary problems with stone formation, and heart diseases. High-quality foods include beef, horsemeat, chicken, and lamb. Corn, wheat, barley, eggs, milk, corn oil, and soy beans are good examples of foods containing high-quality protein.

I believe that a cat should have some fresh meat at least once a week. Organ foods such as liver, kidney, sweetbreads, lungs, brains, tripe, giblets (either cooked or uncooked depending on your cat's preference) are very nutritious and furnish vitamins and minerals.

Normal Eating

Adult cats usually feed once every twenty-four hours, although many house pets prefer to be fed twice a day. Growing kittens and lactating queens require several meals a day.

Most cats are creatures of habit and dislike any drastic changes in their feeding schedule or type of food, which is why it is a good idea to make a varied diet the norm rather than the exception. If it is necessary to alter the feeding schedule, try to bring about the change gradually.

Water

Clean fresh water should be available at all times, and especially for cats on dry and semi-moist diets. Although cats are not avid water drinkers, a minimum amount of fluid is necessary each day for the proper functioning of the kidneys and to avoid dehydration. Some cats will get water from dripping faucets, vases, toilet bowls, etc., but do not let this keep you from putting out fresh water every day. The water in vases may be toxic from the flowers, and the water in the toilets may contain disinfectant chemicals which are toxic, so your cat should not be left without an alternative.

If a cat does not like the water you put out, it may be that it contains distasteful minerals or that it is polluted, and the cat will most likely end up not drinking even the necessary minimal amount. If this appears to be the case, bottled water would be a wise investment. Also, soups, broth, and tomato and clam juice can prove to be a tasty supplement.

Excessive drinking, either suddenly or gradually, is always an indication of an illness and veterinary attention is essential. Kidney disease is the most common cause of notably increased drinking. A sudden increase may also indicate dehydration, fever, anemia, and other pathological problems.

Finickiness?

I'm sure you don't have enough fingers to count the number of times you have "discovered" a food your cat has found irresistible—for a couple of meals. In the meantime you have stocked up on this latest favorite only to be looked at with disdain at your stupidity in assuming it had the slightest interest in that particular food. And quite often you have probably gotten the same scornful look when the food dish contained a really old favorite.

None of this is necessarily honest-to-goodness finickiness because so many factors affect the appetite of the cat.

At the top of the list is odor. The sense of smell is so acute in the cat that a repugnant odor or the inability to smell could cause the animal to starve to death. For example, I know of one colony of cats that stopped eating because the detergent used in cleaning their food dishes had been changed. Also, any infection in the upper respiratory tract will prevent a cat from eating simply because it cannot smell the food. Since healthy cats can go without food or water for very long periods, they can steadfastly refuse food they dislike almost to the point of starvation. And many cats do get bored with the same food day in, day out.

Food consistency is important to many cats. Some like hard foods and others like soft. Also, a cat with a sore mouth or tongue will eat any food very gingerly, if at all.

The immediate surroundings at mealtime can ruin a cat's appetite. More light and noise than usual and extra people around will send most cats scurrying for a quiet, secluded spot. Even raised voices between master and mistress or other members of the family cannot be tolerated by most cats.

The temperature of the food can also be a factor. Most cats do not like cold food, so it should not be served directly from the refrigerator. Brought to room temperature, or with a little warm water added to it, it will be much more palatable.

Another reason for lack of appetite could be that the diet is deficient in vitamin B_1. This can be remedied by sprinkling a little brewer's yeast on the food.

Uneaten food that has become soggy and contaminated should be thrown out. It is unacceptable to any self-respecting cat. And any food that is unfit for human consumption should *never* be offered to a cat.

It is said that finicky eaters are not born but made. But whenever a cat refuses food for more than forty-eight hours, it is a warning that something is wrong. Loss of appetite is one of the earliest symptoms of most ailments and diseases and the presence of parasites.

Commercial Foods

Although cat-food companies continue to improve their products and add to the varieties and flavors available, none of these foods—despite any claims to the contrary—provides a "complete" diet. You must supplement your cat's commercial diet with other foods as described below, because these commercial foods, if they constitute the cat's entire diet, may be injurious to its health.

What Is Ash Content?

In choosing a brand of cat food, it is important to read the analysis of the ingredients carefully and to be especially aware of the mineral residue or ash content. The ash content should not exceed 4 percent in the moist foods, which is equivalent to 12 percent in the dry foods because of the different processing procedure. Excessive ash is known to be a major cause of cystitis, a painful and dangerous ailment (see page 194). Many veterinarians believe that an excess of ash in the

food is a factor in bladder stones in the urinary tract. For years veterinarians have been issuing warnings about these dangers. Unfortunately, some cat-food companies are now omitting reference to ash content in their analysis. You might infer from this that these companies have something to hide—and avoid the brands that will not offer this information.

The Dry Foods

Research has shown that cats fed a certain amount of dry food each day have healthier gums and teeth than those fed exclusively soft, moist diets. This least expensive and most convenient form of pet feeding is perfectly healthful if you take the following precautions:

Dry foods are deficient in fat, and some essential nutrients are destroyed by the high heat used in the manufacturing process. Compensate for this by adding cooking oil, animal fat, or butter to dry food. Brewer's yeast is an excellent and economical way to replace the lost nutrients. It is most important that an ample supply of fresh water be available at all times. Check to be sure that the ash content doest not exceed 12 percent.

Semi-moist Pouch Foods

These handy and increasingly popular "TV dinners" are also quite acceptable when certain precautions are taken. Although these foods are not as deficient in fat as the completely dry food, your cat will benefit if you add a bit of additional fat to its diet each day. Here, as with dry foods, a constant supply of fresh water is a necessity.

Because of the high bacterial content, once the pouch is opened the food deteriorates quite rapidly even when refrigerated and should be thrown out if not eaten within twenty-four hours.

When this type of food constitutes the main

WHAT TO LOOK FOR IN COMMERCIAL CAT FOOD

Type	Protein Content	Fat Content	Ash Content
Dry foods	30%	not less than 6%	not to exceed 12%
Semi-moist	not less than 20%	not less than 7%	no figures available
Canned foods	not less than 12%	not less than 2%	not to exceed 4%

diet, it is wise to vary the flavors so the pet does not get "hooked" on one dish. And beware of overfeeding. Some cats are so fond of this bill of fare that they go at it the way some of us attack nuts or potato chips.

Canned Foods

Some of these foods can provide the best of all diets, and some the very worst. And even the very best, if served exclusively every day, can prove detrimental to a cat's health—for example, fish. Since canned food is the most expensive way of feeding a cat, the owner should be especially wary of the content analysis. The ash content should not exceed 4 percent. The cheaper foods usually contain too much ash and low-quality proteins—gristle, entrails, skin—and make up a great deal of their weight in water. Some of them contain such large fish bones as to be actually injurious to the digestive system. Others contain only a single ingredient. As for vitamins, the heat used in processing the cheaper foods destroys most of their potency.

With canned cat food, the owner should strive for variety, a full range of animal by-products, and palatability.

Dog Foods for Cats a No-no

Most commercial dog foods are deficient in taurine, a substance necessary for proper feline nutrition. Cats that continually and wholly eat dog food will suffer from eye trou-ble caused by retinal degeneration, which is caused by an absence of taurine.

The best rule of thumb is to look for the greatest number of nutrients for your money.

Countless cats lead perfectly healthy and happy lives exclusively on commercial diets. I do feel, however, that a combination of the three types should be considered, and that the precautions I have outlined above should be followed in order to avoid potential deficiencies and subsequent ailments.

For those who have trouble finding commercial foods palatable to their pets or who wish to do a little pampering, there are also certain nutritional guidelines which should be followed.

The sample diet on the following page is not intended as the ultimate in a nutritional program for any particular cat but as a guide consistent with the following dietary requirements.

Basic Dietary Requirements

Calories—Proteins, Fats, Carbohydrates

In this era of sometimes obsessive diet-watching, what we should be most aware of for our cats is that we feed them enough, in a proper balance.

Calories are a measurement of energy, and every bit of activity in an animal requires

SAMPLE WEEKLY DIET

Morning:	Two days	Raw egg yolks
	Five days	Dry commercial cat foods
Evening:	Two days and not more than three	Raw organ meat such as heart, liver, or kidney. Second choice is raw horse-meat or hamburger
	Five days	A variety of commercial canned foods
Occasionally:		Cheese, cooked muscle meats, cooked fish, meat-type baby foods, yogurt, cooked vegetables and cereals, soups, tomato or clam juice, milk (if tolerated), and a large bone to chew
Vitamin and mineral supplements:	As recommended by your veterinarian	
Fats:	One teaspoon daily	Cooking oils, bacon fat, or butter
Water:	Always available, always fresh	

energy. Calories are fuel for the body in the same way that gasoline is for the automobile. Also, calories are required to keep the body temperature normal.

Active cats need more calories than the ones who catnap all day. The cat's temperament affects its caloric requirements; the high-strung pet requires more calories than the placid, easygoing one. More calories are required in cold weather. During gestation and lactation the queen needs more calories. Growing kittens require about twice as many calories as adult cats. A small cat requires more calories per pound of body weight than a large cat. The larger the cat, the less its caloric requirement per pound of body weight.

Fats furnish more than double the calories per gram than do carbohydrates or proteins. The calories of fats and carbohydrates should be used for energy, and the calories of proteins for tissue building and the maintenance

of body functions. Cats need more proteins than any other animal—about 30 percent of the diet for adults and 40 percent for kittens.

Vitamins and Minerals

Generally, the commercial foods contain sufficient vitamins and minerals for the average adult cat, but for lactating queens, growing kittens, and older cats, I feel that extra amounts should be added to the diet. Supplements can be found in liver, egg yolks, and some vegetables.

What to Do about Vitamin Deficiencies

Vitamin A deficiency results in infected and running eyes, poor appetite and growth, and skin lesions. A good supplement is egg yolk. Vitamin B_1 deficiency causes loss of appetite, nervousness, or convulsions and other neurological symptoms. Brewer's yeast is an excellent source of this vitamin, as are whole-grain cereals, liver, egg yolk, milk, and green vegetables. Lack of vitamin B_2 usually results in diarrhea, ulceration of the gums, and watery, bloodshot eyes. Good sources of this vitamin are yeast, wheat germ, liver, meat, fish, poultry, egg yolk, milk, and green vegetables. A deficiency of nicotinic acid is responsible for ulcerated mouth and black tongue (this corresponds to pellagra in human beings). This can be found in the foods that contain vitamin B_2 except for milk, egg yolk, and green vegetables. Vitamin D is essential to bone formation and the prevention of rickets in kittens. It is found in oils such as fish-liver oil. Vitamin E is said to aid in fertility and reproduction, in healing minor cuts, and is beneficial to skin and fur. It is present in egg yolk, wheat-germ oil, and green leafy vegetables such as lettuce, cabbage, and spinach.

If you wish to give your cat vitamins in pill or capsule form I recommend that you measure out one fourth the recommended adult daily dosage.

Vitamin C

Until recently, Vitamin C was considered an unnecessary additive for cats. However, it is now known that cats, although they are capable of manufacturing their own vitamin C, do not produce all of this nutrient that they need—particularly in times of stress. Although it has been common veterinary knowledge for years that vitamin C is useful in the treatment of respiratory and liver diseases and in arthritis, the latest research indicates that a high intake of vitamin C is helpful in the *prevention* of these diseases, and in cystitis.

Vitamin C is found in fruit juices and vegetables. Since many cats like the taste of tomato juice, a little each day would be helpful in preventing the above-mentioned problems and in keeping the urine acidic so as to prevent cystitis. Spinach and rhubarb are also

good sources of this important vitamin, but not every cat will eat them.

Vitamin Overfeeding

Because of the availability of high-potency supplements at low prices, some people give extra amounts of vitamins, believing that if a little helps, more is even better. Fortunately, the healthy adult cat will eliminate the extra amounts without harmful effects, but there can be problems.

The most commonly overused and most dangerous is vitamin D. Found in oils such as fish-liver oil, it is oil-soluble and is difficult for the body to eliminate. Any slight excess is eliminated through the kidneys, but in greatly excessive amounts the vitamin acts in a negative way; calcium is deposited in soft tissues and mineralization of the bones takes place.

The overfeeding of some vitamins has not been proven harmful but it is still in question. I would not feed a cat an excessive amount of any vitamin unless instructed to do so by your veterinarian.

Vegetables and Canapés

Though they are not essential, many cats find certain vegetables much to their liking. This is all to the good because they are a fine source of vitamins and minerals. Raw vegetables—the ingredients we toss into our salads—are avidly munched on by countless cats and supply a semblance of the live greenery our indoor pets are deprived of. Some cats like fruits as well and enjoy a bite or two of apple or cantaloupe.

Just as many other cats find the "happy hour" a special time of day for them. These are the cats who eat exotic foods because their human families do and they love to wander among the platters of shrimp, caviar, cheeses, and olives. Although I don't believe there is any food we eat that will harm a cat, once it becomes acquainted with gourmet morsels a cat tends to refuse commercial cat foods—and becomes in a sense addicted to much more expensive delicacies. You should discourage this because it will greatly interfere with your cat's normal feeding habits.

Cats and Greenery

All cats require greenery. Nibbling on leaves and grass helps remove hair balls and aids the digestive processes. This is why many indoor cats cannot be kept from attacking potted plants around the house, generally to the distress of their owners.

Since many plants are poisonous to cats and should never be accessible to them (see Chapter 17 for a listing of the toxic plants), a pet garden is the safest and sanest solution to this dietary need. Pots or planters around the house could contain sprouts of oats, wheat, rye, parsley, and even plain grass from the backyard. Some people also grow catnip and allow their pets to munch on it when they need a pick-me-up (see page 144).

Signs Of Nutritional Deficiencies

☐ Dry, scaly skin
☐ Excessive shedding
☐ Stunted growth
☐ Running eyes
☐ Rickets (bent legs)
☐ Black tongue and mouth ulceration
☐ Infertility
☐ Nervous disorders
☐ Anemia (listlessness, pale eye membranes and gums)

If any of these symptoms are marked in your cat, a trip to your veterinarian would be in order.

Some Hazards and Harmful Feeding Practices

Liver

Although liver is an excellent food, feeding it exclusively or even every day will eventually cause lameness due to the effects of excessive vitamin A on the bone structure.

Canned Fish

An exclusive diet of fish, especially tuna, will cause a disease called steatitis. This is caused by a vitamin E deficiency and shows itself in listlessness, loss of appetite, and soreness all over the body. It can prove fatal.

Raw Fish

Excessive feeding of raw fish is especially bad. There is an enzyme in raw fish which destroys vitamin B_1. The resulting deficiency manifests itself in loss of appetite and weight, heart disorders, and eventually convulsions and paralysis. Also, raw fish may transmit tapeworms. Cooked fish is the simple solution for the health and safety of your your cat. Be especially careful to remove all the bones.

Egg Whites

Egg whites also destroy certain vitamins when eaten raw. Skin problems are the result. Since cooked whites have no nutritional value, although they are perfectly safe, raw or cooked yolk is the best form in which to serve eggs.

Milk

While perfectly nutritious for most cats, some adult cats cannot digest milk and suffer diarrhea and allergic skin reactions from it. Cheese is a good milk substitute and one or the other is necessary if the cat is on an all-meat diet. They provide the calcium supplement for the prevention of bone disorders.

Bones

Small or brittle bones such as fish bones or those of chicken, pork, veal, lamb or rabbit should be avoided because the splinters can injure a cat's throat and intestines. But large bones are excellent for both the diet and the condition of the gums and teeth.

If you have a pressure cooker, it is possible to make use of even those taboo small bones. Pressure cooking takes the brittleness out of the bones, and when they are thoroughly soft, they will not harm the cat. The nutritional benefits, especially from the marrow, are excellent.

Special Feeding Situations

Weight Watching

Quality, not quantity, in food is important in keeping the cat's weight at a proper level.

When an animal is gaining too much weight, the amount of carbohydrates must be lowered and higher-protein food (eggs, meat, fish) given to cut down on the caloric intake. If your cat has been getting eight ounces of food a day, cut the daily ration to six ounces (or from seven to five, or from six to four). Referring to the sample weekly chart on page 134 should be helpful in figuring out what would be best for your cat. The diet should be at least half protein; the rest should include essential nutrients. The purpose of a reducing diet is to cause a gradual loss in body weight without serious side effects. The cat should have ample amounts of all nutrients.

For extreme cases of obesity there is a prescription diet called RD (reducing diet). Scientifically prepared, it is a complete, well-balanced diet, satisfies hunger, and yet reduces weight.

In any reducing program there will be no significant loss in weight for at least two weeks—the time it takes for the cat's body to use up excess fluid. Also, dieting will not work if the cat is not given exercise.

A recent survey has revealed some interesting facts regarding overweight cats:

□ Females are more commonly obese than males, because they are less aggressive and less territorial and therefore less active.

□ Overweight rises sharply in both sexes toward middle age, and tends to decrease after twelve years.

□ Obesity is more prevalent in cats fed on dry foods, table scraps, or home-prepared foods; less in those fed canned products.

□ Overweight is higher among cats owned by obese people and also among cats owned by middle-aged and elderly persons.

□ Thirty-one percent of owners with obese cats considered them normal in weight.

Invalid Diets for Sick Cats

You should ask your veterinarian whether your ailing cat requires a specific diet. Sick and convalescing cats need bland diets to allow nature to heal the affected organs. The normal diet is too harsh and irritating to the stomach and intestines, and all commercial cat foods should be removed from the diet. Baby foods are excellent and can be spoon-fed if necessary, or actually inserted into the mouth, small amounts at a time. Egg yolk mixed with milk and Karo syrup makes a life-sustaining mixture which can be fed with an eye dropper if need be. This solution can keep a critically ill animal from dehydrating while fighting the ravages of a disease. When a cat is ill and desperately needs food for survival keep in mind what you know are its favorite food fancies. The sick cat doesn't want to eat, but IT MUST. (See Chapter 14.)

Feeding at the Boarding Kennel or Hospital

When taking a cat to a boarding kennel let the management know what brand of food the cat is accustomed to. And an especially fussy cat generally settles into a kennel easier if you take its own water dish and feeding bowl along.

When taking a cat from the hospital or kennel, let it have several hours of peace and quiet at home before giving it anything to eat or drink. Overexcitement causes nausea.

13 · Year-Round Care

Vital Statistics · Grooming · Exercise · Traveling

Cathood Vital Statistics

Female breeding age (onset)	6–7 months
Male breeding age (onset)	6–7 months
Breeding span of female	4–5 years
Breeding span of male	5–7 years
Estrus cycle (heat period)	12–15 days per year
	3–4 days each time
Gestation (conception to birth)	58–69 days (average: 63)
Litter size	1–8 (average: 4)
Birth weight	4–4.5 ounces
Weaning age	6–8 weeks
Begin feeding cat food	4–6 weeks
Weight of adult female	4–8 pounds
Weight of adult male	4–10 pounds

139

During their ancestral days, cats naturally made adjustments to the elements, and they were able to withstand nature's hardships much more easily than today's pets. Pet cats have no need to race across ice packs or the hot desert sands. They have lost their heavy protective covering and are much more refined.

Since many of our pets stay indoors most of the time, in heated houses during the winter and in air-conditioned, low-humidity dwellings during the summer—contrary to what nature intended—we have to make various adjustments for them to help nature along.

Today's cats need special care with their coats, skin, claws, exercise-play periods, and general well-being. And they have to be handled differently each season.

Intranasal Vaccination

Recently, a new type of vaccination against respiratory diseases of cats has been introduced to the veterinarians. The first intranasal vaccine to prevent rhino-tracheitis and calici-virus infections is available and has proved to give a very strong immunity. It is very simply done by placing a drop of vaccine in each eye and a few drops on the nose.

In extensive trials, the vaccine showed no reaction, no temperature rise, and did not cause the cats to go off feed. The entire process is so quick and gentle that even a more aggressive cat normally responds with only a flick of its head.

Intranasal vaccination is advised at twelve weeks of age and annual boosters thereafter.

Winterizing

During the winter months, when sickness and disease are especially prevalent, the cat's health should be under constant surveillance. Health is dependent upon housing, diet, exercise, and general treatment.

By keeping the cat healthy, natural resis-tance to disease-producing germs is increased. Annual booster vaccination against distemper, rhino-tracheitis, calici, and pneumonitis each fall is especially recommended to fully protect a cat during the winter months.

Also, never keep a cat in a cold, damp, or drafty place or it will be extremely prone to respiratory problems.

Summerizing

During hot weather, cats are subject to many more skin conditions because fungus is more in evidence, and fleas, ticks and lice are more plentiful.

Fleas are the greatest cause of summer eczemas. A recent survey lists the flea as the cause of over 70 percent of summer skin problems. Preventive measures include the use of flea collars, flea sprays and powders, and periodic baths with a flea shampoo.

About 50 percent of all cats are acutely sensitive to flea bites and such cats will itch and scratch incessantly from a single bite. See Chapter 16 for treatment for fleas.

Grooming

Cat grooming does not require a lot of time or professional training, and most of the techniques of a good grooming program can be learned in a short time. Most cats enjoy the special attention they receive in grooming, and look forward to it. A regular program of grooming—if possible, initiated in kittenhood—is essential to health and well-being.

Care of the Coat and Fur

Three types of hair coats have to be considered in grooming: (1) short hair, which is relatively easy to keep well groomed; (2) long hair, which needs combing and brushing quite often; and (3) semi-long hair, which needs more care than short hair and less than long hair.

The aim of fur grooming is to maintain a full, glossy coat. It is much easier to prevent matted hair by frequent brushing than to try to restore a coat that is full of tangles. In extreme cases of matting, clipping is necessary.

Shedding

In cats in the wild state and in domestic cats who live much of their lives outdoors, the lengthening of the hours of sunlight in the spring activates shedding of the cat's heavy winter coat. However, for indoor cats, artificial conditions—constant thermal control, air conditioning, and electric lighting—rather than strictly seasonal changes affect the shedding process. Therefore, some indoor cats will shed all year around.

The indoor-outdoor cat will normally begin to shed at the onset of hot weather. The undercoat of dead hair comes out in great rolls. To help this process along (and to cut down on the amount of hair that is shed in your house), you should comb out the loose hair each day. Old dead hair may cause skin irritations. A silky, shiny coat makes a cat look beautiful and is the best insulation from the hot rays of the summer sun.

Occasionally unnatural brownish-red spots appear on a cat's coat. This is a condition known as "rusting," and darker-colored cats such as blacks and blues are most susceptible, although cream coats may also be affected. Rusting is caused by dampness, food stains, too much sunlight, or too much licking. These discolorations can be eliminated by the use of "color" shampoos found in pet stores.

Combing and Brushing

Special cat combs and brushes can be purchased at pet stores. Start at the head and work down toward the rear, combing or brushing in short strokes. At the same time, look for any evidence of fleas or skin problems. It is important to get out all the tangles and mats. There are excellent tangleproof solutions on the market which help soften the knots and ease the combing problem. Otherwise, if the mats will not comb out, snip them out carefully with blunt scissors, cutting away from the cat's body.

You can also remove excess hair by rubbing the cat with a piece of chamois leather or a rough cloth. The more old fur you remove, the less chance your cat will have problems with hair balls in the stomach.

Some cats who will not tolerate combing and brushing have to be taken in hand periodically for the removal of tangles and mats. Tranquilization or complete anesthesia are necessary for the most difficult cases.

In long-haired cats, a problem occasionally arises in which a cat gets hair entangled across its lower canine teeth. The owner will notice the cat pawing at its mouth and salivating excessively. The hair can be readily be taken off with eyebrow tweezers.

Bathing

Normally, cats wash themselves and do not need baths. Bathing washes away the protective natural oils in the fur. But sometimes a cat will get dirty and will not be able to do all the cleaning alone. Under no circumstances, however, should a cat under three months of age be bathed.

Bathing a cat can be quite an experience and a battle of wits, so before beginning you should understand all aspects of the procedure. Since most cats basically dislike water, you can expect a lot of resistance, and you should be gentle and patient.

The cat's head should not be submerged in the water for even a second. But there probably will be some splashing, and a bit of soapy water could get into the eyes and ears. To avoid irritation to the eyes, put a drop of mineral oil or Vaseline around them. And to avoid possible infection from water in the ears, a little cotton in each one will keep them high and dry.

Bathe only in a warm room. Use two tubs, one containing warm soapy water, and the other clean warm water. The water should be only to the cat's shoulder, so that it can stand and move without swallowing or inhaling water. If it is a cold day, or a cold room, or you have no warm water, do not bathe the cat. Use only soap recommended for cats, or a gentle baby soap, but *never* a dog soap. Gently lower the cat—facing away from you, the back toward you to avoid clawing—into the soapy water and rub the suds into the fur. Avoid getting soap or water near the head and the eyes and ears. Do the job quickly. Rinse your cat in the other tub and dry with warm towels. Keep the cat inside and warm for an hour or two afterwards.

Care of the Cat's Ears

Never poke or probe in your cat's ears, and never wash the ears out with soap and water. Instead, apply a small amount of baby oil or a 3 percent solution of peroxide on a cotton swab and gently rotate the swab, wiping only as far as you can reach without using pressure. Do not probe too far into the ear, for there is a risk of permanent damage to the ear canal. Be sure to have someone hold the cat so that it doesn't squirm and resist your probing too much.

If the ear appears dry, you might wipe it gently with baby oil. If the surface seems too moist, a dusting with BFI powder might be helpful.

Watch out for: black caking around the ear canal, shaking of the head, pawing at the ear, which usually indicate ear mites. If your cat holds its head at a strange angle and there is a strong odor this usually indicates an infection in the ear canal.

Nail Clipping

A house pet that has been well trained to a scratching post will still need to have its claws clipped. This is not so much for the protection of furniture as for the protection of people and other pets. There are many situations in which a cat may inadvertently inflict rather painful cuts. The Burmese and Siamese breeds, for example, are excellent jumpers and are easily trained to jump into the owner's arms or onto his shoulders. This can be an agonizing experience if the cat's hold is not secure and it decides to dig in. If the nails are long, the evidence will be substantial.

Nail clipping is seldom necessary for the outdoor cat with opportunities, and hard surfaces, for keeping the nails in condition. Moreover, for the outdoor cat the nails are an essential defense weapon. With both the indoor and the outdoor cat it is usually not necessary to clip the back claws, as the cat generally keeps them filed down.

The clipping procedure is actually much easier with cats than with many dogs, primarily because the cat's claws are translucent and the veins can be seen readily. Clipping should begin in kittenhood. If you initiate the procedure with an older cat, you will be met with resistance, and you should probably consult your veterinarian before you attempt the job. If you are very nervous about undertaking this aspect of grooming, it might be better to have your cat's nails clipped by your veterinarian.

Use only special pet nail clippers because scissors and clippers intended for human nails will pinch and hurt the animal. Since cats generally object to this procedure, it might be wise to have an assistant hold your pet. The best time for nail clipping is when the cat is relaxed and somewhat sleepy. Speak soothingly and handle the animal gently but firmly. If the kitten offers slight resistance, a gentle flick on the nose, paired with a verbal reprimand—"No!"—should bring the situation safely under your control.

Hold each paw to the light, press the pad gently to cause the cat to extend its claws, and cut, *only the slightest bit,* the white or clear-colored part of the nail. Where the clear color ends and the nail becomes pink is the quick. If the quick is cut, a blood vessel will be cut which bleeds quite badly. If you should cut into the quick and blood appears, alum powder or a styptic pencil should be used to stop the bleeding. Good eyesight and firm holding are necessary for this operation.

Declawing

There is much public sentiment against declawing cats. I certainly do not recommend the operation for outdoor cats, as they need their nails for protection. However, in some households it may be necessary in order to prevent destruction of household objects. But this should be the solution *only* after attempts to train the cat to a scratching post have failed (see page 104).

Normally only the front paws of the cat are declawed because the hind claws are not as destructive. Declawing is a minor surgical procedure but requires general anesthesia and a short stay in the veterinary hospital.

There is a compromise operation which removes only the middle two nails. This reduces the destructive effects of scratching somewhat and still leaves the animal with some climbing and fighting ability. If this operation is not satisfactory, the remaining nails can always be removed.

Although I do not generally advise this, some breeders and veterinarians recommend declawing kittens between three and fourteen days of age. They claim it is less painful at such an age—similar to tail docking in puppies. The surgery is performed under a gas anesthetic and the kittens are back nursing their mothers within ten to fifteen minutes. The paws are completely healed in a few days.

I should add here that declawing a cat will not inhibit the instinct to scratch, and there are cases of declawed cats whose toe pads develop calluses which are as effective as claws in destroying furniture.

Schedule of Vaccinations Against Disease

	AGE TO BEGIN	BOOSTER VACCINATIONS
Distemper (panleukopenia)	8 weeks	annual
Rhino-tracheitis	10–12 weeks	annual
Pneumonitis	10–12 weeks	annual
Calici-virus	10–12 weeks	annual
Rabies	6 months	annual

Vaccinations

For the year-round health and well-being of your cat, annual vaccinations are extremely important. The preceding chart should prove helpful in scheduling your necessary yearly trips to your veterinarian.

Exercise

Inside Toys

The scratching post is the best toy and piece of furniture for inside cats for both exercise and scratching. When purchasing a post, even for a kitten, I would advise getting one tall enough for a mature cat—the kitten will soon outgrow a small one. For details on how to build a scratching post, and how to train your cat to use it, see page 104.

Retrieving is a favorite game for cats, and splendid exercise. Use an old sock, a Ping-Pong ball, anything you can throw (but not chewable rubber objects or cellophane). You may be able to teach the cat to retrieve it on command and give it a reward on its return.

A flashlight can be an amusing diversion for a cat. Darken the room and the cat will follow the spot of light for hours. This is an especially good method for those cat owners who cannot get about easily.

Catnip

Catnip toys are always fascinating to cats, for they apparently get quite a "trip" from catnip. It is considered to be very similar to marijuana. Catnip serves as a mild nerve stimulant and does no harm to most cats (although it is not recommended for cats with kidney ailments). It is the odor, not the taste, that produces the ecstasy.

Cats high on catnip act so much like sexually aroused queens that the herb was thought to be an aphrodisiac. However, scientific tests have indicated that it is not a love potion.

Catnip arouses even lazy and bored cats and stimulates valuable exercise.

Traveling

The Summer Deathtrap: The Car (see also Chapter 18)

Invariably, every summer cats are brought to me either dead or just about gone from heatstroke caused by leaving them too long in a car. On hot days a car is a very dangerous place to leave a cat. Park the car in the shade with the windows open, but not wide enough for the cat to jump out if it is not in a carrier.

Air-conditioned cars are a great help but dangerous when the motor is stopped and the air-conditioning is off. Some people go away for a "few minutes," only to find the cat in distress or dead upon their return.

The early signs of heat prostration are staggering, panting, gasping. Put cold packs on the cat's head, pull the tongue forward to keep the cat from choking on it, and quickly get to a veterinarian. If the cat is in bad shape, a spot of brandy or black coffee may be given as a stimulant.

Sometimes these animals can be saved, but unfortunately there is often brain damage from the high fever and with the ensuing complications they will not survive.

Vacation Trips

Before going on a long trip, visit your veterinarian for a health certificate (in some states, and in Mexico and Canada, this is required), and get any booster shots that are falling due.

Make sure you have a suitable carrier in which your cat can ride in safety and comfort.

144

Do not rely on a cardboard box or the arms of a traveling companion. In warm weather a wire cage is a good idea because it allows ample air circulation and with the cat inside the cage you can keep the car windows lowered whenever you have to leave the cat alone in the car.

A few days before you depart, set the carrier on the floor and let the cat get used to it with short periods of confinement.

Most cats curl up and sleep during a long car ride. However, there are some excitable animals who need sedation, and your veterinarian can prescribe a tranquilizer that will keep the cat quiet and prevent drooling or vomiting.

Take along plenty of fresh water and offer it often during the trip. But feed the cat only at the end of each day.

The cat should have a collar with an identification tag. When not in the carrier the cat should wear a figure-eight harness with a leash and be under the control of a capable person. Never turn a cat loose in a strange area—that will most likely be the end of the cat, for you.

Moving to a New Home

One out of every five American families moves its household each year and so a large number of cats are moving too. To a cat this can be bewildering and often terrifying.

One of the most common myths about cats is that they love places more than people. Thus some ill-advised cat owners have had their cats put to sleep rather than take them along when they moved. This is absolutely absurd. Cats want more than anything else to be with the people they love.

When you have arrived at your new home, confine the cat to a room with fresh water and food until all the moving commotion is over.

Then the cat can be introduced to the old familiar furniture in the new house or the old toys that came along for the ride. Keep all doors and windows shut. You might spread butter on the cat's paws. While licking it off, the cat will pick up the new scents in the house. An old theory—that works.

The American Humane Association recommends that cats be confined for several weeks until they become accustomed to their new homes, because of their tendency to wander off and try to return to their original homes. In my opinion, this depends on the way the transition is handled and on the bond between cat and owner.

Shipping a Cat by Air

There are many advantages to shipping a cat by air and most of the time the trip is uneventful. When a problems occurs, it is usually due to carelessness or inexperience on the part of the shipper. Here are some simple precautions which will avoid a lot of grief.

□ Make a reservation on as direct a flight as possible—a minimum of changes, nonstop if it can be arranged.

□ It is a good idea to ship something as valuable as a cat collect. There is the chance that better care will be given.

□ Health certificates are required by airlines. When this is obtained from your veterinarian you should seek his advice on the use of a tranquilizer.

□ Feed the cat very lightly before the trip.

□ Use a sturdy wooden or plastic container. These are available from most airlines.

□ Wait with the cat at the freight office until it is taken out to the plane. Being reassured of the flight, you should then call the people receiving the cat so that they can be waiting at the air terminal for the flight upon arrival. And it should be a bon voyage.

Part 4
The Ailing Cat

14 · Nursing, Medicating, and Force-Feeding the Ailing Cat

Nursing Care

The first thing one of my professors in veterinary school told me was that the doctor's job is to help nature along, not to impede it, and that if we interfere with nature, we are not doing our job as doctors.

Even with antibiotics, new drugs, the latest in laboratory equipment, and expanding medical knowledge, the value of nursing care cannot be overestimated. A cat can be given every known drug and yet not respond until tender, loving care is instituted. Penicillin will not cure a lonely heart. There has to be a combination of veterinary supervision and tender nursing care to stimulate the cat's response to the drugs and to restore it to health.

At the Hospital

There are some conditions that definitely require hospital care, such as surgical cases, cases which require oxygen and blood transfusions, and animals so critically ill that constant supervision is necessary to keep them alive.

The first intensive-care unit for animals was established at Cornell University Veterinary College. Its equipment is comparable to the best units in use for humans. This laboratory machinery enables the staff to pinpoint the precise ailment within one minute. Included in the unit is a "blood-gas" machine, a cardiac defibrillator, an electrocardiograph, an instrument to measure arterial blood pressure, a respirator, and an oxygen tent. Quick diagnosis and help often save the lives of many patients who otherwise would not have made it. Eventually, intensive-care units will be set up in most good, progressive veterinary hospitals.

Fortunately, the average cat does well in a veterinary hospital. It is quick to respond to the gentle voices of the attendants and to the

149

soothing treatment. For animals who are highly emotional and need the human touch, most up-to-date veterinary hospitals have veterinary nurses in attendance who give individual attention and try to substitute the tender, loving care pets miss from their owners.

Visiting Sick Animals

Visting is not generally advisable, because it gets the animals unduly excited and they tend to be quite disappointed when the visitors leave, but there are some cases when visiting should be allowed. Sometimes a critically ill cat will seem to give up, not caring whether it lives or dies. Such a cat needs an emotional lift, and at this point I usually ask the owner to come to the hospital and bring some favorite tidbit. In rare cases I have allowed an owner to stay overnight in the hospital with the animal.

Some veterinary hospitals have special rooms where the owner can visit a critically ill cat away from the rest of the patients so that the hospital routine is not interrupted.

There is the occasional cat who will not respond to anyone but its owner, and for such a problem child I recommend home treatment, even if it involves daily or even twice-daily trips to the veterinary hospital.

Plastic Surgery

Veterinarians nowadays often concern themselves with the physical appearance of the animal that has been seriously injured in an accident and are employing many techniques commonly used on human beings by plastic surgeons. Disfiguration may be avoided in many cases, and cosmetic surgery is a daily routine in most good veterinary hospitals. For instance, a cat with a broken jaw can have it repaired with wires so that instead of having a protruding row of teeth and misshapen jaw, it can look (and function) normally again.

Recently a kitten was brought to me that had been severely burned by chewing a hot electric wire. Part of the tongue was burned off and also one side of the cheek and lips. The cat required surgery to help control the muscular action of the tongue and cosmetic surgery was needed to restore its appearance. After a series of plastic-surgery operations, the animal was restored to a normal-looking and normal-acting kitten. Unfortunately, this kind of operation can be very costly. When expense is a major consideration, the owner should discuss with a veterinarian the advisability of such surgery.

Amputees

At times, amputation of a cat's limb is necessary because of a badly broken bone, an infected leg, or a bone infection that has already degenerated into gangrene.

It is amazing how well cats adapt to a life on three legs. They adjust much more readily to a missing leg than humans do. By the day after surgery, they are walking around. After a few days they are running and playing and even climbing as if nothing ever happened. They can lead a normal life for years to come.

Common-Sense Care of Your Cat at Home

Although love itself will not cure a sick animal, the close affection between a cat and its master, combined with the proper medication, will often overcome a dangerous disease. In nursing a sick cat, persistence and patience are of the utmost importance.

Most people try home remedies when their animals first show signs of illness and then seek veterinary help when the aspirin or the milk of magnesia doesn't seem to work. If the illness is such that the animal can be treated

150

at home, the veterinarian will prescribe drugs that can be administered along with rest and quiet and tender, loving care. Fortunately, few animal diseases are contagious to humans, so that exposure to sick cats will not endanger the owner.

Nursing care is twenty-four-hour duty, and most people will stay up day and night nursing a sick pet. But they must follow the veterinarian's advice. Some people, upon returning home with the animal, disregard instructions. It is not fair either to the animal or to the veterinarian. If the animal doesn't recover, the veterinarian will likely be blamed even though the nursing care is what was lacking.

The Bed

The bed should be warm and free from drafts. The bedding should be kept clean so that when the cat relieves itself it does not have to lie in a wet or dirty box.

For a cat who cannot move about, bed sores become a problem. It should be turned from side to side every few hours and kept clean with a washcloth so that its urine doesn't burn its legs. It will need enemas or suppositories to aid in elimination (see page 152). Comfort is always important for recovery.

Peace and Quiet

The sick cat should have peace and quiet with as little handling and with as few strangers to excite it as possible.

Exercise

Never allow the cat to go outdoors in extremely cold or wet weather if it has a cold or fever. And don't allow it to overexercise when it is recuperating. Avoid overexposure to the elements and dry the cat thoroughly if it has gotten wet. Any convalescent cat is quite susceptible to secondary pneumonia.

Taking the Pulse

The inexperienced owner will find it difficult to take his cat's pulse. It is taken on the inside of the cat's thigh, where the femoral artery can be felt. The femoral artery pulsation determines the pulse rate. A normal rate is about 110 to 130 per minute, but it varies with age, exercise, excitement, and condition of the cat. In shock, it is very fast and weak. A normal cat's *heart* beats 90 to 100 times a minute.

The Temperature

When nursing a sick cat, you should check its temperature frequently. The normal temperature is 100 to 101.5 degrees. A temperature below 100 is a serious sign that the body is weakening and emergency treatment is necessary. The cat should be wrapped in warm blankets with a hot-water bottle or an electric heating pad until it can be taken to the veterinarian. A stimulant—brandy or any other alcoholic beverage—should be administered: one teaspoon of water with one quarter teaspoon of brandy.

Any temperature over 102 degrees should be regarded as fever, and if there is a high fever a veterinarian should be consulted. Some diseases such as distemper can cause fever as high as 105 or 106 degrees. High fevers often result in convulsions, as seen in brain diseases such as meningitis.

In taking a cat's temperature, an ordinary rectal thermometer may be used. A thermometer should never be inserted into a cat's mouth. Naturally, while the temperature is being taken the cat must be held securely. Lubricate the end of the thermometer with either mineral oil or Vaseline to prevent irritation and gently insert it into the cat's anus. Leave it in about two to three minutes. Remember, anything over 102 degrees indicates trouble.

How to Give Your Cat an Enema

Occasionally, when laxatives do not work and your cat is in dire distress, an enema is called for. This is not an easy task and it is the work of a minimum of two people. Sometimes a third person is needed if the cat is strong-willed.

Lukewarm water, either plain or soapy, should be used, and a human enema bag with a rubber syringe will work well. For the average cat, a pint of water is usually sufficient to give relief.

You can also purchase a prepared disposable enema syringe called Fleet Enema at your local pharmacy. It is easy to use and less messy than the soap-and-water routine.

Symptomatic Nursing

Although I use all the drugs available to the veterinary profession, I am still old-fashioned enough to believe in symptomatic treatment. For example, the use of a vaporizer with a drop or two of tincture of benzoin or camphor in the water is beneficial in the treatment of pneumonia, distemper, or a chest infection. Vicks salve or something similar on the nose is helpful because the cat will lick it, and it is soothing to the throat and is a good expectorant, useful in bringing up phlegm from the chest.

If a cat has pneumonia, rubbing its chest with camphorated oil or some other liniment and covering with a sweater or chest protector will help the animal breathe more easily.

For an irritated-throat condition, pure honey is soothing and is a good food as well. However, if infection is present, antibiotics and other drugs should be administered simultaneously, but only under the direction of a veterinarian.

Symptomatic nursing involves what common sense tells one to do. If a cat's nose is running, it should be kept washed and protected with soothing ointments. A boric acid or warm salt water solution can be used to keep the nostrils clear, and baby oil or Vaseline can be used to soothe them. If the cat has diarrhea, the condition should be treated with Pepto-Bismol or Kaopectate. If constipation is present, a laxative (such as milk of magnesia), a suppository, or an enema should be given. Continual diarrhea can cause dehydration, and constipation can cause discomfort, gas, and a toxic condition.

Bandaging: Protecting Against Licking and Scratching

If the cat is scratching an area of skin with its hind legs, we make booties out of gauze, bandage, and tape. Because cats scratch themselves, if the nails are covered the wound may clear up by itself.

If the lesion is on the body around the chest or rib cage, a sweater or towel wrapped around the body and pinned securely will protect it from scratching and licking.

If an area cannot be bandaged, an "Elizabethan" collar can be made to prevent the cat from turning around to lick a certain area. Simply take a piece of plastic or cardboard and attach it to the collar around its neck.

Medicines
The Medicine Chest

A medicine chest is essential for every cat owner. There are many times when drugs are needed for minor ailments or until your veterinarian can be reached in an emergency. I advise discussing the matter with your veterinarian; he will be pleased to tell you what preparations to stock.

The following can serve as a basic guide:

absorbent cotton
adhesive tape
cotton swabs
enema tubes; Fleet (disposable)
gauze bandage
nail clippers (for pets)
rectal thermometer
scissors

alcohol
ammonia (aromatic spirits of)
bicarbonate of soda
calamine lotion
camphorated oil
charcoal (activated—antidote for poisoning)
disinfectant (such as Clorox)
Epsom salts (to soak minor infections)
hydrogen peroxide
iodine
Kaopectate
Metaphen or Mercurochrome
milk of magnesia
mineral oil
sedative (by prescription only)
shock formula (see page 225)
soap (germicidal, such as tincture of green)
styptic powder (to stop bleeding)
talcum powder (medicated)
Vaseline (but not carbolated)
zinc oxide

How to Administer Some "Common-Sense" Household Medicines to Your Cat

Mineral Oil

Mineral oil can be added to food but never administered by spoon or dropper. Since it does not stimulate a strong swallowing reflex, the cat may unknowingly allow it to trickle down his trachea, and thus become a victim of fatal foreign-body pneumonia. Mineral oil also interferes with absorption of fat-soluble vitamins and can cause deficiencies if overused.

Vaseline (Petroleum Jelly—Non-carbolated)

Vaseline is effective in the relief of constipation, especially that caused by hair balls. It is an excellent substitute for mineral oil, readily swallowed with no danger of pneumonia. Administer it by rubbing one half to one teaspoon of Vaseline on the cat's paws and the cat will lick it off.

Commercial Hair-Ball Medicine

Each time a cat grooms itself, it ingests a great deal of hair which forms into a ball in the stomach. In short-haired cats these balls are generally quite small and are easily eliminated. In long-haired cats the hair balls are larger and harder to eliminate. Although most cats regurgitate the hair balls, for those who have difficulty hair-ball preparations should be given at regular intervals. The medicine should be administered between meals so as not to interfere (like mineral oil) with proper absorption of essential vitamins. Most of these preparations are well tolerated by cats.

Aspirin

Aspirin, although helpful in reducing fever and alleviating pain and discomfort, can be fatal if given consistently to a cat. An occasional small dose (one-fourth of an adult aspirin) will not hurt a cat, but if given daily for a week or so can cause grave symptoms and possible death.

It has recently been proven that in both animals and humans aspirin can cause ulceration of the stomach and intestines if taken in too large quantities over too long a time.

Some Warnings about the Misuse of Medicines

Most human medications should be used for a cat only on the advice of a veterinarian. For example, some human laxatives contain strychnine, which can be fatal to cats. Also, some drugs deteriorate with age and either lose their effectiveness or increase in strength and can be harmful. Medicines should not be kept more than one year.

Any sudden change in a sick cat, such as fast breathing, spasmodic coughing, bleeding from any body cavity, swelling of the head, welts on the body, sneezing, or rubbing of eyes, should be reported at once to the veterinarian, because this could indicate a drug reaction. An animal occasionally shows susceptibility to a drug and can quickly go into anaphylactic shock, an allergic reaction.

Antibiotics

Some cat owners believe that a shot of penicillin will cure anything. By indiscriminate administration of antibiotics, they decrease resistance to certain drugs and cause some cats to develop a drug sensitivity. Before any such drug is used a veterinarian should be consulted.

The dangers of indiscriminate use of antibiotics are many: Germs become immune to certain antibiotics over a period of time, and the animal will be helpless when an antibiotic is really necessary; continual use of antibiotics will destroy the normal bacteria in the intestinal tract and some cats will develop diarrhea; vitamin deficiencies appear in some cats; some combinations of drugs are dangerous.

Pregant queens should never be given antibiotics unless a veterinarian so recommends; these drugs go through the bloodstream and can affect the unborn kittens. The antibiotic tetracycline can cause kittens' teeth to turn yellow, but fortunately the permanent teeth come in white and structurally healthy.

No one but a veterinarian or other professional should attempt to inject antibiotics because faulty administration can cause abscesses or, if the needle should hit a nerve, partial or complete paralysis.

Hormones

I heartily approve of the use of male and female hormones, under the guidance of a veterinarian, for many conditions discussed in this book—spayed queens, castrated males, and certain ailments—but I deplore the excessive and indiscriminate use of hormones.

The misuse of hormones to keep females out of heat has ruined much good breeding stock by making it necessary to perform hysterectomies to save the lives of queens because of infections of the female organs.

There has also been misuse of hormones to bring females into heat. When they come into heat, they don't ovulate and don't conceive.

However, there is a valuable fertility drug, which has been used in human medicine to help sterile woman conceive. This drug is often used in cats to help them ovulate, and otherwise barren queens have been able to conceive and raise litters of healthy kittens.

There is a place in veterinary medicine for the *proper* use of hormones, but never without a prescription.

Tranquilizers

Tranquilizers have transformed many a bad cat into a manageable one, but, like any other drugs, when used incorrectly they can adversely affect an animal's personality. Occasionally a cat reacts badly to tranquilizers and changes into a raving man-hating beast.

Stimulants

Benzedrine ("goof balls") and other stimulants are dangerous to the cat and can even cause death. They are too hard on the heart and other vital organs. Some cats go into convulsions, and others are permanently affected with lifelong epileptic seizures or similar muscular conditions. Giving stimulants to show cats is frowned upon by the Cat Fanciers Association. If a cat ever needs a stimulant, I advise nothing stronger than a teaspoon of black coffee or brandy. Any artificial stimulation should be used only on the advice of a veterinarian unless emergency treatment is being administered.

Cortisone

Cortisone has an important role in veterinary medicine because of its value in the treatment of arthritis, skin diseases, traumatic injuries, shock, snake bites, and anaphylactic shock, but it should be used only upon the advice of a veterinarian. Overdosage and prolonged use cause a toxic condition and are very detrimental to the kidneys. The symptoms are excessive water drinking and urination, and some bloating. There is increase in appetite and an increase in weight with retention of fluids.

Medicating and Force-feeding the Ailing Cat

Since this lifesaving subject has driven many a cat owner to near despair, this section is intended to take some of the distress out of the treatment.

It is assumed that the most important step has already been taken: that a veterinarian has been consulted and that he has prescribed the medications and special diets. He will also

ascertain whether the cat is too sick for home care. If so, he will take care of the force-feeding intravenously. But once the cat is over the critical period, it will usually respond and recover much more quickly under the tender, loving care of its owner. And now *the real treatment is up to you.* The cat *must* ingest the medication and food in order to resist the ravages of the ailment or disease—and to survive.

The initial problem to be faced is that a cat normally rejects any unknown taste or object forced into his mouth.

The second strike against the cat owner is the basic cat instinct of fighting restraint. No matter how ill, a cat will fight, and even die fighting, rather than give in. Therefore, if the pet is not handled correctly, the added stress of fighting will lower its chances of recovery and perhaps cause a relapse.

Most important of all, treat your cat with gentleness, firmness, patience.

How to Administer Medications

If you need to medicate or force-feed your cat, the cat should always be on a table, a counter top, or your lap (on the floor, you have less control and the cat has more room to maneuver).

For maximum control you can drape a towel around the cat—from the neck down, and with its front legs and feet encased. A pillowcase (in it up to its neck and tied, but not too tightly) is an excellent restraint for an especially active cat.

Pills or capsules can be moistened with a bit of butter or oil to make them slip down more easily. Hold the pill or capsule in your hand between your thumb and index finger. With your other hand, tilt the cat's head up to at least a 45-degree angle and gently press open the corner of the mouth. Move your fingers around to the front teeth and press the lower jaw down until the mouth is open

enough to pop the pill in, as far back on the center of the tongue as possible. Quickly close the cat's mouth and hold it shut while keeping the chin pointed upward. With the other hand, gently stroke the throat to stimulate swallowing. To further stimulate the swallowing mechanism, a sudden puff of air into the cat's face might shock it into gulping.

If at first you don't succeed, please, please do not give up. Frustrating as it may be for you, it is perfectly normal for the cat to try to spit out the pill which it so badly needs. And with a little patience and practice you should soon master the technique.

If you seem to have trouble getting the pill far enough back on the tongue, you might try pushing it down the throat with your finger. *But be very careful because:*

1. You might have your finger badly bitten or even lose part of it.

2. The pill could go down the wrong way, into the windpipe. If the cat coughs or gags,

stop immediately! Let go of its head so it can cough the pill up. If it seems lodged, hold the cat upside down until the pill comes free.

If the pill-giving technique proves utterly impossible, all is not lost. You can pulverize the pill or take the powder out of the capsule and mix it with a highly favored food (and preferably highly flavored, to mask the medicine taste). This is where getting to know your cat and what it most likes to eat is rewarding. Even a little caviar at a time like this is more than worth the price.

However, if the cat is completely off its feed, which so many ailing cats tend to be, you can treat the pulverized pill or capsule powder as a *liquid* medication. Add it to an egg yolk, pour in a little Karo syrup, and beat the mixture well. This can be given to the cat with a medicine dropper made of *plastic* (not glass—it breaks too easily). Prepare and posture the cat as for the pill-giving procedure to administer any liquid medicine, but make

157

sure the head is only slightly tilted upward (not more than 45 degrees) to keep the liquid from getting into the windpipe (if it does, it will end up in the lungs and possibly cause a foreign-body pneumonia). Take the filled medicine dropper, and holding the head with the other hand, insert the dropper between the rear teeth and squirt the contents to the back of the tongue. Keep the head tilted and massage the throat until the liquid is swallowed (or else the cat will try to spit it out). Give the cat a few seconds to regain its aplomb before the next dropperful. Proceed slowly and gently until all the mixture is consumed.

Here, too, it is important to stop *immediately* if the cat starts to cough or gag. It means that some of the liquid may be getting into the windpipe.

Force-feeding

Food is a very important element in curing sick animals. In the early stages of sickness a cat with an upset stomach or a fever will likely refuse food, and this is good because the cat will be prone to nausea and a full stomach will aggravate its condition. However, if it persists in refusing food and liquid, it will dehydrate quickly. A kitten is critically prone to dehydration, and if it goes without food and water for as little as twelve hours, it will dehydrate to the point of death. If food continues to nauseate the cat then it will have to be fed by injections of saline and glucose, and other nutrients will have to be given intravenously.

If the cat refuses to eat but the food doesn't seem to nauseate it, don't hesitate to force-feed it. Bits of food every fifteen to twenty minutes will often stave off dehydration and prevent the cat from going into coma and shock. Some people simply take the food away if a sick cat refuses it, thinking to starve the animal into eating. Others will sit by the

hour feeding their cats piece by piece minute amounts of food. Obviously, the more patient cat lovers are much more likely to save their animals.

Dehydration in the sick cat is a symptom which especially has to be watched for. Also called "drying out" or becoming "hide-bound," it is usually caused by diarrhea and vomiting, when more fluids are lost than are taken in. For survival the dehydration must be treated and the vomiting and diarrhea must be stopped. Normally the loose skin on the back of the neck will quickly bounce back into place when pulled out, but with dehydration the skin remains pulled away from the neck and returns very slowly. In the clinic, the veterinarian combats dehydration with intravenous administration of saline and glucose and with injections to stop vomiting and diarrhea.

When a cat is sick, its diet must be changed. It generally will refuse its normal food; the regular commercial foods are too harsh for a sick or convalescing cat. Don't hesitate to try many combinations of food until one is found that seems to stimulate the cat's appetite. Some cats will eat the strangest things when they are ill, and every bit of food that they ingest is that much in their favor, for they need the strength to fight off the germs and the aftereffects of the illness.

If your veterinarian did not give you a specific diet, the first step is to try to tempt the cat in every way possible. Present it with its very favorite food—its "special treat" food. If the cat walks away from it, you might try some of the things it never or rarely gets— liver, kidney, heart, raw or cooked. If this tactic fails, the cat may be taken in by tidbits you may normally scold it for "stealing"—raw or rare roast beef, expensive canned salmon, chicken-liver pâté, tuna, lobster, caviar. If all these fail, then force-feeding must be resorted to.

(Incidentally, because cats tend to eat what they like the smell of, upper respiratory infections and diseases cause the greatest feeding problems. The sense of smell is so impaired that the food presented to them has to be extra "smelly" to tempt them.)

A good guide to follow in force-feeding a cat who will not be tempted by food is (every twenty-four hours):

    1 jar of baby-food meat
    1 egg yolk mixed with
    1 cup of fluid—broth, milk, or water

A sick cat can be maintained indefinitely with this amount of food. A ten-pound cat requires ten ounces of food per day.

To force-feed, it is best to prepare the cat as in the medication procedure (with a towel or pillowcase). If the cat is especially docile it might prefer your lap to a table or counter top. And needless to say, there should be a minimum of excitement and confusion.

To feed a cat baby-food paste, hold its head and open its mouth with one hand. With the other hand, dip the paste onto the index finger, open the mouth further with the middle finger, and put the paste on the roof of the cat's mouth. What paste does not cling to the roof will come off on the tongue, teeth, and lips as you withdraw your finger. Allow the cat to breathe and rest a bit between mouthfuls. Never give too much too quickly, as this could cause gagging and vomiting and open the way for foreign-body pneumonia. A good timing rule is about two ounces of food every couple of hours during the day. If there are any signs of stress such as panting or coughing, *stop* for a rest and try again in fifteen to thirty minutes. Even just a few bits every little while. Every bite counts.

To feed the cat liquid food, follow the same procedures outlined for the liquid medications.

One of the greatest lifesaving formulas for the very ill cat who cannot tolerate any food is an eggnog made up of the following ingredients, well-beaten:

    1 cup of milk
    1 egg yolk
    1 teaspoon of Karo syrup

This life-sustaining, body-building mixture has brought many cats through many serious illnesses.

Finally, and it cannot be repeated too often, *the ailing cat has to have medicine, food, and liquids, at regular intervals, in order to survive.*

15 · Ailments and Diseases

Abdominal Disorders · Allergies · Anemia · Bone and Joint Disorders · Cancer; Leukemia · Cysts · Diabetes · Ear Disorders · Eye Disorders · Feline AIDS · Female Disorders · The Heart · Hepatitis · Intestinal Disorders · Male Disorders · The Mouth · Nervous Disorders · Rectal Disorders · Respiratory Disorders · Skin and Fur Disorders · Spinal Disorders · Tumors · Urinary Disorders

Abdominal Disorders

Bloat

Occasionally, we find a cat with a very distended abdomen, caused by a stomach that is filled with gas under pressure. The animal is in acute distress, and unless immediate relief is given, the stomach can rupture and death will follow.

The tension from the gas-filled stomach can be relieved by passing a stomach tube. This requires the services of a veterinarian and speed in treatment is necessary for survival. Until a veterinarian can be reached, give the cat a teaspoon of milk of magnesia, which will alleviate the pain somewhat. The earliest symptoms are extreme restlessness and swelling of the abdomen. The swelling is rapid and acute; the stomach will stretch to two or three times its normal size within an hour.

It is not known what causes bloat, although rapid gulping of large amounts of food and excessive exercise immediately after eating can be contributing factors.

Allergies

Although allergies—in the form of asthma, hay fever, and eczema—have been known for many years to be a major cause of human discomfort, it is only in recent years that the same allergy syndromes have been identified with feline discomfort. They show up in itching; in the skin, in welts and lesions; in the intestinal tract, in diarrhea and vomiting; in the head and other parts of the body, in hive-like swellings; in the nasal passages, in excessive sneezing; and in running eyes and swollen eyelids.

161

Allergic reactions in the cat can be caused by various foods; by certain insects; by vegetation and pollens; and by hundreds of different agents, such as flea collars and powders, house dust, floor polishes, woolen articles, nylon rugs, chicken feathers, tobacco, and even occasionally catnip.

A recent breakthrough in veterinary medical research has produced tests for determining causes of allergic reactions and has developed protective antigens. When an allergy is suspected, skin areas are shaved, tests are made, and within two to three days the veterinarian can read the results. When a test is positive, it is correlated with the cat's history, surroundings, habits, care, and food; when the cause of the allergy reaction is removed from the cat's environment, fast recovery usually occurs. If the cause is ever-present, the cat can be vaccinated to desensitize it to the object(s) (there can be more than one irritant) it is allergic to. Cats allergic to trees, grasses, pollens, etc., will have seasonal reactions.

Allergic Symptoms

- ☐ Scratching
- ☐ Coughing
- ☐ Sneezing
- ☐ Running eyes
- ☐ Eye rubbing
- ☐ Skin lesions
- ☐ Hive-like swellings
- ☐ Diarrhea
- ☐ Vomiting

Discussing any of the above symptoms with a veterinarian will save a pet many hours of needless suffering.

Dietary

Just as with humans, not all cats can assimilate all foods; they have their idiosyncrasies too. Some pets can digest only "people" food and in fact develop colitis, a chronic inflammation of the intestines, when given commercial cat foods. With some cats, the simplest deviation from the normal diet will produce diarrhea with or without vomiting. Some cats seem sensitive to milk and will develop diarrhea if they drink it, while for other cats a new food may produce hive-like swellings. The occasional cat is born with an allergy to fish, which manifests itself in a condition called fish food dermatitis. The animal develops lesions around the neck and on the back by the thighs and the base of the tail, and eventually all over the body.

For determining dietary allergies a basic diet is used. The cat is taken completely off its regular diet and is put on a relatively allergy-free diet—lamb and rice. Foods are then added, one at a time, until an allergic response tells which food is the causative agent. Protein sources should be tested first—fish, liver, kidney, chicken, beef, veal, egg, whole milk—followed by cereal products.

Flea

Hypersensitivity to flea bites is a fairly common allergic reaction. In cats with this allergy, the bite of the flea produces intense itching. The animal scratches frantically, often injuring the skin and predisposing it to secondary skin infection. For pets with this sensitivity, injections with flea antigens are used. The antigens rid the cat of the allergic response; they do not destroy or banish the fleas.

Some cats are allergic to flea collars and/or certain flea powders. Flea-collar sensitivity produces lesions around the neck; with the slightest indication of such a condition, the flea collar should be removed. Constant sneezing and running eyes would indicate a flea-powder reaction. In this event, flea powders should not be used; permanent lung damage could result.

Hives

Hives in the cat are characterized by swelling of the head, usually around the eyes and mouth. The animal is uncomfortable and experiences severe itching. Hives are usually caused by an allergy to a certain type of food not generally a part of the regular diet. Antihistamines are prescribed. Cold packs are used to relieve the itchiness and swelling, and in most cases the best treatment is a good laxative or enema to wash the intestinal tract of the causative agent. Hive-like swellings can also be caused by a bee sting. In snake bites the enlargement is much more dramatic.

Skin

White and light-colored cats seem to have a special susceptibility to skin allergies. (Of course, this is true in humans too; blond, light-skinned people seem to have greater skin sensitivity.) The initial symptom is itchiness with redness and inflammation. Scaliness follows, and the hair starts to fall out, from either scratching or dryness, leaving bare patches. Baby oil or lanolin rubbed on the irritated areas will soothe and relieve the skin, but to effect a cure the cause has to be determined.

A dietary allergic dermatitis readily causes a secondary skin infection. The cat scratches and licks the skin, producing chronic ulceration (veterinarians call it "lick granuloma") of the affected parts. Whenever the skin is involved, even after the cause has been determined, treatment of the secondary infection is very important for full recovery.

Cat Allergy in People

Some people show a sensitivity to cats, showing allergic symptoms such as itchy eyes, sore throat, running nose, and, in severe cases, asthmatic wheezing.

The allergy is due to the dander of the cat, which is a mixture of cat's hair, saliva, and shedding of skin. It usually affects children more than adults, and often these children outgrow this sensitivity.

Anemia

Anemia is a condition of the blood in which there is a reduction in hemoglobin. It is characterized by pale gums and loss of energy. Usually the cat becomes listless and weak, sleeps a lot, loses its appetite, and vomits. It loses weight and after a time becomes emaciated and dehydrated. Instead of a healthy-looking red color, the gums show a paleness which goes from a light pink to a blanched white. The tongue also becomes pale-colored. The whiteness of the gums and tongue is indicative of an extreme loss of blood and is a serious condition.

The most common cause of anemia is infestation of hookworms, lice, or ticks. Other causes are coccidiosis, enteritis, poisons (e.g., lead or antifreeze), a disease called feline infectious anemia, nutritional deficiencies, malignant tumors, chronic nephritis, liver damage, steatitis, mycotic (fungus) infections, hemorrhage, coal-tar products, bite wounds, feline distemper, and leukemia.

In the treatment of anemia the cat should be fed liver and red meats, along with supplements of iron, malt, and vitamins, especially vitamin B_{12}. In severe cases the cat has to be given blood transfusions until its body can produce more blood cells.

Feline Infectious Anemia

Also known as haemobartonella, this may occur in either acute or chronic form. It is caused by protozoa, carried by parasites, which destroy the red blood cells of the infected cat. Because of the symptoms, it is often compared to malaria in humans, but be assured it is not contagious from cat to human.

It is similar to malaria in that some days the cat appears perfectly normal, and other days, depressed and feverish. The earliest symptoms are loss of appetite, excessive thirst, and lethargy. As the condition progresses, the animal becomes severely anemic, emaciated, and jaundiced (yellow discoloration of all the body membranes). These cases usually prove fatal. The danger signals of anemia are paleness of the gums, tongue, nose, and claws.

This form of anemia usually attacks adult cats from one to three years of age, but newborn kittens can also be stricken if their mother was infected while pregnant with them.

The highest incidence is found in warm, moist areas of the country where there are many insects. The protozoa are carried by fleas and other biting insects, but it is thought that they may also be transferred from one cat to another through bite wounds. Cats with other ailments or diseases, or infested with worms, can easily become victims of this infectious anemia.

Diagnosis is made by the veterinarian through examination of blood smears. Treatment consists of antibiotics and vitamins. In critical cases, blood transfusions and intravenous feeding are necessary to save the animal.

Once a cat has had infectious anemia it can become a carrier and hence a source of infection for other cats. Under your veterinarian's care, the cat should be quarantined for two to three weeks. Also, as with malaria, the symptoms can reappear at future times. Therefore, cats who have recovered should have their blood tested every few months for at least a year, and the owner should be constantly on the alert for any telltale symptoms.

For prevention, fleas should be controlled at all times since they are the host carriers from cat to cat. Needless to say, a well-balanced diet is one of the best preventives against sickness.

Bone and Joint Disorders
Arthritis

Arthritis is an inflammation of the bone in a joint; it occurs more frequently in dogs than in cats. The end of the bone develops calcium deposits, and movement is painful. A veterinarian may prescribe injections of cortisone, which can be beneficial. Also, heat gives relief.

Arthritis should be suspected when the animal shows pain in getting up from a lying position and in walking.

Bone Tumors

Fortunately bone cancer is rare. The tumors spread to the lungs, and the condition is considered inoperable. Limbs affected by bone tumors can be amputated if the tumors are detected early enough—before they have spread to other parts of the body.

Bursitis

Bursitis in an inflammation of the joint capsule in the leg. Any movement of the limb can cause extreme pain. Treatment involves heat and steroids.

Rheumatism

This can be seen in middle-aged and older cats. It is an inflammation of the joints and muscles similar to arthritis. On cold and damp days cats tend to show more signs of the affliction; so warm, dry living quarters are prescribed for preventing repeated attacks. Heat is also helpful.

Cancer

Since cancer is one of the diseases man has in common with his pets—with similar frequency and with the same results—researchers are working round the clock for linked clues. There is no evidence that cancer is transmissible between pets and humans. A sensational news item in 1969 labeled cats as the main carrier of the cancer virus, but it was completely repudiated by virologists the world over. Since then, scientists have taken a giant step forward in cancer research by isolating a virus in feline leukemia, although as yet they have not been able to isolate a virus in human leukemia.

Presently there are 128 reported new cases of cancer per 100,000 cats each year. Skin cancer is the most common form; leukemia is second; and cancer of the digestive system is third. When breast tumors appear, they are generally malignant and usually spread to the lungs. Incidentally, breast tumors rarely occur in the spayed queen, so if the cat is not to be used for breeding, spaying her before one year of age will most probably eliminate the possibility of these tumors occurring.

Leukemia

Leukemia is cancer of the blood-forming tissues. Although all domestic animals are susceptible to this disease, it is most common in the cat. A virus called the feline leukemia virus (FeLV) has been found to cause leukemia in cats. This virus attacks the white blood cells, causing them to multiply at a fantastic rate and to replace the normal cells and tissues.

There are over 1 million cats in the United States alone that have active forms of the infection. About 83 percent of those cats will die within three years from cancer or related diseases.

The virus can also cause other diseases such as pernicious anemia, distemper-like disease, fading kitten syndrome, fetal abortion, and cancerous tumors (lymphosarcoma).

The virus destroys the cat's immune system,

much like the AIDS virus does to humans. Subsequently, bacteria, viruses, or funguses take over and overwhelm the cat.

Exposure to the FeLV virus does not always mean the cat will become sick. About 40 percent of cats seem to have a natural immunity while the remaining 60 percent become carriers or die of the infection. In female carriers that become pregnant, they can pass the infections on to their newborn kittens, which usually results in death of the kittens.

What are the signs of leukemia in cats? The symptoms of leukemia in cats are varied, but in the early stages the disease does not cause abnormalities that can be detected by physical examination. In the later stages there is always anemia, weight loss, poor appetite, and weakness. Secondary infections may cause coughing and difficult breathing—the cat may breathe with its mouth open due to the tumors and fluid accumulation in its chest.

It will be reluctant to lie down and will lie on its chest rather than its side. The cancer may spread not only to the lungs but also to the kidneys, causing eventual kidney failure and uremia.

The warning signs below do not necessarily indicate that the cat has leukemia or any other cancerous condition. They do mean that all is not well with your cat and that the animal should be taken for a complete physical examination, as appropriate diagnosis and therapeutic procedures are needed.

☐ Poor appetite or complete refusal to eat
☐ Chronic weight loss and emaciation
☐ Chronic diarrhea
☐ Chronic vomiting
☐ Progressive weakness, feverishness, and lethargy
☐ Difficult respiration and coughing

Any cats showing vague and chronic recurrent illnesses should have a blood test for FeLV virus. In order to make a definite diagnosis, your veterinarian may perform further laboratory tests, such as a complete blood count, a bone marrow examination, or a biopsy of the lymph nodes. Cancerous cells must be found in the blood, bone marrow, or lymph nodes in order for a definite diagnosis of cancer to be made.

How is leukemia transmitted from cat to cat? The means of transmission of the FeLV virus is by direct contact. The virus is shed in saliva, urine, and feces. It is transmitted through licking, biting, and sneezing. The FeLV can enter a cat's body through the mouth, nose, or eyes. Feeding utensils and litter pans can be a likely source of infection among cats. The virus itself is short-lived outside the body and is readily destroyed by disinfectants.

Certain cats will show a positive FeLV test but will have no symptoms of leukemia. These cats are carriers of the disease, infected with FeLV but resistant to its symptoms. If one cat in a household of cats gives a positive test, it is a potential threat to any other cats that it comes in contact with.

There is no current evidence to indicate that the leukemic cat is a threat to the health of the owner.

Following exposure to the FeLV virus, the cat may respond in several ways:

1. It may not become infected at all due to antibodies formed from a previous exposure.

2. It may become infected, rapidly develop immunity, and revert to a noninfected state.

3. It may become infected and after a period of nine weeks to three years develop cancer or a related disease.

4. It may become infected and not develop the illness but continue to carry the virus for an indefinite period, becoming a potentially dangerous carrier for other cats.

When should you test for FeLV? If your cat shows symptoms of FeLV infection, you should definitely have a veterinarian give it the FeLV test. This should be done as a routine check before breeding your queen or tom, and if you are buying a cat from a cattery, be sure that the cattery has been certified free of the virus.

In a household of more than one cat, if one is found to be FeLV infected, that pet must be immediately isolated from the others. Because your other cats are known to have been exposed to the virus via the infected cat, they all should be tested twice, the second test occurring after three months of possible incubation have elapsed. Avoid exposing your cats to any other cats during that period until your veterinarian is certain that they are not infected.

Throw out all the toys, bowls, and litter boxes and disenfect the areas of the household that the cat had access to. After thirty days, a new cat can be brought into the family without danger of infection.

Is there a cure for leukemia? Unfortunately, leukemia is a fatal disease; treatment will usually prolong the cat's life, but it will not be curative. The same anticancer drugs that are used in human leukemia are used to treat cat leukemia, but they ultimately prove ineffectual. Supportive treatment such as antibiotics, vitamins, and blood transfusions are helpful. Leukemic cats can go into short remissions and appear cured only to have a subsequent relapse.

Is there a vaccination to prevent leukemia? Fortunately, in recent years, an excellent vaccine has been developed to protect cats against the leukemia complex. After your cat is given two initial vaccine doses, a single annual booster shot is needed to ensure full protection against this dreaded disease.

Cysts

Cysts are growths varying in size from a pimple to an orange. They can be found on almost any part of the body, but mainly there are four different types of cysts found in five different areas:

on the ears, on the ovaries, under the tongue, under the neck, and under the skin.

Blood Cyst/Ear Hematoma
(see page 169)

Ovarian

Cysts which grow on the ovaries of queens cause frequent and prolonged heat periods. In some cases, hormones, by injection, can be used successfully, but in severe cases surgical removal of the ovaries is the only relief. If the cysts appear on only one ovary, that ovary can be removed and the queen still can be used for breeding.

Ranula

This is a cyst which grows under the tongue. It increases in size until it pushes the tongue upward and to the side and causes extreme distress. Affected cats show loss of appetite, salivation, and frequent pawing at the mouth. Surgery is the only correction.

Salivary

A salivary cyst develops under the jaw along the neck. It appears as a small growth, and if untreated can grow to a large size. It is caused by a blockage of the salivary duct. the salivary gland secretion cannot be discharged into the mouth and forms a sac or cyst. These cysts are difficult to treat, and the only complete cure is surgical removal, which is a complicated and delicate operation.

Sebaceous

See Skin Disorders, page 191.

Diabetes

As in humans, diabetes is a disease of the pancreas. Because of improved diagnosis, it is being seen more frequently in veterinary hospitals. Although it is more common in the older neutered tom, it also occurs in queens.

The symptoms are: extreme thirst, frequent urination, emaciation, and eventually coma.

Many diabetic cats are leading healthy and happy lives with their daily insulin injection. Oral insulin is usually not effective in cats, although there have been cases in which insulin tablets have proven successful. The use of either medication is up to your veterinarian and his diagnosis. If injections should be necessary (they are not expensive), he will show you how to administer the daily dosage. A special diet is very important. It should be completely sugar free and low in carbohydrates.

Ear Disorders

Next to smell, hearing is the cat's most acute sense—about 140 percent more acute than the auditory sense in humans, and likely keener than in dogs because, when hunting, cats depend more on hearing and sight than on smell.

As in humans, the cat's ear is divided into three sections: outer ear, middle ear, and inner ear.

Also like humans, cats have ear-wax problems, but since a certain amount of wax should normally be present, very frequent cleaning is not advised.

167

Anytime a cat is seen shaking its head persistently, or frantically scratching at its ear, it indicates that the ear needs attention. Often there is an odor emanating from the ear which is diagnostic of trouble, usually caused by ear mites.

In a severe middle-ear infection, the cat will circle continually to one side, either right or left, until the condition is treated.

Ear canker, a term covering most ear infections, is a serious condition of the middle ear. As the infection progresses, it goes into the inner ear, which is close to the brain. When it infects the inner workings of the ear, the cat holds its head to one side and walks in circles, with a loss of equilibrium. This can prove fatal if the brain is damaged.

Ear canker is caused by either bacteria or ear mites. Ear mites are parasites which live in the cat's ear; infestation leads to a chronic irritation of the ear canal. The irritation predisposes the ear to infection from bacteria or fungi. Kittens can be born with ear mites, and a large percentage of kittens carry ear mites which they acquired from their mothers.

It is easy to diagnose ear mites: on looking into the ear one can see black, crusty, foul-smelling debris, sometimes actually moving about. Under a microscope or magnifying glass, small legs can be seen.

The symptoms are headshaking, ear scratching, and rubbing the ear against objects. The cat cries in pain when the ear is touched.

In the treatment for ear mites, the debris is first washed out. Cotton swabs with alcohol or hydrogen peroxide can be used, and if the mass is caked, mineral oil will help soften it. But the mites must be killed; your veterinarian can supply you with an ear-mite preparation which kills mites, bacteria, and fungi. Because the mites lay eggs in the ears, the treatment must be continued daily until all the eggs as well as the mites are killed, to prevent further infestation. As the mites don't always confine themselves to the inside of the

ear but often take a stroll around the head when the host is resting, and because the headshaking spreads the mites around the house, the treatment may have to be continued for some time. Also, the mites bury themselves under the skin in the inner side of the ear flap, and are difficult to treat and irritating to the skin of the ear membrane. For complete treatment, the life cycle of the mite must be broken. Even the house must be disinfected because the cat can be reinfected, and mites are very contagious from one cat to another. For a fuller discussion of ear mites, see Chapter 16.

Inner-ear infection must be prevented by proper treatment of the ear at the first signs of distress. In serious cases of middle- and inner-ear infection, external treatment alone is not sufficient; internal antibiotics are needed as well. Sometimes the condition is so stubborn and resistant to medical therapy that the veterinarian has to resort to surgery, removing part of the ear canal and in extreme cases removing the entire canal right down to the skull.

Deafness

In checking hearing in a human, the person is asked if he hears sounds in different tones and intensities. Since these subjective tests are not possible for animals, their ability to hear must be judged by their actions, that is, how they use their ears in response to sounds. In general, their hearing is discriminating as well as acute. Many cats are able to distinguish the varied footsteps of members of their household and even the engine of the family automobile. In checking a cat's auditory responses, be alert to the fact that it may be compensating for a hearing loss with sight and scent.

Deafness can be caused by severe ear canker and inner-ear infections. Tumors growing deep in the ear canal can interfere with hearing. As a cat approaches ten to eleven years of age there is a decrease in the acuteness of its hearing, since the nerve controlling the hearing degenerates. There is no cure. Eventually the cat is unable to hear voice commands. High-pitched whistles can then be used for calling. A deaf cat can also be directed by stamping on the floor. It feels the vibrations and responds to them.

Deafness seems to run in white cats and inherited deafness is prevalent. While it is not true that *all* white cats are deaf, a high percentage of white cats with blue eyes are born deaf. Almost all white cats with multi-colored eyes can hear.

Hematoma

Constant headshaking can lead to a blood cyst, known as a hematoma. It is caused by a broken blood vessel—the result of an injury, a blow on the ear, or continual headshaking and ear scratching. The blood vessel ruptures between the layers of the skin and starts filling up.

A hematoma needs intervention by a veterinarian. The only cure is surgical. If the cat does not stop shaking its head, the bleeding will continue, so a stocking or bandage should be put over its head while it is being taken to the veterinarian. Sticking a needle or knife into the soft painless swelling will not effect a cure; the ruptured blood vessel has to be treated. Also, the predisposing cause, ear mites, must be dealt with when the hematoma is treated so that the headshaking will stop.

Tumors

Warts and tumors sometimes grow in the ear canal, and these have to be removed surgically. They are irritating and can be serious. They can block the ear canal, allowing infection to develop in the canal's inner recesses.

There are cancerous tumors which grow on the ear flaps of cats. Fortunately, these malignancies are not common and the patient can be saved if the tumor is removed at an early stage.

Cleansing the Ears (see page 142)

Eye Disorders

Fortunately, the protective reflexes of the cat are so well developed that eye injuries are not a major ailment. But as the eye is such a sensitive and vital organ, treatment of an abnormal eye must be very carefully administered. The normal eye has a slight clear-colored discharge, and normally the tear duct in the inside corner of the eye drains into the nostril and carries away the normal discharge. Whenever there is any trouble, there is a significant increase in the amount of discharge, and its color and consistency noticeably change. The excessive discharge is more than the tear duct can carry, and the mucopurulent matter spills over the outside of the eye and runs down the face.

If the abnormal discharge is the result of a mild irritation to the eye caused by dust, dirt, smoke, or smog, a simple washing with warm water, or mild salt solution (a pinch of salt to a cup of water), or a collyrium wash, should be sufficient to eliminate the irritation. However, if after two days the eye has not cleared up, it should be looked at with an ophthalmoscope for something more serious, such as a scratch on the cornea, an ulcer, or a foreign body. Excessive discharge can also be caused by a deficiency of vitamin A, which can be due to inadequate diet or to a severe case of worms. Sometimes simply worming the cat will clear the eyes. In all cases of eye trouble, foods rich in vitamin A, such as eggs and carrots, should be added to the diet.

When a cat's eye is irritated, sometimes it will try to paw at it and rub it. This can result in scratches on the eyeball and cornea, so it is highly advisable to tape the claws on the front legs to prevent injury.

Bulging, Protruded Eye (Prolapse of the Eyeball)

This emergency condition is treated in Chapter 18.

Cataracts

Cataracts are a partial or total opacity of the lens of the eye. They are most often seen in older cats but, fortunately, are not very common. This condition is also seen in aged neutered male cats with diabetes.

There is no adequate medical treatment for cataracts except excision of the lens so that the animal may perceive light. With the removal of the cataracts, these blind cats are given additional years of sight. The eyesight is not perfect—the cat cannot focus—but at least it can discern shadows and objects in its path.

Conjunctivitis

This is an inflammation of the tissues surrounding the eye and of the tissues of the inner circle of the eyelid. The inflammatory condition can be caused by foreign bodies, dust, dirt, smog, different types of pollen, or bacterial infection. Along with an excessive discharge, the cat does a lot of blinking.

A treatment for simple conjunctivitis is a drop or two of cod-liver oil in the eye daily; this relieves the irritation and helps to heal the eye. If a foreign body is in the eye, a collyrium solution may wash it out, but if it is embedded in the tissues, professional help should be sought to remove the object. Amateur probing in the eye can do irreparable damage.

There is a follicular conjunctivitis in which the follicles on the inside of the third eyelid enlarge and become irritated. This can be contagious to other cats. A substance is secreted that continuously drains out of the eye. The veterinarian will usually have to put the animal under anesthesia and scrape the follicles or possibly remove the third eyelid.

Entropion

Entropion is an inverted or inwardly rolled eyelid. The condition is usually congenital and often hereditary, but it could be caused by a wounded eye. The eyelashes continually scrape the cornea or the eyeball, causing severe irritation. Over an extended period, ulceration and permanent defects result. The only correction is surgical: the eyelids are pulled outward, with good results cosmetically. Until surgery is performed, a lubricating ointment or oil should be kept in the eye to protect it from the irritation.

Film or Membrane over the Eyes (Prolapse of the Third Eyelid)

A film or membrane (the third eyelid) covers part of the eye in most types of eye irritations—nature's way of protecting the eyeball. The important point is that this is not normal, it is a symptom, and it must be treated. Prolapse of the third eyelid can indicate: a simple to serious irritation or infection of the eyes; an ailment or disease in any other part of the body; or worms. In other words, any weakened condition can be the cause. The extent of the "covering" can vary from hour to hour. The complementary symptoms would include listnessness, lost of appetite, and possibly vomiting and diarrhea.

This condition must not be ignored. In treatment, the cause must be discovered and cured.

Glaucoma

This is an enlargement of the eyeball due to an increase of fluid inside it. Because of the abnormality the fluid can't escape, and pressure builds up. Glaucoma often starts in one eye and sympathetically spreads to the other eye. The condition can be helped, but there is no permanent cure. Some cats respond to an eyedrop treatment, and the pressure lessens. For others there are diuretic tablets which draw the fluid from the eye. There is also a surgical technique which provides continuous drainage for the pressure. It is a delicate operation, but it can be used with good results.

Feline glaucomas most often result from displacement of the lens of the eye due to an injury. They are rarely congenital.

Keratitis

Often called "gray eye" or "blue eye," this is an inflammation of the cornea, the outside covering of the eyeball. It usually starts with an inflammatory condition of the cornea, and then if there is constant irritation, there will be a graying or a bluing of the eye. In serious cases, the eye becomes completely opaque—a whitish-gray color. The animal is unable to get any light and is temporarily blinded in the affected eye.

Keratitis is usually caused by a foreign body, an injury, or an allergy. It could also be due to a nutritional deficiency. It should be treated by a professional, and the first step is to remove the cause.

Ulcers

Since cats are so pugnacious, ulcers of the eye are quite common. An ulcer is dangerous; it can result in the loss of the eye if not treated quickly. Even a slight pin scratch on the eyeball can enlarge and penetrate into the inner eye, in which case the eyeball has to be removed surgically. It is painful, and the animal will try to scratch at it. The eye ointment used should contain a local anesthetic to help relieve the pain, and often a sedative is necessary.

Other Conditions

White-colored cats and cats without coloration of the hair around their eyes seem to have more problems than pigmented cats. Light-colored hair does not refract the rays of the sun, whereas dark hair protects the eyes from the sun and helps reduce the glare.

Some cats develop tumors on their eyelids. Pimples or pustules, such as sties in humans, are not uncommon. These require professional treatment.

There is a congenital eye ailment in which the upper lateral eyelid fails to develop. The animal will suffer from conjunctivitis. This condition is operable and the best time for surgery is between three and four months of age. Since it is hereditary, the cat should be sterilized.

When cats go blind, they adjust more quickly to their environment and with fewer emotional problems than humans do. It takes them only a day or two to relearn the location of doors and furniture. When the cat went blind in a cat-and-dog family I know, the cat continued to go about as before—but always close to the dog, who immediately assumed the seeing-eye role.

Female Disorders
Metritis

This is an infection of the uterus seen in middle-aged and older queens. It can be either acute or chronic. The veterinarian can determine the severity of the infection by the white blood count. When the count goes to a certain point, surgery is essential to save the cat.

Often mild attacks of metritis occur after heat periods; the infection may appear anywhere from two weeks to two months after the cat goes out of heat. Antibiotics can be helpful and can often avert surgery.

If the animal has many attacks, the veterinarian likely will advise a hysterectomy. It is recommended that the operation be per-

171

formed while she is still in good physical shape; if emergency surgery has to be performed during an acute attack, the chances of survival are less favorable.

Ovarian Cysts

This condition is discussed under Cysts.

Prolapse (Protrusion) of the Uterus

This is a breakdown of the muscles of the vagina and uterus which allows the uterus to protrude from the vagina. It can be caused by severe straining during delivery of kittens or by tumors. Upon palpation of the vaginal tract the veterinarian can determine the cause.

In some cases the uterus can be pushed back into the pelvic area—with the possibility that it will come out again in a few hours. In other cases a partial hysterectomy can be done to remove the mass. In severe and repeated attacks I advise a complete hysterectomy for the queen's future health and well-being.

Vaginitis

This is an infection found in the vagina of the queen, and when she is bred some of the bacteria is transmitted to the stud. It does not cause sickness in the male, but when he breeds with another female, he passes the bacteria on to her.

Nor does the female show signs of sickness. However, when she is in season, she gets very wet under the tail; this wetness contains the bacteria.

When the kittens of an infected queen start to open their eyes, you will notice that they are pus-filled. Immediate medical attention is vital in order to save the kittens and their eyesight. (See page 84 for further discussion.)

The Heart

Cats have fewer heart disorders than dogs, and when they occur it is generally in older animals (discussed in Chapter 9). However, cats of any age can have heart problems, including kittens born with a condition like that in the human blue baby.

A main symptom of heart trouble is shortness of breath—gasping with any exertion. Extreme exercise will produce pronounced symptoms, with the gums turning cyanotic (bluish), because the animal can't get enough oxygen to the lungs. In certain types of congestive heart failure there is usually a cough due to the presence of fluid in the lungs caused by inadequate heart valves. Sometimes there is a vibration in the chest which can be felt by putting a hand on the rib cage over the heart.

In extreme cases there is a collapse or fainting; the cat is unconscious for a few moments. This calls for emergency treatment. The heart should be massaged by gently pounding on the ribs and artificial respiration given (see page 224). Mouth-to-mouth resuscitation is helpful. These cats need professional care to digitalize the heart. Digitalization (the administration of digitalis) strengthens the muscles for more efficient heart functioning. With proper care these pets can have long and happy lives.

Heart Disease

Possibly the reason cats have heart disease less often than dogs is that they are more placid in temperament, less anxious to please their owner, less excitable than canines.

With the advances in veterinary medicine and the advent of adequate drug therapy and controlled diet, many of these cats are helped by reducing the effects of heart failure, and they live contentedly for a nearly normal life span.

When heart disease does appear in felines,

it resembles heart disease of humans. Cats may suffer embolism, which is a plugging of the arteries thought to be caused by fragments that break off from the diseased lining of the heart and are then carried into the bloodstream.

The first symptoms the cat will display include abnormal breathing, swelling of the abdomen or chest, and lameness. The veterinarian, with his stethoscope and electrocardiograph, can confirm any suspicion of heart trouble.

Cats seldom suffer from scar tissue on the valves of the heart, a problem frequently found in humans and dogs. Research has shown that big cats in the zoo have the same type of heart trouble as house cats.

The veterinarian probably will digitalize the cat's heart to strengthen the muscles and then prescribe heart pills. When heart patients are under treatment, there is often dropsy—an accumulation of fluid in the abdominal cavity—accompanied by coughing, another symptom of congestive heart failure. There are drugs to relieve the coughing and diuretics to help pass the excess fluid from the body. The fluid develops not only in the abdominal cavity but also in the lung tissues and causes the coughing. Getting at the cause of the cough, strengthening the heart muscles, and reducing the fluid are all paramount in treatment. Also, emotional excitement is bad for the heart patient.

If a cat has had severe cardiac failure, there should be a minimum of movement in getting it to the veterinarian. Oxygen is critical in saving the life of the animal.

Low-sodium diets for heart-diseased cats. A cat with heart disease is allowed the following foods: beef, lamb, rabbit, veal, chicken, turkey, freshwater fish, salt-free cottage cheese, egg yolks. Rice, wheat, macaroni, spaghetti, and noodles can be used as fillers for the meat products. Gravy can be used to flavor the food and whet the cat's appetite. Some cats will eat fruit and vegetables, especially tomatoes, which are helpful in keeping the urine acid. The vegetables may be fresh or frozen as long as they are salt-free (some frozen vegetables contain salt—avoid these). The fruit may be raw or cooked.

Foods to avoid are: heart, liver, kidney, hot dogs, ham, bacon, shellfish, baby foods, processed cheese, and luncheon meats.

Congenital Heart Disease

The use of X rays to diagnose feline heart diseases has been greatly extended in recent years. Congenital anomalies such as patent ductus arteriosum (PDA) and ventricular septal defects can be corrected by surgical intervention. In PDA an abnormality connects the aorta and the pulmonary artery which simultaneously fill with blood. Ventricular septal defects cause a heart murmur due to the blood flowing through the opening from the left to the right ventricle under high pressure.

Your veterinarian can detect many congenital heart defects upon stethoscopic examination of the kittens.

Hepatitis

This is a bacterial or viral infection of the liver. The most common form seen in the cat is *toxic hepatitis,* which is a damaged liver caused by the absorption of toxic substances such as phenol compounds, coal tar products, etc. *Parasitic hepatitis* may result from invasion of the liver tissue by toxoplasmosis or roundworm larvae.

Any interference with liver metabolism results in severe consequences. Icterus (or jaundice)—a yellowing discoloration of the body tissue—is a sign that the liver is damaged and the prognosis is grave.

Intestinal Disorders
Coccidiosis (see also Chapter 16)

Although this disease is caused by a protozoan parasite, its symptoms bear a resemblance to feline infectious enteritis. (It can be differentiated upon laboratory examination.)

Kittens are especially susceptible to coccidiosis (just after weaning when they are no longer receiving the natural immunity provided by the mother's milk). The critical signs are intense abdominal pain, diarrhea (with mucus and blood), nasal and eye discharge, loss of appetite. The cat becomes physically depressed and dehydrated, with progressive emaciation and anemia. Secondary infection produces a fever.

Unsanitary quarters where the cat comes into contact with infected feces is the principal cause. And since there is no preventive vaccine, proper sanitation is the best prevention.

Your veterinarian can prescribe drugs which can effectively combat this disease. Good nursing care under sanitary conditions, along with proper diet and control of diarrhea, is essential.

Colitis (Chronic Enteritis)

Colitis, an inflammation of the large intestine, usually appears in chronic form. It should not be confused with feline infectious enteritis, which is a serious disease commonly called "distemper" (see page 175). But colitis can be a sequel to feline infectious enteritis and it is seen more frequently in the older cat.

Although the precise cause is unknown, we know that emotional tension and excitability are contributing factors. We also suspect allergic reactions to certain types of foods. Some traits, such as shyness, insecurity, and anxiety, can bring on various psychosomatic illnesses, including colitis attacks. We see it often in pets who stay in close confinement with their owners and who have close emotional interactions with them.

The symptoms are diarrhea with mucus and vomiting. Blood in the stools usually indicates an ulcerated condition. Ulcers form on the lining of the large intestine and occasionally bleed.

Colitis tends to recur, so we must try to eliminate the predisposing factors. In other words, don't let your cat worry; anything that seems to disturb it should not be allowed in the house. The diet should be bland—cooked cereals and eggs, lean meat, and other soft foods. Animals with colitis usually have trouble digesting commercial cat foods; these are rough and harsh to a sensitive intestinal tract. Colitis may be caused by a certain food, so it is advisable to experiment with a bland diet, adding foods one at a time (see Allergies). Above all, the cat should be kept quiet during an attack.

Constipation

The most common cause of constipation is hair balls (see page 153), but improper diet, overfeeding, and lack of exercise can also bring it on. Too many bones will tend to cause an impaction of the intestinal tract. A change of diet can upset the intestinal balance. Also, impacted anal glands (see Rectal Disorders) can cause constipation because of the pain involved when the animal tries to relieve itself.

If the cause is hair balls, this can be easily remedied by an occasional laxative—mineral oil or milk of magnesia, or Vaseline rubbed on the paws. There are also laxative jellies which most cats like to lick, and there are hair-ball pills which are easy to administer. Sometimes compensatory foods that loosen the bowels, such as milk and liver, give relief. Of course, proper combing (see page 141) is the best means of preventing problems caused by hair balls.

Some cats have a chronic constipation which results in protrusion of the rectum from constant straining. These cats should receive mineral oil once or twice a week as a preventive. And here again, fresh liver should be given quite often.

Although the condition is unusual, some cats are born with a deformity of the rectum and/or colon (called megacolon). This is an enlarged colon which causes the food wastes to collect. Because the waste matter is unable to pass through the colon or rectum, the animal becomes severely impacted. The veterinarian can diagnose this condition with barium X rays and it often has to be corrected by surgery. But here again, laxatives can be the answer.

An important point on laxatives. Cats with chronic constipation—like people—can become dependont on laxatives, some of which are habit-forming. However, there are laxatives (we call them bulk-type laxatives) which are non-habit forming and very safe. The main ingredient of these laxatives is methylcellulose, a compound that concentrates the fluid in the intestinal tract of both people and animals, thus stimulating evacuation. These laxatives can be given on a regular basis—without fear—to a cat with chronic constipation.

Diarrhea

Diarrhea can occur in cats from such simple causes as change in diet or excitement, or from more severe causes such as distemper (feline infectious enteritis) or poisoning. Diarrhea is extremely debilitating and can quickly cause death if unattended. In a kitten, one loose movement should be attended to immediately; diarrhea weakens and dehydrates these little creatures so quickly that there is not a moment to lose.

If it is not simple diarrhea—that is, if it does not respond to treatment over a forty-eight-hour period—professional help should be sought.

Some cats cannot digest milk properly and will get diarrhea from it. If your cat has diarrhea, always remove milk from the diet.

Fading Disease (see page 81)

FELINE AIDS (FIV) (Feline Immunodeficiency Virus)

Feline Immunodeficiency virus (FIV) recently has been recognized as an infectious disease in cats. The virus affects the cat in a way very similar to the way that human immunodeficiency virus (HIV) affects humans. Therefore, the name, FELINE AIDS.

The disease causes the cat's immune system to weaken, thus making it susceptible to other diseases. Scientists find no relation to the human virus and agree that the cat virus is not transferable to humans or other animals. Researchers believe that the FIV virus is transmitted through bite wounds. Thus, adult male cats are at the highest risk and also any cats that are exposed to these outdoor roaming individuals. It is estimated that the infection rate is 5% in outdoor cats.

The earliest signs to watch for are fever, lethargy, loss of appetite, and loss of weight. It is usually accompanied by persistent diarrhea, sores around the mouth, and eventually other infections appear such as skin, urinary, and upper respiratory diseases.

At the present time there is neither a vaccine to prevent FIV nor a cure for affected cats.

Your veterinarian can make a diagnosis by the clinical signs and results of an FIV antibody test that is available. It is important to know if your cat has FIV because of the possibility of transmitting the virus to other cats. Once your cat is infected with the virus, it carries the virus for the rest of its life.

Confinement of FIV-positive cats is recommended so that other cats will not be exposed to the infection. It is also for the best interest of the affected cat so that it is not exposed to other diseases.

Prevention is the best method of protecting your cat. Keep cats indoors and neuter male cats.

Have your veterinarian test any new cat or kitten for the FIV virus.

Your cat should have semiannual checkups by your veterinarian, and treat any disorder in the early stages, however minor it may appear.

Feline Panleukopenia (Distemper)

The seriousness of this most widespread and devastating disease of cats is further compounded by a confusion of names and symptoms. It is also known as distemper, cat fever, cat plague, and yellow vomit, and the initial symptoms are often mistaken for poisoning.

Even though the highly contagious virus which causes this intestinal disease—even in unborn kittens—is almost 100 percent fatal to kittens and about 90 percent fatal to older cats, it is preventable, treatable, and controllable. The latest research on this virus indicates that it causes degeneration of the retina and that eyesight may be permanently impaired.

The actual virus was first isolated in a snow leopard in 1964 (wild members of the feline family also appear to be susceptible to this disease). As a result, there are many good types of vaccines available.

Here, as whenever possible, prevention is the best solution. Vaccine can be given to the kitten anytime after eight weeks of age. Generally two shots are given; the second ten to fourteen days after the first. Then, as there is no "lifetime" immunity, an annual booster shot should be given.

If a cat has not been vaccinated, very early detection of the disease is of prime importance in saving the life of the animal. The incubation period is from two to nine days,

usually less than six days. The onset is very sudden and some cats may die without any signs of sickness.

A typical symptom of this disease is vomiting—colorless at first, and then a yellow bile-like fluid. There is also a yellow diarrhea (later streaked with blood). The cat is extremely thirsty, and a symptomatic posture is holding its head over the water bowl without attempting to drink. Other symptoms include high fever (the temperature drops to below normal preceding death), loss of appetite, matted unkempt fur, a film over the eyes, the abdomen becomes tender to the touch, and there is extreme emaciation. The cat may lie flat on its abdomen, head on the floor, in a spread-eagle position. Any of these symptoms should trigger an immediate visit to a veterinarian. The only sure diagnosis is a blood count (the disease destroys the white blood cells). With the use of antibiotics and good nursing care, many cats survive, *if treatment is started early enough*.

Feline panleukopenia is extremely contagious. Infected cats can spread the virus through body secretions such as eye and nasal discharge, urine, feces, and blood. Food dishes used by an infected cat can pass on the disease to other cats. And even humans can be carriers by importing the virus on their clothing. Lice, fleas, and other blood-sucking parasites can also transmit the disease. Once it establishes itself, the virus is very difficult to get rid of and it can live in a house or cattery for as long as three months.

Normal sanitation and good housecleaning practices are the only way of helping to rid the house of contamination. Normal household disinfectants do not kill the virus.

Gastritis

This is an inflammation of the stomach characterized by nausea and vomiting. Sometimes overeating or eating the wrong foods will cause this condition. It can also be caused by certain diseases such as feline panleuko-penia, leptospirosis, uremia, nephritis, and metritis.

When a cat is suffering from indigestion or nausea, it eats grass to empty its stomach or to serve as a laxative. If the cat does this repeatedly it should be examined to find out the cause.

Along with the grass eating, the cat is very thirsty and demands water to soothe its inflamed stomach. However, the more water it drinks, the more it vomits, so the water should be restricted. Substituting a few ice cubes in the water dish is a good idea. Kaopectate and Pepto-Bismol are both soothing to an inflamed stomach; in a simple case only three to four doses are needed. Use a bland diet with soft foods until the inflammation subsides.

Pancreatitis

Fortunately, this rarely occurs in the cat. It is an acute or chronic infection of the pancreas, a very important gland which helps to furnish digestive ferments that aid in the breakdown of foods. In the acute form, there is a high fever, abdominal pains, and persistent vomiting. In the chronic form, an intermittent vomiting usually presents itself. Dietary control is an important part of the treatment. Cats cannot digest all fats, so the diet should be free of any fried or greasy foods. A simple bland diet is essential.

Peritonitis

Bloat is the main characteristic of this insidious, chronic, and often fatal disease, the virus of which has not yet been isolated and for which there exists no vaccine. There is a gradual accumulation of fluid in the abdomen, sometimes in the thorax, and the abdomen begins to swell, giving a potbellied appearance.

While it is easy to diagnose, there is no effective treatment or prevention. The diagnosis consists of a laboratory examination of the blood. But unfortunately the germs are resistant to most antibiotics. This is a painful, debilitating disease, and the majority of cats will not survive.

Toxoplasmosis

This is one of the few diseases which can be passed between cat and man, and recent magazine articles on the subject of toxoplasmosis unduly alarmed many pregnant women living in cat-owning households. It is indeed important to realize that cats can carry this disease and that when it is transmitted to a pregnant mother it can cause miscarriage or birth defects (such as blindness or brain damage) in the baby. But it is also important that all the facts should be thoroughly understood before the family pet is given away or destroyed. Research has shown that families who don't have a cat have almost the same incidence of toxoplasmosis as families who do.

The symptoms of the disease in the cat include fever, labored breathing, coughing, loss of appetite, emaciation, jaundice, and nervous disorders. Actually, any of these symptoms should be of enough concern to a cat lover to call for an immediate trip to the veterinarian.

Caused by a parasite—a protozoon—it appears not only in cats but also in mice and other small animals all over the world—even in birds. These animals acquire the disease from eating contaminated food and from contact with infected nasal discharge or feces. Young animals and kittens are most susceptible. The disease is then transmitted to humans through contaminated food (infected by houseflies and roaches carrying the parasite, which they picked up from infected animal feces) or through eating raw or undercooked meats (especially mutton and pork). The chances of this are negligible if commonsense sanitary rules are followed.

In other words, it is important that the pregnant woman, with or without a cat in the house, be advised not to eat raw or under-cooked meats. The household should also be rigid about following the basic rules of sanitation and keeping all foods and liquids covered and/or refrigerated and safe from contamination.

If there is a cat in the house, there are only a few additional rules. Since the feces of the cat could contain the parasite, someone other than the pregnant woman should be assigned litter-box duty. And since the parasites do not become infective until three days after they are excreted, daily disposal of the litter provides additional protection. An extra protection against the cat's getting toxoplasmosis would be to eliminate all raw meat from its diet (stick to commercial cat foods).

If your cat does show symptoms of the disease, your veterinarian, through laboratory tests of the blood and feces of the animal, can diagnose the presence of toxoplasmosis.

To prevent a cat from getting toxoplasmosis, feed only dry, canned, or cooked foods—never raw meat. And don't allow the cat to eat wild birds, mice, or other prey.

Treatment is possible. There is a drug that is given for several weeks until microscopic examination gives a negative finding of toxoplasmosis in the feces.

Male Disorders
Orchitis

This is a condition in which there is an abnormal enlargement of one or both testicles. It requires professional treatment because the testicle may abscess or may even have to be removed.

An enlargement of the testicles can also mean a tumorous growth. In cats, orchitis is usually the result of a fight wound inflicted by another tomcat.

Prostatitis (see pages 91–92)

Penis Hair Ring (see page 54)

Stud Tail (see Skin Disorders)

The Mouth
The Gums

Many cats suffer from gum infections. The gums bleed easily, swell, become ulcerated, and ooze pus. The accompanying putrid odor is caused by either tartar formation or infection working under the gums.

This pyorrhea-type of infection causes loosening of the teeth, and the cat becomes toothless at an early age.

The gums should be massaged with a good antiseptic, such as salt and soda, and painted with tincture of iodine. Hydrogen peroxide, Bactine, and other mouthwashes are also good. This treatment should be repeated at least once a week for badly infected gums.

Gum Tumors. A benign tumor of the gums, called an epulis, is seen in some older cats. When these tumors become large, they can interfere with chewing of food. Removal is recommended. Malignant tumors of the gums are rare in cats and are usually too advanced for treatment.

Trench Mouth. Trench mouth, an inflammation of the gums and mouth, is caused by germs that are formed in the mouth of cats. The gums bleed readily, the breath is offensive, and a brownish saliva may be seen in and around the mouth. Fortunately, your veterinarian can treat this condition and it responds well to antibiotics.

Halitosis

This problem usually comes from the same source as in humans—an unclean mouth and the resulting decaying particles among the tooth crevices. Tartar and infected gums or teeth are the prime cause of bad odor. It could also be a sign of nephritis, leukemia, or a vitamin B deficiency.

Cats who are confined inside the house (not allowed to hunt) and live on soft foods from cans soon develop tartar and the subsequent mouth odors. When a cat is five to six years old, usually a lot of tartar has built up. Teeth should be regularly cleaned and scraped by a veterinarian to prevent gum infection and deterioration and premature loss of teeth.

An odor from the mouth can also be due to an intestinal or stomach problem caused by excess gas being produced. This could be a dietary condition or could be caused by worms.

Lip Infection (Rodent Ulcer)

This is an unsightly sore that appears on a cat's lip (usually between the nose and the lip).

It is difficult to treat because the cat licks off any medication applied to the sore. Fortunately, the advent of antibiotics has given the veterinarian much-needed help in combating this ailment. Cortisone injections are used, along with surgical and chemical cauterization and X-ray therapy for more stubborn cases.

Teeth

The normal cat is blessed with a much stronger set of teeth than is the normal human. The tooth structure is stronger, the enamel is thicker, and the teeth have much more resistance to cavities. Dental caries is very rare in cats who receive proper diets.

The adult cat has twenty-eight teeth. Kittens normally begin cutting their deciduous, or baby, teeth at about three weeks of age and finish at about six weeks. All the baby teeth are shed and replaced by the permanent teeth at between five and seven months.

Abscessed Teeth. An abscessed tooth gives the cat many moments of pain and fever. It will be reluctant to eat and will exhibit all the symptoms of a person in extreme difficulty

with an infected tooth. Its jaw may swell over the area of the tooth, and there is usually swelling under the eye. When this swelling appears, the tooth has to be extracted. Once the tooth is pulled, the abscess drains into the mouth, and the swelling subsides. Occasionally an abscess erupts through the skin of the cheekbone under the eye, and we have a chronic fistula that continually exudes pus. Once the tooth is removed, this disappears and clears up.

Broken Teeth. This is fairly common in tomcats because of their habit of fighting. Many a tooth has been broken off and left in the muscles of an adversary. Chipped, broken, or loosened teeth can sometimes be corrected by capping or filling, but this is not very practical.

Cavities (Dental Caries). Although cats rarely develop tooth cavities (possibly because they do not normally eat much sugar), they are seen occasionally. Your veterinarian can fill cavities, but owners seldom wish to go to this expense. Root-canal work is also being done on cats.

Tooth Defects. Discolored or pitted teeth are seen in some cats. This can be caused by several diseases, nutritional deficiencies, and parasites occurring during the first two months of life, when the teeth are developing. Drugs such as tetracycline given at this young age can cause yellowing in the kitten's teeth.

Inherited Defects. The practice of dentistry on felines has progressed far in the past decade. There are even cats in the show-ring with caps on their teeth, and this is allowed if it can be proven that the cat's tooth was broken, that the defect occurred after birth and was not congenital. The correction of any congenital defect is frowned on by the Cat Fanciers Association.

There are inherited tendencies of the mouth and teeth that must be carefully watched for in breeding. These are undershot jaw, overshot jaw, and missing, loose, or misaligned teeth. There is a good possibility that if an animal with any of these defects is bred, the offspring will show the same defects.

The hereditary defect that breeders are primarily concerned with is that of missing teeth. Some breeds are born with missing tooth buds. This can hurt the cat's chances in the show-ring but it has no health significance.

Misalignment of teeth is becoming more and more of a problem among purebred cats. There is a tendency for these imperfections to be inherited. Orthodontia—realignment of teeth—is being tried, but it must be done when the animal is still under one year of age. Also, it is difficult to get a cat to cooperate with the type of metallic braces that children wear.

Tartar. The commonest cause of dental problems in the cat is tartar formation. The tartar attaches below the gum line and causes oozing of serum from the gums. The tartar progressively builds up over a period of several months, and as it worsens it causes bad breath, sore gums, pus formation, loose teeth, abscessing of the roots, and general ill health. Eventually the teeth will fall out.

Along with bad breath, signs of tartar would be teeth turning brown, dropping food while eating, quivering jaws, and red and inflamed gums.

Cats who eat soft foods that require no chewing often have tartar formation and loosening of the teeth at an early age.

When the teeth are loose in the sockets, they give a lot of pain and may cause the cat to stop eating. I have had to remove eight to ten teeth at a time in some cats, leaving them almost toothless and doomed to a life of soft-mashed foods. Periodic checkup with a veterinarian at least every six months can prevent a lot of these problems, as he will check the mouth and scrape off any tartar.

In its early stages tartar may be removed by a solution of salt and soda (a teaspoon of salt and a teaspoon of soda in a cup of water). This is an excellent solution that can be rubbed on the teeth and gums (with a piece of cotton) at frequent intervals. For some cats, once a month may be sufficient, but in others once

a week may be necessary. Some people use toothbrushes and regular toothpaste, but most cats put up a lot of resistance.

For the prevention of tartar formation, the feeding of hard or semi-hard foods, which require chewing, is recommended. There are excellent kibbles on the market. A large bone once a week will give a cat many hours of enjoyment and will help its teeth and gums.

Teething. The owner must keep close watch on the kitten's mouth to make sure that the baby teeth fall out when the permanent teeth appear. Should the baby teeth interfere with the normal position and alignment of the permanent teeth, unless they are removed by the age of seven to eight months they can affect the mouth structure of the cat for the rest of its life.

During the teething process there will probably be periods of fever, swollen throat glands, mouth hemorrhages with or without loss of appetite, and even diarrhea. If the symptoms persist for more than twelve to twenty-four hours at a time, a veterinarian should be consulted.

Prevention of Dental Problems

1. Yearly checkup of teeth and gums by your veterinarian.

2. Feeding the cat some dry food daily or allowing the cat to chew bones that do not splinter readily.

3. Weekly wiping of the teeth and gums with a salt and soda solution (one teaspoon of salt and one teaspoon of soda in a cup of water). This makes an excellent mouth antiseptic and is tolerated by most cats.

The Tongue

The tongue of the cat is the frequent site of infection caused by injuries and wounds, or tumors.

The most common ailment is tongue irritation from licking irritant materials, such as lime, creosote, and other chemicals used in fertilizers, weed killers, and even household cleansers (see Chapter 17).

Although most cats will not directly drink or lick such chemicals, their meticulous cleaning habits cause them many tongue problems. Upon examination, you may find an ulcerated area or an abscess on the surface of the tongue. You may even find a wood or bone splinter or a roll of thread with a needle attached.

Symptoms are excessive salivation, refusal of food or water, and sometimes a clicking of the jaws due to the pain involved. As the infection progresses, a putrid odor develops and there may be a blood-stained saliva. The cat becomes lethargic, physically depressed, dehydrated, and develops a fever.

These conditions are all serious and require immediate medical attention. There is also a cystic condition (a ranula) which develops under the tongue (see Cysts). This requires professional care.

Nervous Disorders

Nervous disorders lead to many distressing symptoms, such as fits, convulsions, shaking, twitching, paralysis, and various frightening exhibitions of hyperexcitability. The causes are many and varied, ranging from a highly emotional animal's upset over the presence of strangers to diseases affecting the brain such as distemper, meningitis, and rabies. With the rapid advance of neurological research on animals, the practicing clinician will soon know more both about the effects of disease on the brain and spinal cord and about emotional factors in relation to the cat's brain. There is usually a cause for any nervousness in a cat, whether it be a mild fever, a sore throat, a stomachache, or a severe case of worms. Any deviation from normal should be thoroughly checked and the condition corrected.

Chapter 11 dealt with abnormal behavior that arises from external circumstances. This section discusses the various physically induced nervous disorders.

Cerebella Ataxia

Recent research has discovered this distemper-like disease which is characterized by incoordination and difficulty in walking. Formerly it was thought to be an inherited disease; it is now known to be caused by a virus which attacks the brain of a kitten while it is in the mother's uterus.

Unfortunately, it is incurable and the brain damage is irreparable. Although some of these kittens live, it is advisable to have them put to sleep, because they would forever be completely incoordinated.

Convulsions and Fits

Convulsions and fits can be caused by worms, high fever, overexcitement, poisons, head injuries, internal parasites, and congenital types of epilepsy. Viruses in some cases attack the brain and cause an encephalitis which results in fits and then generalized convulsions throughout the body. There is a complete change in personality from a docile cat to a vicious animal that bites everything in sight.

Encephalitis

This is an inflammation of the brain from an infection with many causes. It could be bacteria, a virus, parasites, or a poison, specifically lead poisoning.

The symptoms are high fever, dilated pupils, vomiting, and convulsions. These are accompanied by incoordination, dilated pupils, then paralysis and death.

To save the cat, extreme therapeutic measures are necessary. The animal will need a quiet, dark room and tranquilizers. Your veterinarian will give the pet steroids and antibiotics to reduce the inflammation.

Unfortunately, there is a grave danger that

the cat will be permanently brain-damaged. If this is very severe, you may have to face the question whether it would be best to put the cat to sleep. You should talk this over with your veterinarian.

Epilepsy

We are seeing more and more epilepsy in cats. The cause is not known. For no apparent reason the animal goes into severe convulsions, frightening both the owner and itself. These seizures can occur several times a day or every week or two. Epileptic fits in cats are controlled by the same drugs that are used for human epilepsy, and many cats with the condition live out their years in health and relative comfort.

When the cat is in the midst of a seizure, it falls over on its side, chomps its jaws, and froths at the mouth and drools. There is no danger of its swallowing its tongue. Do not put your hand in or near the mouth or you may be bitten. Leave the cat alone during the seizure. A period of unconsciousness (lasting about five to ten minutes) usually follows. When the seizure is over, the cat lies quiet for ten to twenty minutes and then will get to its feet, usually when fully conscious. It may be wobbly for a short time afterward but will soon be normal-acting in every respect.

Your veterinarian will recommend a carefully supervised dosage of anti-epileptic drugs which will control the disease and contribute to a normal life span.

An epileptic cat is usually healthy in all other respects. However, should the fits become frequent with resultant brain damage, euthanasia is advised.

Incoordination

This is a nervous disorder characterized by staggering. It is usually due to an inner-ear

infection or brain tumor. Sometimes long-standing chronic ear infections go into the inner ear and affect the brain. The cat holds its head to one side and walks in circles. It is a serious condition, and when there is brain damage, it usually leaves the cat with a permanent disability. However, there are excellent drugs at the disposal of the veterinarian for combating the infection. Sometimes radical surgery is necessary. Ablation, or removal, of the entire ear canal is performed and the diseased part of the inner ear excised. The operation gives dramatic results in some critically ill patients. (See also Ear Disorders.)

Meningitis

This is an infection, caused by either a virus or bacteria, that affects the covering of the brain or the spinal cord.

It is very contagious (but only to other cats) and is contracted by direct contact with an infected animal. Quick treatment is needed if it is going to be at all possible to save the animal. It is rarely diagnosed in cats. Early symptoms are extreme pain, listlessness, fever, and loss of appetite; later on there are convulsions.

Poisoning

There are some types of poisons that affect the nervous system, causing extreme nervousness or convulsions. Strychnine is a prime example. It produces a severe convulsion type of syndrome similar to the epileptic fit. However, in strychnine poisoning the animal does not recover in five to ten minutes as in epilepsy but continues to worsen as long as the poison is in the bloodstream.

When sensitive cats are overdosed with some of the insecticide poisons (such as DDT and lindane), there will be a trembling which increases in severity to a shaking and then convulsions. Unless these animals are given antidotes, they soon succumb. (See Chapter 17.)

Rabies

Although rabies, or hydrophobia, has been known to man since the days of Aristotle, there is more confusion about it than about almost any other disease, human or animal. The virus of rabies infects all warm-blooded animals, including man. Infection with the virus is 100 percent fatal in all species with the possible exception of the bat, which is a common carrier of the disease. It produces an infection of the central nervous system which leads to a most horrible death.

Rabies is not a hot-weather disease, as is commonly thought. Although it is more in evidence during the spring and summer months when animals tend to roam more, it is a year-round disease.

It can be contracted only from an animal with the disease, and for the disease to develop, the saliva of the rabid animal must get into the bloodstream of the victim through a lesion in the skin, a bite, or a cut. In other words, a scratch from a rabid cat does not mean exposure to rabies, unless saliva and/or a bite is involved.

The most obvious symptom of rabies is a drastic change in behavior. The entire personality of the cat changes. It becomes wild and ferocious, clawing and biting at everything and everybody in its path. There is a wild expression in the eyes—with dilated pupils. Because of paralysis of the throat, the voice becomes deep and hoarse, and the cat has difficulty swallowing. As the disease progresses, the animal becomes more and more uncontrollably frenzied.

Even thought the percentage of cats with rabies is smaller than that of dogs, there is always danger of exposure to the disease. The hunting and prowling habits of cats bring them into contact with many animals which serve as reservoirs for rabies.

Unfortunately, there is not compulsory rabies vaccination for cats as with dogs. I must stress here that any cat allowed outside must be vaccinated for the protection of the animal and its owner. Kittens can be vaccinated between five and six months of age. But once is not enough—or twice. *Annual vaccination is an absolute necessity!*

Rabies is preventable in the initial stage. If a person is bitten by an animal, or an animal is bitten by another animal, professional help should be sought immediately, as the necessary steps for the control of rabies should be instituted as soon as possible. For a bite on the face or head, emergency measures should be taken at once because the closer the bite is to the brain, the more rapidly the symptoms will develop. Wash the wound out immediately and thoroughly with soapy water.

If a cat bites someone both confinement and observation for ten to fourteen days are essential. At the present time there are no tests that can be made on a living animal to determine if it is in the early stages of the disease. If no symptoms develop in the cat for fourteen days after it has bitten a human or another animal, it is almost certain that it has no rabies virus in its saliva.

If, however, the cat does show symptoms of rabies within the fourteen-day incubation period, *there is still time enough for the human to receive treatment*—fourteen prophylactic injections of rabies given at daily intervals, the Pasteur treatment. For some people the injections might be painful, or there might be an anaphylactic reaction, but the injections are absolutely essential.

When an animal has bitten a person, the animal should be placed under the observation of a veterinarian so that the earliest symptoms can be noted and the person's physician notitified so that treatment, if neessary, can be started at once. Contrary to a common belief,

183

these vaccinations generally are not painful and do not have dire consequences. If one is bitten by a rabid animal, there is no choice in the matter—the treatment has to be taken if the person is to survive. The same procedures apply for a pet bitten by a rabid animal, and there is a similar treatment.

A suspected animal should under no circumstances be destroyed until the disease has been permitted to run its full course. The veterinarian has proper facilities for the confinement of these animals, and public health laboratories throughout the country have an accurate method of diagnosis for rabies, which entails making slides of the brain cells. If the animal is killed too soon, the lesions in the brain cells may not be developed and a false negative may be signaled.

Even when a vaccinated cat bites a person, the cat is legally required to be quarantined for ten to fourteen days to make sure the vaccine took. Rabies vaccine is as close to perfect as any vaccine can be, but there is always a chance of error.

Tetanus (Lockjaw)

Although this is rarely seen in cats (they seem to have a natural immunity), it is good to be aware of the symptoms. There is a general paralysis. The legs stiffen, the tail stands straight out. The throat becomes paralyzed, making it impossible for the cat to chew or swallow, and causing it to emit a moaning sound.

Bacteria in any wound can cause tetanus.

Unfortunately, there is no cure in the latter stages of the disease.

Rectal Disorders
Anal-Gland Impactions

Anal glands are two sac-like organs on either side of the anus which discharge their contents into the rectum. They are sometimes called skunk glands, because they are the same glands which produce such wicked results in the skunk when used as a weapon of defense. However, in the cat they are just vestigial organs and not really needed.

The anal sacs normally secrete a viscous, malodorous liquid ranging in color from light gray to brown and in consistency from water to paste. Occasionally blood or pus is seen; this indicates infection, and a veterinarian should be consulted. If there is no infection present, the veterinarian can treat blocked or distended sacs by exerting gentle pressure to expel the secretion.

If an anal-gland impaction is left unattended, injury to the anus with subsequent infection of the surrounding skin is possible. Occasionally segments of tapeworm migrate into the ducts of the gland, causing a blockage. Anal-sac infection can progress to such an extent that an abcess of the anal gland results; this requires surgery to relieve the pressure. At times we see a generalized infection manifested by an itchy, dry skin. In several cases I have found that the licking of the discharge from infected anal glands was the cause of throat infections and chronic intestinal infections.

Anal Infection

Sometimes bacterial and fungal infections develop in the anal ring and cause severe irritation. In mild cases of anal infection, Vaseline or baby oil can soothe the irritation, but the condition should really be corrected under medical supervision.

Foreign Objects

Sometimes foreign bodies pass through the alimentary tract and become lodged in the rctum. The subsequent infection is usually painful. Generally a veterinarian can remove these foreign objects manually.

Prolapse of the Rectum

In this condition a large mass of intestine protrudes from the anus. The predisposing cause is usually a severe case of diarrhea which breaks down the tissue holding the rectum in place.

In cases where the rectum has protruded for a long time and there is extensive injury to the tissue, gangrene often sets in. Sometimes we have to excise part of the rectum and insert what remains back into the pelvic canal. The cause of the diarrhea has to be corrected before a permanent cure can be effected.

Rectal Tumors

Rectal tumors usually are not malignant and can be removed surgically. However, if they are allowed to remain and grow, they can obstruct the passageway and cause severe impactions and chronic constipation and eventually can become malignant. Any growths around the rectum should be checked by a veterinarian.

Respiratory Disorders

Cats are especially susceptible to respiratory diseases. For some of these diseases, fortunately, there are preventive vaccines. But for those without, the earliest possible detection and treatment are vital to the pet's survival. There are many causes, but the symptoms are similar: sneezing, coughing, nasal discharge, eye discharge, labored breathing.

Most of these diseases are contagious and spread rapidly from cat to cat. Transmission is either by direct contact or by such indirect means as airborne viruses, clothing, feeding utensils, and parasite-carrying feces. In all of these diseases, proper sanitation is of the utmost importance, as is good ventilation—an even, non-drafty flow of air (dank and dark areas are especially good breeding places for diseases).

The most common cause of respiratory diseases in cats is virus infection. Although still in its early stages, research may show that humans, cats, and dogs share the same respiratory viruses. At least thirty different viruses have been isolated as being infectious to cats. They are highly contagious and can result in serious illness or, in some cases, death. Feline viral rhino-tracheitis (FVR) and feline calici-viruses are the major feline respiratory diseases. Together they account for approximately 80 percent of respiratory illnesses of cats. New vaccines have been developed by several drug companies which offer combined protection against distemper, rhino-tracheitis, calici-virus, and pneumonitis. These four diseases are a vital concern to cat owners and veterinarians alike.

Parasites are also responsible for respiratory diseases in cats—lungworms, lung flukes, roundworms, and the toxoplasmosis protozoon (see Chapter 16).

There are certain bacteria which cause pneumonia, especially the streptococcus and staphylococcccus bacteria. And there are some fungi which can cause severe respiratory problems.

As with all other illnesses cats are prone to, the best prevention is vaccination for the immunizable diseases and consistent good health practices.

Colds

Cats are subject to colds very similar to the colds that human beings contract, although there is no conclusive evidence that there is a correlation between the human head cold and the feline cold—nor does it seem that they are transmissible. The cat will come down with a running nose, red and running eyes, red throat, and fever. It may sneeze or breathe with difficulty. This is an ailment that responds best to common-sense home nursing (see Chapter 14). Keep your cat inside the house, and keep it quiet. A baby aspirin (or a quarter of an adult aspirin) administered only once should be helpful in reducing fever and alleviating the symptoms. A bit of vitamin C and a dab of Vicks or Mentholatum applied to the nostrils will help clear up the stuffy nose. When a cat has a cold (or any respiratory ailment) its appetite will suffer because the sense of smell is impaired; therefore it is very important to be sure that your cat eats properly. Force-feeding may be necessary (see page 158). A cold should clear up within a few days with proper care. If it does not, and a fever persists, consult your veterinarian.

Emphysema

This is an abnormal distension of the lungs with air, characterized by coughing and difficult breathing and wheezing. It is similar to the emphysema suffered by human beings. Any respiratory disease or disorder can result in emphysema, for which there is no medical cure. Cough medicines are useless and sometimes contraindicated.

The best way to help a pet with this condition is to keep it quiet. Rest, proper diet, and avoidance of excitement and strenuous exercise are necessary.

Pneumonia

This is an infection of the lungs or the lining around the lungs, and it can be as serious in the cat as in the human. The patient has a difficult time breathing and will hold its head in an extended position trying to get oxygen into its lungs.

Well-equipped veterinary hospitals have oxygen cages which help the animal breathe, along with medicinals which are projected through the air into the cage. The oxygen and medicinals help the cat symptomatically while the antibiotics which it receives destroy the infection.

Foreign-body Pneumonia

This is congestion and infection of the lungs caused by unnatural materials gaining entrance into the respiratory system. The inhalation of toxic fumes or smoke, the ingestion of fluids, medicines, or even food going into the windpipe can cause this serious condition.

Breathing will be difficult and labored.

Pneumonitis (Chlamydia)

This highly infectious disease affects cats of all ages. Fortunately, it is less often fatal than some other respiratory diseases. Prevention is available in an excellent vaccine and is the wisest measure in combating the disease.

Cats with the disease should be treated by a veterinarian as quickly as possible to avert the dangerous secondary infections; the virus lowers their resistance to other diseases. Recovery usually takes a long time, particularly in younger cats.

Pneumonitis is similar to a bad cold in the human being. The symptoms are sniffling and sneezing, nasal discharge, and swollen watery eyes, with fever and sore throat. The first indication of pneumonitis will usually be the occurrence of a conjunctivitis condition affecting one or both eyes. The clinical signs of the disease usually persist for four to six weeks. The accompanying loss of appetite should be treated with force-feeding to prevent dehydration (see page 158). The cat's impaired sense of smell and sore throat will cause it to shun food.

Rhino-tracheitis and Calici-virus

Rhino-tracheitis and calici-virus are the most severe of all the respiratory diseases of cats, and both are highly contagious. It has been shown that a cat can be a carrier of both viruses.

Calici-viruses (FCV virus disease) principally affect the lungs, causing pneumonia. In some instances, the pneumonia may be severe enough to result in death. Signs to watch for are: ulceration of the tongue, lips, and nasal surfaces as well as fast, difficult breathing.

Feline viral rhino-tracheitis (FVR) principally affects the upper respiratory tract and the sinuses of the head and eyes. Cats with this disease salivate profusely, have spasmodic bouts of sneezing and coughing. Excessive discharges appear in the eyes and nostrils. Breathing is very difficult and labored.

This very serious disease is caused by a herpes virus which is host-specific and cannot infect other animals (other than cats) or humans. Kittens and young adult cats are especially susceptible and the mortality rate is quite high. If the disease strikes a pregnant queen, miscarriage or generalized infection of the newborn kittens may occur. A queen should be immunized regularly, as she may be a carrier and throughout lactating stress may weaken and shed the virus at the time that the kittens' maternal immunity is fading. An outbreak can wreak havoc with an entire colony.

Care by your veterinarian is needed to save any cat with these diseases. Supportive therapy and good nursing are the main ingredients of the cure. Antibiotics are used to prevent possible secondary infections. A chronic sinus infection is not uncommon in cats who recover from these diseases.

Your veterinarian can protect your cat against all the major respiratory diseases (rhinotracheitis, calici, chlamydia) as well as panleukopenia (distemper) in one vaccine. Vaccinations should begin no later than three months of age, followed by annual revaccination.

Sinusitis

This is a nasal disorder whih can cause a cat much distress. The symptoms include sneezing, nasal discharge,watering eyes, and if an infection is present, loss of appetite.

Sinusitis can be caused by:

☐ An allergy to a type of pollen or other vegetation—similar to human hay fever.

☐ Infected teeth can result in an abscess in the sinus cavity. The diseased teeth must be removed and drainage from the sinus established.

☐ Head injuries can result in broken bones in the sinuses. Infection usually follows.

☐ Foreign objects can sometimes work their way into the sinuses; either debris accidentally embedded, such as twigs and grass, or such things as peanuts and bits of plastic toys stuck into cats' noses by small children.

☐ Nasal tumors.

☐ There is a parasite that is occasionally found in the frontal sinuses.

The first step in the treatment of sinusitis is ridding the pet of the causative agent. Antibiotics, antihistamines, and steroids are used at the discretion of the veterinarian. Unfortunately, most cats cannot tolerate nasal sprays and nose drops.

Chronic Sinusitis (Rhinitis, "Snuffles")

Chronic sinusitis is a distressing condition encountered quite frequently in cats of all ages. It usually follows an upper respiratory infection.

There is a thick purulent type of discharge from the nose. Frequent sneezing attacks occur, often of an explosive nature, much to the discomfort of both the cat and the owner.

Treatment is very difficult and at times unrewarding. Continued use of antibiotics is recommended, and in extreme cases surgery is the only recourse. The veterinary surgeon will drill holes in the skull and flush out the sinuses, instilling antiseptics and antibiotics directly in the sinuses.

Occasionally, foreign bodies such as the awn of the wild barley have been found in the sinuses. Tumors and parasites (types of worms) in the nostrils have also been found to cause this disorder.

Tonsillitis

The tonsils are two small glands in the back recesses of the throat which are troublemakers in some cats.

The causes of tonsillitis are many and varied—from a chill in a drafty room to getting wet, either out in the rain or in a bath given at the wrong time of day. Some cats are unable to stand a sudden change in temperature or moisture. In feline infectious anemia (see page 163), tonsillitis is one of the early symptoms.

Symptoms include crouching with frequent gulping and licking of the lips. Excessive salivation, and refusal of food because of the pain involved in swallowing, would also be indicative.

Treatment requires antibiotics and soft foods.

Because of the similarity in symptoms, tonsillitis is sometimes confused with a foreign body lodge in the throat.

Tracheo-bronchitis

This is an inflammation of the upper respiratory tract, specifically the windpipe and the bronchial tubes. It is an infectious condition and contagious from one cat to another. It can spread rapidly.

There is a persistent dry hacking cough which becomes more severe with excitement or exercise. The animal may seem normal in other respects, with a normal temperature and a healthy appetite.

No specific causative agent has been isolated. It is thought to be a bacterium, but this has not been firmly established.

Treatment is both difficult and prolonged. The disease runs a course of two weeks to two months. I've seen catteries affected by this "bug" for as long as two years. Complete isolation of infected animals and strict sanitary procedures are essential for its control. One helpful treatment is vaporizing the cat room with antibiotics and expectorants. In stubborn cases a veterinarian can inject an antibiotic and cortisone directly into the windpipe.

Tuberculosis

This disease is very rare in cats and appears to be of diminishing importance, probably due to the decline in both human and bovine tuberculosis.

Cats can contract tuberculosis in two ways: from the bovine strain (drinking milk from infected cows) and from close association with a human suffering from the disease. When a cat has had association with a tubercular human, it should be checked for any symptoms of the disease.

The symptoms are listlessness, occasional vomiting, diarrhea with blood-stained stools, anemia, emaciation, coughing as the lungs are affected, and a colic as the intestinal tract is affected.

Most cats with tuberculosis are put to sleep because of the danger of possible infection of human beings.

Skin Disorders

Skin ailments are common among our feline population, and the causes are multitudinous. When one sees a scratching cat, the first thing one usually thinks of is fleas or some other external parasite. Actually the scratching can be due to any of the countless allergies, or a diet deficiency, or a fungus infection; and there are hundreds of causes of internal disarrangement.

All the same, the most common cause of skin infection is the flea. Once the cat starts scratching and digging its claws into the skin to rid itself of the flea, it gets a secondary infection, and then it licks and bites, causing more irritation, and this sets off a chain reaction. By using the excellent flea collars on the market, and the flea soaps, sprays, and powders, and by grooming regularly during the flea season, we can rid our cats of this cause of skin disorders.

All cats suffering from skin conditions should be kept out of direct sunlight—which irritates the skin—until the condition has cleared up.

Blackheads (Black Chin)

Blackheads are skin infections found on the chins of cats—usually short-haired cats—caused by food caking on the skin. They resemble coffee grounds and are sometimes called this. Cleansing with a surgical soap such as tincture of green soap or betadine will usually clear up the blackheads. In chronic conditions, keep the chin greased with Vaseline or mineral oil, which seems to keep the blackheads from taking root in other areas of the chin and prevents food from touching the skin.

Chin Infection in Cats

Cats drinking out of plastic pans can develop a chin infection.

The Coat

The general health of the cat has much to do with its skin and coat. The hair of the cat is hollow, containing air and blood, and since the hair root gets its nutrition and sustenance directly from the bloodstream, disorders of the skin and coat have to be treated internally even more than externally.

Alopecia (loss of hair). This is usually caused by an internal condition—a dietary or hormonal imbalance. In many cases I've found a hypothyroid condition (underactive thyroid gland) to be the cause. Thyroid extract or thyroid stimulating drugs usually help cure the baldness. It is also seen in some spayed females and castrated males, the result of hormone deficiency. These conditions can only be cured internally.

Dandruff. Flakiness of the cat's skin usually has an internal cause, such as insufficient oils or fats in the diet, and we usually advise adding these to the food, along with wheat-germ oil.

Dandruff is common in house cats who stay inside most of the time. They don't get enough fresh air, and the skin dries out.

One of the main causes of skin flaking is too frequent bathing, especially with strong soaps. The bathing washes away the natural oils which keeps the cat's skin healthy.

A common cause of dandruff in kittens is worms. Worms deprive the cat of needed sustenance. After worming, the dandruff usually disappears.

In the treatment of dandruff, we should first find the cause and then try to prevent it. In symptomatic treatment, we apply a bland oil or a hair tonic containing lanolin. We give the coat an oil rubdown once a week, massaging the oil right into the skin. In cases of dandruff it is not the hair but the skin that needs treatment.

Shedding. Some cats shed the year round and others only in the spring. Nature has provided animals with the light of day to control shedding. As the days get longer, with more daylight, the hair stops growing and starts to fall out. As the days shorten, new hair grows and replaces the old.

Cats who stay inside are exposed to electric lights all year and therefore shed all year. For them, the electric bulb has replaced nature. The cat who remains outside will carry a heavy coat from fall to spring, commencing to shed in April or May.

To prevent excessive shedding, you must see to proper grooming. The dead hair must be brushed out. The more you brush the hair and skin, the healthier they will be. Bathe your cat occasionally (not more than once a month) with a bland soap. At times rub it down with oil on your fingertips. I advise the addition of wheat-germ oil to its diet. Vitamin E, which is in wheat germ, is excellent for conditioning the skin (as well as for treating minor cuts), and many show cats are kept on vitamin E to keep their hair beautiful.

189

Eczema

Eczema is a condition of the skin which covers many varieties of nonspecific dermatitis, has hundreds of different causes, and includes all types of skin infections. It is divided into two general types: moist eczema and dry eczema.

In moist eczema—commonly called "hot spots" and sometimes "weeping mange"—we see a red and angry pustular-looking area which can arise in hours. It itches terribly, and the cat licks it if it can be reached, or scratches it, and spreads it quickly and furiously all over its body. To relieve this condition we give the cat tranquilizers or sedatives, and we use cortisone preparations and soothing healing ointment on the eczema. A good drying powder, such as BFI, is also soothing and helpful. If possible it is wise to bandage the affected area; keeping the animal's tongue and paws away from the infection is half the battle. (See page 152 for suggestions on bandaging.)

In dry eczema the skin is dry and scaly in appearance. As in moist eczema, it is usually itchy, and the same treatment is prescribed, including bandaging to prevent secondary infection. Something oily like lanolin or baby oil rubbed on the skin will relieve the itchiness, but the origin must be found.

One of the major causes of dry eczema is dietary imbalance—not receiving enough of the proper foods, or too much of one kind and not enough of another. Some diets don't have enough fats or oils—for example, those limited to some types of commercial dry cat food, which cause the hair of some cats to become dry and dull-looking and then start to shed. The simple addition of fats or fish oils to the diet will often correct the dry-eczema condition.

Another cause of dry eczema is hormonal imbalance. In spayed females we sometimes get this type of eczema with itching and shedding. The addition of female hormones clears the skin. We also see this condition in older cats, both male and female. By giving hormones we can usually help these animals and relieve their itchy skin.

Dry eczema is also seen when there are certain organic imbalances, such as underactive thyroid glands, kidney disorders, or digestive disturbances. Certain toxins are released into the bloodstream. A cat with nephritis often has a severe eczema which usually clears up along with the kidney dysfunction.

Another cause is psychosomatic in origin. Eczema often occurs when a cat is envious of another cat or pet in the family. It will take to scratching to gain attention and literally scratch itself into a bad skin condition (see page 109, on psychosomatic ailments).

Summer eczema is a condition some cats develop in early spring as soon as the weather starts to get warmer, and they scratch and itch until the frosts of early winter. The prime cause of summer eczema is fleas, along with other external parasites; ear mites and ear infection also cause a cat to scratch, with subsequent eczema or skin infection developing around the ears. The second most persistent cause is fungus infection. In some areas of the country there are types of fungus which live in grass, weeds, and other vegetation and which infect certain cats (some cats are allergic to the vegetation itself). A cat may have to be kept indoors to effect a cure, since the heat of the summer and the sun make the skin more susceptible to the fungus. During the early-morning dew and late at night when the grasses are wet, the cat should definitely be kept inside.

Treatment of summer eczema requires medicated shampoos at regular intervals, antihistamines, and cortisone. But we must find out the cause, and then try to eliminate it. The indiscriminate use of cortisone is dangerous to a cat's health. Cortisone can cause serious kidney disorders; it should be used only under the supervision of a veterinarian.

Mange

Mange is of two types: demodectic (or follicular) and notoedric. Fortunately, although it does occur, demodectic mange is extremely rare in cats.

Demodectic mange is characterized by shedding of hair, reddening of the skin, bare spots around the eyes, a thickening of the skin, and eventually a bloody pustular discharge. The lesions may be localized on the head, elbows, hocks, and toes or may be spread over the entire body.

The only way to find out if your cat has mange or some other skin condition is to have your veterinarian examine a skin scraping under the microscope.

Sarcoptic or notoedric mange is the more common form seen in cats. The condition is characterized by intense itching, thick and dry skin, scabs, and loss of hair. The condition usually begins on the cat's head, around the eyes, ears, and muzzle. However, it may also appear on the lower abdomen, on the chest, under the front legs, and at the root of the tail. Positive identification of the mange mite is made by a microscopic examination of a skin scraping.

Treatment of both types of mange consists of frequent baths and applications of salves until the mange mites are destroyed and the normal hair is restored.

Ringworm

Ringworm is a skin disorder caused by a fungus infection which involves the hair and hair follicles. It is contagious to other cats and to human beings, but kittens and young children seem to be most susceptible. Not only is the cat a potential source of ringworm in humans; the cat can also be a carrier without showing any symptoms. Fortunately, this fungus condition in cats is not nearly so prevalent as people believe. Nor is it as dangerous as it once was; it is now easily cured with medication.

Ringworm is caused by one or two parasitic fungi. It can be contracted from the ground, from droppings of other cats, from household effects that have been in contact with an infected cat, and from manure fertilizer.

The presence of ringworm is indicated by ring-shaped, usually red-colored patches covered with scales. In some cases the red patches form honeycomb-like crusts over the hair roots and give off a distinctive moldy odor. There is progressive enlargement of the lesions.

Early diagnosis of any lesion or loss of hair in a cat is important because if it is ringworm the person handling the cat could also get it. There is a three-week incubation period between the time of exposure and the time the condition becomes visible. The fungus infection itself has a life span of from thirteen months to five years. The spores are quite resistant to normal cleansers and disinfectants and can live on the animal as well as on sinks, stoves, refrigerators, doors, windows, anywhere in the house. If the spores are in clothing, the clothing has to be boiled in Clorox or burned for complete elimination. Silks and wools and other delicate fabrics can be sealed into a plastic bag along with blotters soaked in formaldehyde. The vapor will permeate the clothing and kill the spores. When the garments are taken out of the bag they should be hung out in the fresh air for a day.

The treatment of ringworm was revolutionized several years back with the development of an oral tablet that works efficiently in both humans and animals. Fulvicin (griseofulvin) is a very potent drug; given orally, it goes directly into the bloodstream and attacks the ringworm fungus at the root of the hair follicles. This is used in conjunction with external medication. It takes a minimum of one month to rid the cat's body of the developing spores. A Clorox solution (one part Clorox to ten parts water) is about the only household cleanser capable of ridding the kitchen of the spores and keeping them under control.

191

Stud Tail

Although all cats have sebaceous glands on the tail, sexually active tomcats are the most prone to problem conditions in this area. Excessive secretion from these glands results in an accumulation of brownish waxy material. This condition, known as stud tail, may develop into an infection, blackheads or pustules may form, and eventually, if it is untreated, the hair on the tail may fall out.

Washing with a medicated shampoo such as Sebbefom (Winthrop) should help relieve this condition. If the tail becomes secondarily infected, your veterinarian will prescribe antibiotics. Hormone treatment will *not* help. The treatment is important because the condition may spread if the cat licks the infected area.

If you have your cat neutered, the problem will be eliminated.

Sebaceous Cysts

Although sebaceous cysts are the most common type of cyst, this condition is seen less in cats than in dogs because the cat's sebaceous glands secrete less sebum. These cysts are caused by infected sebaceous glands in the skin. Antibiotics are somewhat helpful, but surgery is necessary for a complete cure.

Skin Tumors

Skin tumors appear in both malignant and benign form. Anytime there is a chronic ulcerated area of the skin that will not heal, a skin tumor should be suspected. The tumors are difficult to treat because they itch badly and the animals can't leave them alone. A chronic skin ulcer that doesn't respond to medication should be removed surgically, and a biopsy made for detection of malignancy. Skin tumors are seen especially on the legs, and as the cat will chew and lick the infected area, it can quickly grow from pin-point size to the size of a flea or larger.

In treatment of long-haired cats, it is usually necessary to clip the hair so the skin can be treated more efficiently.

Spinal Disorders

The spine is a sensitive part of the body. The symptoms of a disorder at first may be ambiguous—the animal may refuse to jump onto its usual couch or chair or will not walk up or down stairs. A spinal disorder may go unnoticed until the animal refuses to move or moves gingerly. As the condition progresses, that cat will cry out in pain when it tries to move into a certain position. It may hold its head either straight outward or to one side if the injury is in the region of the neck.

In any painful condition of the body in which the animal refuses to move in its usual fashion and will not jump, an injury to the spine should be considered. In such injuries there is incoordination in the rear legs, and gradually the animal goes down on its rear legs and begins dragging. There is severe pain when the back is touched.

A definite diagnosis can only be made with X rays. There are several methods of treatment, and sometimes surgery is the only recourse.

Accidents

If a cat is hit by a car, it sometimes suffers fractured bones in the spine. These can be repaired surgically if the spinal cord has not been severed. If there is a complete severance of the spinal cord, there is no hope for recovery, as the cord will not regenerate itself.

Sometimes there is temporary paralysis of the spine due to bleeding inside the spinal canal caused by the heavy blow.

There is also a syndrome called "shock paralysis" in which the animal lies paralyzed for several days owing to the shock of being hit by a car or some other trauma. Cats in this condition often show signs of recovery within two or three days and complete recovery sometimes within two to three weeks.

Slipped or Ruptured Disk

Spinal disks are paddings between the vertebrae. Sometimes when there is strenuous movement or an injury to the back, the disk slips out of place or is completely ruptured ("slipped" disk; "ruptured" disk). This condition is rarely seen in cats.

Spinal Arthritis (Spondylitis)

In this extremely painful arthritis of the spine, small calcium deposits (spurs) develop on the vertebral column. Any excessive motion in any direction will cause pain and in severe cases can result in paralysis. There is no cure, but Butazolidin and cortisone give some symptomatic relief. A diagnosis can be made only by X ray.

Tumors (see also Cancer)

Tumors can appear on any organ of the body, and each presents a different challenge. There are two types of growth or tumor: one is benign, or harmless, and the other is malignant, or cancerous. It takes professional skill and medical facilities to distinguish between the two, and I certainly advise seeking the help of your veterinarian if you discover an enlargement. In my opinion, early removal of all tumors is absolutely necessary, as it usually will forestall further complications in other parts of the body. Cats may also develop a leukemia similar to that which afflicts humans and tumors of the lymph glands, which are always malignant, spread rapidly, and are usually fatal. We can hope that the fruits of the extensive medical research in progress will soon be available to help both humans and animals. In the meantime surgery is the only complete answer for any type of tumor.

The Head

Cats can develop tumor of the brain. The symptoms are very gradual incoordination, circling, head to one side, and the tumors are hard to diagnose. X ray and EEG can determine their presence, and if the tumors are benign, the cat can be saved.

Tumors are sometimes found in the ear canal. They are distressful and cause the cat to shake its head continuously (see Ear Disorders).

There are also tumors of the mouth, and unfortunately some of these, either in the hard palate or in the soft palate, are malignant. Sometimes they attack the bones of the mouth and continue to spread if not detected in the early stages. Tumors can also appear on the gums. These benign masses can be effectively removed with electric cauterization (see The Mouth).

Tumors sometimes appear in the nostrils and the sinus passages, either on one or on both sides. They are usually malignant and have a poor prognosis. If there is a discharge of blood from one or both nostrils, be suspicious of a tumorous mass in the sinus cavities.

Mammary Tumors

Mammary tumors usually are seen in older unspayed females, and because they increase in size after the heat period, they are believed to be correlated with an excess of female hormones. Cats do not develop breast tumors as frequently as dogs.

In some cases, we treat breast tumors with male-hormone injections at periodic intervals; this seems to control their size.

Eliminating the heat period in older cats is the most desirable approach to treatment. I therefore advise spaying older queens; this helps to keep down the spread of mammary tumors and also averts metritis, an infection of the uterus.

One fact seems to be established: if a queen

is spayed when she is under one year of age, it is most unlikely she will develop mammary tumors. If surgery is performed after the age of one, the cat will have about the same chance of getting a tumor as an unspayed queen. If the cat is to be kept only as a pet, I advise spaying between six and seven months of age.

When one breast is affected, often the adjoining breasts begin to develop masses around them too. In such cases, when we have to resort to surgery, we remove two or three breasts in a row. Usually the lymph nodes are also removed to make sure that the growth will not spread through the lymphatic system to other parts of the body.

Mammary tumors can be either benign or malignant. If they are malignant, they can spread to other organs. If an X ray reveals that the tumors have spread to the lungs or elsewhere, removing the breast growths will not help the patient.

Other Tumors

Tumors in the lungs usually have a poor prognosis. If a cat is suffering from bone cancer, often the tumors spread into the lungs, giving rise to chest abnormalities. Tumors of organs such as the liver and spleen are common, especially those of the spleen. The intestinal organs also can be affected. Tumors of the kidneys sometimes appear, and if only one kidney is damaged, it can be removed with good results.

Urinary Disorders

With improved overall veterinary treatment and a greater life span for cats, urinary disorders in middle-aged and older cats are becoming the most prevalent type of abnormality that we see in our veterinary clinics today. This is a problem that the cat owner and the veterinarian must face together in order to prolong the life of the patient. It is not a simple problem that can be cured with a shot of penicillin. Rather, it is the problem of degeneration of the tissues

of the kidney so desperately needed to support life. The animal can live with only one quarter of the normal kidney tissue functioning. When more than three quarters of the tissue is destroyed, signs of kidney disease are quite evident. Although there is not yet a complete cure, with adequate diet and care the animal can enjoy life for many years. Veterinary medicine in the future will have artifical kidney machines that can be used on cats in kidney failure. I am sure that we will soon see the transplantation of healthy kidneys to cats with kidney failure, a procedure that is becoming so successful in human kidney disease.

Ninety percent of urinary problems in male cats result from a combination of three factors: neutering, high dry-food intake, lack of outdoor exercise. The outdoor male urinates frequently, and thus avoids the stagnation of concentrated urine and the resulting crystallization and formation of bladder stones.

While dry cat food does not cause feline urinary syndrome, it seems to aggravate the condition when it is present. Thus, cats that have a history of cystitis should not be fed commercial dry cat food.

Bladder and Kidney Stones (see also Cystitis, below)

The principal symptom of bladder and kidney stones is straining to urinate, with the production of only a few drops of urine with traces of blood. X ray and urinalysis should be done immediately.

The causes of urinary calculi are not understood in either feline or human medicine. However, three predisposing factors are known: (1) infection, (2) high concentration of minerals in the diet, and (3) reduced water intake. These conditions set in motion a concentration of crystals in the urine with subsequent stone formation.

Urinary stones are composed of either phosphates or uric acid. We must find out which type of stone is involved—by means of chemical analysis—so the proper prophylactic diet to prevent recurrence can be instituted. If the stones are of the phosphate type, milk, cheese, and other dairy products have to be eliminated from the diet. For uric acid crystals, meat and poultry products should be avoided, and the diet should be made up of vegetables, cereal, eggs, and dairy products.

Any urinary infection should be treated and controlled as soon as possible. Preventive measures are by far the best means of prolonging the life of a cat with bladder or kidney stones.

Cystitis

Cystitis, an inflammation and infection of the bladder, is probably the most serious and most common ailment in the young male cat today. Queens are also affected, but they recover quickly and without the aftereffects that males experience. The stones that form often block the urethral passage in the male cat. The female's urethra is wider and will more readily permits stones to pass. When blockage occurs, the cat is unable to urinate, the kidneys can no longer do their work of eliminating poisonous wastes from the body via the urine, and a condition known as uremia results. Unless this blockage is relieved quickly, the cat will die a painful death.

The precise cause of cystitis is unknown. Veterinarians agree that it is an infection, and recently a virus has been isolated which has suggested a new theory. But though there is no conclusive evidence concerning the cause of cystitis, some predisposing factors are known:
□ Limited exercise.
□ Too little water intake.
□ Retaining the urine for too long a time. This could indicate an obstruction or infection.
□ Foods too high in ash content. Canned fish foods or cheap canned meat foods usually are the worst offenders, as they contain a high proportion of minerals (ash). Any food with an ash content over 4 percent can be a potential danger.
□ A vitamin deficiency caused by too many parasites. Vitamin A is important in keeping the bladder healthy and helping the cat resist infection.
□ Stress conditions such as cold and dampness.
□ An injury to the bladder, such as from a kick to the midsection.
□ A small penis, which usually means a tiny urethra. A very narrow urinary canal tends to catch debris and stones, resulting in a blocked bladder.

The signs of cystitis include the following:
□ A housebroken cat urinating on the floor or in the sink or bathtub.
□ Squatting and straining.
□ Frequent trips to the litter box with only a few drops of urine produced each time.
□ Traces of blood in the urine.
□ A strong ammonia-like odor to the urine.
□ Listlessness and poor appetite. Instead of eating the cat will only drink water.

As the condition worsens, the cat will vomit, become dehydrated and physically depressed, and will develop uremia with a urine odor on the breath. With any sign of uremic poisoning the cat needs immediate attention if it is to survive. Its abdomen will be distended, and if you feel the area of its bladder you will notice a hard lump, actually as large as a lime. The cat's pain will be evident. Once this stage is reached, convulsions and death usually follow within forty-eight hours if immediate medical attention is not given.

In the treatment of cystitis, where there is a blockage of the bladder due to stones, the veterinarian will usually catheterize the cat under anesthesia to make sure the urine can pass freely. He also will flush out the bladder with an oily antibiotic solution to help heal and lubricate the bladder and urethra. He will then usually prescribe antibiotics to heal the infection and also urinary acidifiers to help keep the urine acidic.

195

The procedures in the treatment of cystitis are as follows:

1. Urinalysis, to determine the severity of the cystitis, and blood analysis, to measure the extent of the uremia present, together give the veterinarian the facts needed for an accurate medical forecast for the patient.

2. Culture and sensitivity testing of a sterile urine sample will show what bacteria—if any—are present, and indicate the precise antibiotic to be used in treatment.

3. Antibiotic therapy will be started, not only to combat any bacteria identified in procedure 2, but also to deal with other infections that might flare up.

Diet. The cat will then be put on a special diet. All fish foods should be eliminated and replaced with raw liver, kidney, ground beef, and chicken. Raw egg yolks and cottage cheese are also good. Cereals such as puffed wheat and whole wheat can be given, and dry cat foods, so long as they do not contain fish. In areas where the water is hard and has a high mineral content, distilled water is recommended. Tomato juice is a good substitute for water.

Canned prescription diets. Several cat-food companies make special formula foods for cats suffering from specific conditions. These are prescription diets and are available only from veterinarians. While they cost approximately twice as much as regular canned pet foods, they are much more highly concentrated. Hence, they work out just as economically as regular canned foods in feeding the cat. They also save a great deal of work and worry for owners who do not have the time or inclination to follow the diet regimen outlined above. (These special diets are more expensive because their ingredients and proportions must be carefully controlled to conform to medical standards.) Nonetheless, even these canned prescription diets should be supplemented daily with a small quantity of raw liver.

Home care. A word of caution about picking up a cat with an enlarged bladder. The cat should be picked up with one hand under its front legs and the other under its hind legs to keep the pressure away from its abdomen. Picking the cat up by the middle could cause the bladder to rupture, wtih fatal results.

Home care for the post-cystitis cat involves these general care instructions, to which may be added special instructions for individual cases:

1. Make sure the cat is urinating. Inspect its litter box daily. This is vital.

2. Give all the medication that has been prescribed—usually antibiotics and an acidifier to keep the cat's urine acid.

3. Give vitamin supplements according to directions if these have been prescribed.

4. Don't expose the cat to any stress condition. Cold, damp, or any emotional stress or sudden change in environment are all sufficient to precipitate another cystitis attack.

5. If signs of cystitis reappear call your veterinarian at once.

Leptospirosis

This is an infectious disease of man, cats, dogs, horses, cattle, pigs, rodents, and certain other animals. It is caused by bacteria known as spirochetes, which localize in the kidneys and cause the urine to become infectious. Cats contract the disease through killing infected rodents, especially rats, or drinking water polluted with infected urine. The infected cat should be quarantined, away from other animals and people, and the owner should be careful to avoid any contact with the cat's urine.

In the early stages, the symptoms are similar to those of kidney infection: high fever, loss of appetite, extreme thirst, frequent urination, and vomiting and diarrhea. As the disease progresses, there is loss of weight, stiffness in the legs, and bloodshot eyes. One of the typical symptoms is the color of the urine. It darkens sometimes to a deep yellow or orange and has a strong odor, and is specked with blood. Then the membranes and skin turn yellow. This jaundice sign is serious; the bacteria have settled in the kidneys and liver. Also the stools become mixed with blood, the vomitus contains blood, and often there is a bloody discharge from the gums.

It is especially important to catch leptospirosis in its early stages, before there is degeneration of the kidneys and liver. Penicillin and streptomycin are the drugs usually administered by the veterinarian. Unfortunately, as yet there is no vaccine as there is for dogs.

Nephritis

The origin of nephritis, an inflammation of the kidneys, is complex, and the precise cause or causes remain to be found. It is known that some infectious diseases, such as leptospirosis, can cause an acute infection of the kidneys, and in some cases after the disease has run its course it leaves the kidney tissue damaged, so that the animal will suffer from nephritis in the chronic form later in life. Since the kidneys are the excretory organs of the body, any infection, anywhere, is absorbed by the kidneys, ends up in the kidney tissues, and interferes with normal kidney functioning.

One of the first symptoms of nephritis is extreme thirst and especially a craving for dirty or stagnant water. Despite the increased thirst, the cat may not be able to drink due to an inflammation of the mouth, especially when the nephritis is caused by a toxic substance. In such cases, the cat salivates profusely because of the irritated mouth membranes. The average cat ingests a variety of contaminants during its lifetime, and many of them may be highly toxic and damaging to the kidneys.

There are two types of nephritis—acute, which comes on quickly, and chronic. The chief cause of acute nephritis is the virus of feline infectious enteritis, which attacks the tissues of the kidneys as well as other organs of the body. When the condition is severe, the cat is in obvious pain, hunched up and sensitive to palpation on the back. It is reluctant to move around and has a high fever. Treatment is usually more successful than with the chronic form, since the kidney tissue has not been destroyed or damaged.

If the attack is mild and the cat gets over it, it may develop chronic nephritis. Many middle-aged and older cats are showing this deterioration of the kidney tissues, due to a very high-protein diet. When there is a decrease in kidney functioning, the waste products which are normally excreted in the urine begin to accumulate in the body, and we see depression, loss of appetite, and vomiting. As the disease progresses, the cat shows signs of uremia, which is extremely toxic and critical. A cat with a kidney condition should be under the supervision of a veterinarian so that any complications can be treated promptly. Vomiting is one of the first signs of trouble. It means that the kidney functioning is not keeping up with accumulated waste products.

In treatment, besides the antibiotics now in use for nephritis—there are several good ones used in both human and feline urology—diet is of the utmost importance. A low-quantity but high-quality protein diet is essential. There are some prescription diets on the market which have been maintaining many nephritic cats for years with good results. Salt-free diets are important (salt is bad in kidney diseases), and so is free access to water to flush the kidneys of any impurities and waste products. The diet prescribed for cystitis (above) could be used for a cat with nephritis.

Uremia

When a blockage of the urinary tract occurs, the cat is unable to urinate. The kidneys can no longer eliminate poisonous wastes from the body via the urine, and a condition known as uremia results. Unless the blockage is relieved quickly, coma, convulsions, and death follow within about forty-eight hours. It should also be realized that the cat suffers pain from the

197

blockage until coma sets in, and the acuteness of the pain increases hourly. Quick treatment is critical if the animal is to survive. Once the cat is comatose, the medical chances of saving its life are low. Another potential hazard is that the distended bladder may rupture and this is usually fatal.

In severe cases of uremia, an artificial kidney technique may be called for. This is a very time-consuming and costly procedure and can be used only in special cases.

16 · Internal and External Parasites

INTERNAL · Hookworms · Roundworms · Tapeworms · Whipworms · Coccidiosis · Heart Worms · Lung Worms · Toxoplasmosis · Other Worms
EXTERNAL · Fleas · Lice · Ear Mites · Head Mites · Ticks

Internal Parasites

Just because a cat is under the weather doesn't mean it's afflicted with worms. Unfortunately, many cat owners have a tendency to blame worms for almost every feline illness known. Cats have numerous types of worms, and many wrong diagnoses by cat owners have inflicted doses of vile-tasting worm medicines on defenseless pets. Cats should be wormed only if worms are present, and then only with meticulous care, for worm medicines can prove harmful and even fatal unless properly supervised. Many deaths have been the result of overdosage, worming sick and feverish cats, and improper diagnoses.

Intestinal worms are common, and especially in young animals. Although they are a worldwide problem and should be constantly guarded against, they are more prevalent in some parts of the world than others. In the southern states, for instance, the warmer weather makes the soil conducive to the growth of the worm from egg to adult.

Because of the varieties of worms and the dangers involved with worm medicines, a cat suspected of having worms is best taken to a veterinarian. A routine fecal examination will determine whether the cat has worms and, if so, what type. All veterinary hospitals have facilities for microscopic examination for parasites.

Kittens contract worms directly from their mothers or from contact with infested fecal matter. They also can become infested with worms in the womb. A young cat is much more susceptible than an older cat. As a cat gets older its body becomes more resistant to the effects of worms. However, it is still vulnerable to parasites and should be checked at least every six months. Young cats should be checked at more frequent intervals, and kittens under six months of age should be checked at least every month.

The four most common cat worms are: (1) hookworms, (2) roundworms, (3) tapeworms, and (4) whipworms. A cat can have more than one type at the same time. These parasites have complicated life cycles and are resistant to many chemicals. Control of them is best left to a veterinarian.

Every so often I am asked if humans can get pinworms from cats. The answer is definitely "No!" The pinworm that lives in the human does not occur in cats or any animal but man. In fact, no cat worms will live in the human body.

Generalized Symptoms of Worms: Warning Signals

A fecal examination for worms is advisable if a cat has any of the following symptoms:

□ Intermittent or persistent diarrhea with or without blood or mucus
□ Intermittent vomiting
□ Persistent eating of grass
□ Lack of pep or energy—general lassitude
□ Rubbing tail along the ground
□ Bloated stomach
□ Generalized symptoms of anemia, such as pale gums
□ Dry, dull fur with dandruffy skin
□ Persistent watery, running eyes, with the third eyelid forming a film over the eye
□ Gradual loss of weight
□ Unexplained nervousness and irritability

Since any of these symptoms could also be indicative of other diseases or ailments that could be quite serious, a cat showing any one of them should be taken to a veterinarian for diagnosis.

Hookworms

Hookworms are leech-like creatures that suck blood from the intestines. They are tiny worms, about half an inch long, of reddish or grayish hue. A cat can become infested with hookworms in three ways: (1) direct ingestion of the larvae while digging and eating around infected stools; (2) prenatal infection while in the womb; and (3) larval penetration of the skin, usually through the pads of the feet.

The hookworm lays its eggs in the stomach and intestines. The eggs are passed out in the stool and hatch outside the cat in seven to ten days. The larvae are infectious and either are swallowed by the cat or penetrate the skin and subsequently get to the stomach by traveling, via the bloodstream, to the lungs, where they burrow into the air sacs, are coughed up, and are then swallowed. Once in the stomach the cycle starts again; the worms mate and lay eggs.

Adult hookworms are insidious bloodsuckers, and a heavily infested kitten may literally bleed to death. The worms puncture the lining of the intestines and eject a substance which prevents coagulation of the blood. With loss of blood there is anemia and loss of iron. There is also a bloody mucus diarrhea, and sometimes a black tarry stool, indicating blood high up in the intestines. Other symptoms are restlessness, apathy, and stunted growth. If the infestation is severe, a critical amount of blood may be lost. Needless to say, a pregnant queen should be checked for worms and should be in good health before she delivers her kittens.

In addition to clearing up the hookworm infestation, the veterinarian will likely prescribe supportive treatment to help the cat recover from anemia. Blood transfusions and liver injections or iron supplements are used to help the animal gain strength to fight off the effects of the parasites.

Many veterinarians have long considered hookworms a debilitating and killing intestinal ailment—one of the most stubborn and frustrating problems they face. They can kill the worms that attach themselves to the small intestines of the animal, but they have trouble preventing continued infestation. Proper diet and careful sanitary measures are essential in hookworm control. Hookworm infestation constitutes an especially acute problem in crowded catteries with shaded earth runways where young kittens are constantly mingling with cats seeding the area with eggs and larvae. However, even well-kept lawns can be heavily infested.

The ability of hookworm larvae to live in the soil is dependent on temperature, composition of the soil, and amount of rainfall and drainage. They develop best in moist, coarse, sandy soil. Three things will kill hookworm larvae in the soil: (1) A concentrated salt solution (table salt) spilled on the ground at three- to four-week intervals, to break up the life cycle, is effective. (2) A concentrated borax solution, used in the same manner as the salt solution, will kill the larvae. (It will also kill your lawn.) (3) A spray has recently been developed—V.I.P. hookworm spray concentrate—which is proving to be highly effective in killing newly hatched larvae. A second application in fourteen days is advised. (This will not harm your lawn.)

The species of hookworm which affects cats is different from the species which is a major problem with humans in the southeastern states. Feline hookworms cannot be blamed for infesting man. Even though the hookworm larvae can cause a skin irritation in humans—a sort of "creeping eruption" which affects children who play in infected yards or sandboxes where infested pets have deposited their hookworm-laden feces—the cat hookworm will not live inside the human body.

Roundworms

Roundworms are the most common of the worm parasites and are most often found in kittens. They can grow up to five inches in length in the cat's stomach and intestines and are similar in appearance to the earthworm. Alive, the worm tends to curl up; dead, it straightens out. It is not uncommon to see a cat vomit up live, wriggling roundworms.

A good indication of roundworm infestation is the appearance of the third eyelid (like a film) over the eyes. Although this third-eyelid condition can be present in other illnesses, the most common cause is roundworm infestation. A fecal examination by your veterinarian will settle the issue.

The eggs of this parasite are very hardy and can remain alive in the soil for years. The adult roundworm lays her eggs in the stomach and intestines of the cat. The eggs may hatch and the life cycle run its course inside the cat, or the eggs may be passed in the cat's bowel movements, or may be vomited, and develop outside the cat. About ten days later the eggs are infectious to any cat who digs in the soil and eats food or other material on which the eggs are deposited.

It has recently been discovered that large black water bugs transmit roundworm eggs. They deposit the eggs in cats' dishes.

The roundworm eggs can adhere to the nipples and also be present in the mammary tissues of a nursing queen and be ingested by the kittens as they nurse. The eggs hatch inside the body. The larvae enter the bloodstream and travel to the lungs, where they burrow into the air sacs. They are usually coughed up by the cat and then swallowed. Back in the stomach, the worms mate, and once again the cycle begins.

The life cycle is two to three weeks, so treatment for roundworms should be at two-week intervals; one worming will not completely rid a cat of roundworms.

Roundworms can cause diarrhea, anemia, dull coat, and potbelly. There can be serious injury to the lungs, and kittens can develop pneumonia as the worms migrate from the blood vessels to the air sacs of the lungs.

The best prevention for roundworms is proper diet so that the cat will not be hungry and likely to pick up scraps from the ground. The queen should be checked for worms before breeding so that her kittens will not be affected. Her breasts should be washed before each nursing after being outdoors. The litter box should be kept clean and dry and thus unconducive to hatching eggs.

Tapeworms

Four types of tapeworms are seen in the cat:

1. The broad fish tapeworm, contracted by eating raw parasite-infested fish.

2. A tapeworm common to outdoor cats and acquired by eating raw meat and internal organs of such animals as rabbits, hogs, sheep, and beef.

3. The flea tapeworm, acquired by ingesting a flea or a louse; fleas and biting lice serve as immediate hosts. Commonly called the cucumber worm because of its shape, it is the most widely distributed of the tapeworms. It is also the most difficult to remove because the slender neck breaks easily, leaving the small head imbedded in the wall of the intestines, so that a new worm is generated in about a month.

4. The rodent-host tapeworm. This worm is damaging to the cat because the cysts are found in the liver of rats, mice, squirrels, muskrats, and other rodents.

Tapeworms are a common intestinal parasite in cats. In small numbers, they are not harmful, but if the cat is neglected and the worms are allowed to multiply, the cat can become very sick. Heavily infested cats usually lose their appetites and become nervous and irritable. The fur becomes dull and dry, and the skin itchy. The cat may pull itself along on its hindquarters to relieve the irritation of tapeworm segments lodged in the anal glands. You may notice little white worms moving out of the rectum or see them in the stools. The tapeworm is not as harmful as other worms, but it can cause infection in the intestinal tract and chronic colitis, with occasional vomiting. The cat's appetite may be enormous but there will be no weight gain.

The feces and the hair around the cat's anus should be examined for segments of tapeworm by the veterinarian who is making a diagnosis.

The essential thing in treating for tapeworms is the release of the head of the tapeworm from the intestinal tract. Fortunately, the same drugs are effective against all types of tapeworm. *See your veterinarian.* As for home treatment, I warn you that there are some extremely toxic drugs on the market specified for tapeworming. Some of them can make a cat much more violently ill than any group of tapeworms could ever do.

In the prevention of tapeworms, diet and sanitation are important, but ridding the cat of fleas and lice is even more so. A cat cannot become infested with tapeworms directly from another cat, nor will feline tapeworms live in the human body.

Whipworms

Whipworms are slender parasites—not much thicker than coarse sewing thread—which resemble small whips. They have no immediate host. The eggs are laid in the cat and passed out in the feces. They develop in about three weeks and are then infectious. Cats eat the larvae or eggs, and these mature in the cat, living in the caecum (a part of the large intestine). Fortunately, they are not very common.

Whipworms form toxins which cause anemia. They also cause chronic digestive disturbances, such as persistent or intermittent diarrhea. A diagnostic symptom would be a bowel movement that is normal until near completion, and then the mucus appearance of blood. The whipworm is insidious and causes dullness in the fur, excessive shedding, and in some cases there is a cough.

Diagnosis is made by the presence of eggs in the feces. Today, the veterinarian has at his disposal excellent drugs for the elimination of whipworms.

Coccidiosis (see also page 174)

The incidence of coccidiosis is increasing throughout the country. It is an insidious type of infectious disease caused by coccidia, protozoan parasites, microscopic in size, which are often associated with filth. Young kittens are especially susceptible, though adult cats are not immune. In young kittens it weakens resistance to many other diseases. Distemper or any stress factor reduces the kitten's resistance, allowing the coccidia to increase and produce clinical symptoms in the kitten.

Kittens can acquire the infection from contaminated premises or an infected queen. The coccidia are passed in the feces. When sanitation is poor, the animal is constantly reinfected by its own feces, and infection can spread quickly throughout a cattery. Most animals and birds can harbor coccidiosis in the intestinal tract, but each species usually carries its own type of coccidia. Some animals have more than one type, and the parasite is more prevalent in warm climates.

Coccidiosis should be suspected in all cases of continuing unexplained diarrhea and anemia. The first signs can be a mild diarrhea which worsens until the feces become mucoid and blood-tinged. The kitten becomes weak and debilitated. A cough develops, along with running eyes and nose, much as in distemper. The infection progresses until convulsions occur and the cat usually dies.

When kittens recover, they may be carriers, passing the coccidia on to other cats. Even cats in good health can be carriers. Known carriers should be treated, and their quarters cleaned with an antiseptic.

Sulfa drugs, prescribed by your veterinarian, are effective in treating coccidiosis.

Heartworms

Only recently have reports begun to accumulate concerning the natural occurrence of heartworms in cats. Veterinarians are becoming increasingly aware of the fact that cats can be the hosts for these blood-dwelling worms.

Heartworms have been experimentally transplanted from dogs to cats, suggesting the possibility of cross infection between the two.

Although mosquitoes are the main carriers of heartworms, there is some suspicion that other bloodsucking insects, such as fleas, ticks, and flies, may also be involved.

The heartworm larvae are ingested by the bloodsucking insect as it draws blood from a cat with heartworms. When the insect bites other cats, the larvae are injected into their bloodstreams. After the larvae enter the bloodstream, they travel to the heart, lungs, and large vessels, where they mature and eventually produce other larvae. It is not until six to seven months after being bitten by an infected mosquito that larvae may be found in the cat's blood. For this reason, heartworms are rarely encountered in animals under one year of age.

It is the adult worms living in the heart, lungs, and large vessels that cause most of the clinical and pathological symptoms. There is a great variation in symptoms. Some cats appear healthy, while others are anemic, cough, itch, and are dropsical. Any cat showing one or more of the following symptoms should be tested for heartworms: easy fatigue, chronic cough, eczema, anemia with a heavy infestation of fleas, and fainting spells from overexertion.

The treatment and cure of heartworm infestation in cats is possible at this time. In an area heavily infested with mosquitoes, preventive daily doses of medicine should be given to your cat.

Lungworms

There is no such thing as a lungworm per se, but there is a parasite that affects the lungs: the strongyle. Fortunately, this parasite is quite rare. The cat becomes contaminated by eating infected snails, slugs, rodents, and birds.

The larvae of the strongyle attack the lung tissues of the cat and cause a chronic cough. The larvae are found in the feces and under a microscope the larval forms can be seen moving around at a lively pace. Diagnosis is quite difficult, but there are effective drugs to attack these "lung" worms.

Ringworm (see page 191)

Toxoplasmosis (see page 177)

Other Worms
Urinary Worms

These are rarely seen, but when they are present, they cause thickening and infection of the bladder wall.

Eye Worms

These worms, which cause eye irritation, are found mostly in California. They can be observed in the eye and can be removed under anesthesia.

Flukes

These parasites settle in the liver and lungs of cats. Most flukes are acquired when the cat eats infected raw fish.

Ground Rules for Worming

☐ A cat in good condition is less susceptible to worms than a weak cat. Good diet and proper sanitation are important in preventing worms. The same applies to control of external parasites.

☐ If worm medicine is strong enough to kill worms, it is also strong enough to do some damage to the cat's body if used incorrectly. Many cat owners accidentally poison their pets with improper medication. Certain worm medicines can act as deadly poisons when used in overdose, used too frequently, used when not needed, or used for the wrong type of worm.

☐ Never, never give worm medicine to a cat with a fever. Distemper, hepatitis, leptospirosis, and various bacterial infections are sometimes erroneously diagnosed as "worms." Many a cat in the early stages of distemper has died as a result of receiving worm medicine rather than the specific therapy for the condition causing the illness.

☐ Never worm a weak, sickly cat.

☐ Never give worm medicine to a constipated cat, because it will retain the worm medicine in its system too long. If a cat does not have a bowel movement within three hours after being wormed, it must have an enema to empty its intestinal tract.

☐ There are rules that should be followed in properly preparing a cat for worm medicine. For a couple of days before worming the cat should be on a bland diet. Twelve hours before worming, its stomach should be empty. After worming, the bland diet should be continued for a day or two or as long as is necessary to control the intestinal irritation that the worms and the medicine have produced.

External Parasites

External parasites are annoying little bugs that are the bane of many a cat's existence. Not only do they cause extreme irritation to the skin; they carry bacteria and virus infections and, because they suck blood, cause anemia and lower the cat's resistance to many ailments and diseases.

Fleas

Some cats scratch themselves almost as often as they twitch their tails and ears, and although the cause may be fleas, lice, mites, ticks, or a skin disorder, most of the time the culprit is the flea.

Some cat owners tolerate fleas as a necessary evil. However, not only should fleas not be taken lightly, but with so many excellent insecticides on the market, flea control should be given top priority by concerned cat owners. The discomfort fleas cause the cat (and some humans) is bad enough without flirting with the other devastating problems fleas can cause—various skin conditions, internal parasites, and infections.

For combating the flea, a knowledge of the life cycle of this hardy little pest is helpful. Fleas breed and feed on the cat. The female flea produces as many as five hundred eggs in a lifetime. The eggs appear as tiny white dots to the naked eye and are deposited and live in crevices around the house and furniture where there is sufficient organic matter to satisfy the food requirements of the larval stages. Other fleas (the stick-tight type) attach themselves to the cat and lay their eggs under the skin. The eggs spawn and go through the larva and pupa stages of their cycle, during which they can survive for as long as a year. The next part of the cycle is the cocoon stage, from which the adult flea emerges in about four weeks, or the cocoon may lie dormant for as long as a year if conditions are not favorable (too cold, or hot, or dry). An adult flea cannot survive away from the cat for more than ten days. It is the dormant (cocoon) fleas which cause the "swarms" often encountered by vacationing cat owners when they return to their "petless" homes. Footfalls on the floors and carpets are sufficient to cause the scattered cocoons to hatch and "turn on" the blood-hungry newly emerged biters.

Weather is an important factor in the life and emergence of the flea. The adult flea can withstand a certain amount of cold, but the onset of winter drives it indoors. Also during the winter months there is a decline in flea production due to lowered egg production, late hatching, and a high mortality rate for larvae. In the parts of the country where the weather is very hot and dry, fleas live only a short time. It is the warm moist areas of the country that are most conducive to flea and other parasite activity. In such a climate, fleas

multiply rapidly and, with cats as their hosts, can live from six months to three years.

There is considerable variation in the number of fleas a cat can carry before it becomes sensitized. Some cats can endure hundreds of fleas and others only one or two (short-haired breeds appear to be more sensitive). Kittens tend to support more fleas than adult cats, but some older animals develop a tolerance that will permit a moderate flea infestation without discomfort.

Once a cat becomes sensitized to its flea burden, there is decided discomfort and the animal must be treated. The veterinarian can test to determine if a cat's skin lesions are the result of sensitivity to flea bites; and if so, he can inject the cat with a flea antigen. This antigen is helpful, but it merely alleviates the effects of the flea bites and does not rid the animal of the fleas. Therefore, rigid flea control must be practiced to keep the fleas from the cat's body.

Controlling Fleas on the Cat

Flea control depends on the destruction of eggs, larvae, and adults; these must be eradicated from the cat and its environment. With the excellent insecticides now on the market, this is not a difficult procedure.

The *wash,* or *flea bath,* brings the fleas and insecticide into immediate contact and gives rapid relief. Since not too many cats think of a bath as a luxury, fortunately other methods are available.

Flea powders carry the insecticide into the coat, and the fleas come into contact with the toxic dust particles. These same dust particles spread over the various places the cat rests and sleeps and this helps control the flea cycle.

Aerosol sprays are excellent for cats who don't mind being "hissed" at. And a word of caution for cats who will tolerate the sound of the spray. It should scrupulously be kept away from their faces, and especially the eyes.

When applying powders or sprays, start at

the head and work to the rear. This way the fleas will not be able to escape into areas of the head where nothing can reach them.

Even though the *flea collar* is the easiest and most effective means of flea control for most cat owners, some cats react violently to the chemical in the plastic, and others are unable to wear the collar for more than a few days without a local reaction. Use only *cat* flea collars on cats. Most flea-collar manufacturers warn that their collars should not be used on Persian cats, and this warning applies to many other long-haired cats. And there are other "don'ts." Flea collars should never be put on a sick cat and should be taken off if a cat is ailing. The flea collar should be removed from the queen during her nursing cycle (she should be treated with a mild flea powder or spray, only on her head and back; the excess insecticide should be wiped off and none should be allowed near her breasts). Kittens should not wear flea collars until they are at least three months old.

When using a flea collar for the first time, make sure it is not too tight (you should be able to fit two fingers between the neck and the collar), and check daily for any signs of infection or sores under the collar. If the cat shows any skin irritation, or any signs of nausea or diarrhea, the collar should be removed immediately.

The *flea medallion* is proving to be an effective answer for cats sensitive to direct contact with the insecticides in the flea collar. But these too should be watched carefully for the first few days. The cat might react to the fumes of the insecticide; this could be manifested in vomiting or diarrhea. An especially playful cat might find the medallion an enticing object and try to remove it from its neck, only to end up swallowing some of the toxic insecticide.

A *food additive.* A good flea preventive which most cats like is brewer's yeast. The thiamine in the yeast causes the skin to excrete sulfur, which tends to repel insects. If a half teaspoon of brewer's yeast is sprinkled on each serving of food, there is a good chance fleas will shy away from the pet. And even if they don't, this is an excellent additive to the cat's diet.

Controlling Fleas on Kittens

Fleas on kittens are a special problem. Most sprays and powders deemed safe and effective for cats are too toxic for kittens under three months of age. There is a flea powder, Diryl (Pittman-Moore Co.), which is relatively safe for kittens when handled cautiously. It is applied along the back and underside of the kitten and then brushed away. The excess powder must be removed to keep it from being absorbed through the skin or ingested.

Controlling Fleas around the House

For complete flea control, once the fleas have been eradicated from the cat its habitat must be treated. Whereas it is easy to remove fleas from the cat's body, it is difficult to prevent them from returning. Fumigation is the easiest and most satisfactory method of controlling external parasites in the house. But whether it is done by the owner or by a professional, the animal must be removed from the premises until all fumes have subsided.

Fleas can be eliminated by using an aerosol spray in each room, one at a time, applying a generous amount of spray, and then leaving doors and windows shut fifteen to twenty minutes. Everything should be sprayed—cracks and crevices in the floors, walls, and ceilings; along baseboards and cold-air ducts; the edges of rugs; and between cushions of upholstered furniture. Then everything should be vacuumed thoroughly and the sweeper-bag contents burned.

Most insecticides can be poisonous to pets—and humans—if there is overexposure.

206

Follow directions carefully and use only at recommended intervals.

Fleas and People

Some humans are more sensitive to the bite of the cat flea than others. Cat flea bites often result in red edematous swellings, usually around the ankles, where the fleas have jumped from rugs.

Lice

These are small, rapidly moving silver parasites which irritate the skin and cause scratching. They are seen mostly on neglected and poorly fed cats and are easily killed with flea powders and sprays.

Mites
Ear Mites (see also page 168)

Since this is such a common cat parasite, when one adopts a kitten it is more the rule than the exception that it will have ear mites. And they must be dealt with as quickly as possible in order to avoid serious ear problems, and ultimately death.

These mites are very prolific and "contagious." Most cats are infected by their mothers during early kittenhood. They live around and inside the ear and feed on the blood of the cat.

The visible part of the inside of the normal cat ear is a fleshy pink shade and should feel smooth and waxy to the touch. In the early stages of mite infestation, you may see tiny white objects moving slowly about, but more likely you will see the results of their activity—tan-to-brown, greasy, crumbly matter in the inside ear crevices. As the mites continue to ravage the ear, the constant scratching by the cat causes raw areas, scabs, and loss of hair around the ear. The inside of the ear becomes red and inflamed. Occasionally,

there are bacteria or fungus infections that result in the formation of abscesses.

As the devastation continues, the infection worsens and can invade the middle ear and finally the inner ear, causing cerebral disturbances because the infection is now close to the brain. The cat will hold its head to one side, walk in circles, and eventually go into convulsions.

The diagnosis and treatment for ear mites should begin with your veterinarian. He has the proper instruments and solutions for clearing away the canal-clogging debris and will be able to ascertain the damage and the presence of any secondary infection. He will then give you the necessary instructions and medications for the home treatment of your pet.

In the treatment of ear mites, do not overlook the tail. Because most cats sleep with the end of the tail curled next to the ears, there can be mites on the tail to reinfest the ears. So when applying ear-mite medicine, also put some on the tail.

For more advanced stages of infection, daily home treatment will be necessary. In more severe cases, as much as three months of constant care might be required to restore the ears to a clean and healthy condition.

Head Mites

These mites cause a mange which mainly affects the skin around the head of the cat. There is itchiness, and the cat's scratching will cause loss of hair and sores. The treatment is long and difficult, but under the direction of your veterinarian, the mange can eventually be cured.

Ticks

Ticks are not as great a problem for cats as for dogs. When you find a tick (fat and swollen from feasting on your cat's blood), be careful when you pull it out, for the head of the tick can remain buried in the skin and cause infection or an abscess. You can pull a tick out with a tweezer, or forceps or a hemostat if you have one of these surgical instruments handy. An insecticidal spray will cause the tick to detach itself in a few moments. Destroy the tick immediately by burning it or flushing it down the toilet.

17 · Poisons

Both indoor and outdoor cats are exposed to innumerable poisons every day. Fortunately, since cats—unlike dogs—generally are not food bolters, they are not very likely to eat much of anything distasteful. But unfortunately, with their compulsion for personal cleanliness, any toxic materials they should happen to walk through or get on their coats could cause serious poisoning. This hazard is increased by their innate curiosity, which leads them to pry open cupboards (including medicine cabinets) and drawers containing common, everyday items—boric acid, coal-tar products, detergents, human medicines, paints, polishes, sprays—which can prove toxic, and fatal, to pets. Also, bottles can be knocked from shelves and break; tops may be off plastic containers that are upset; there could be residue from a toxic material on a shelf or on the floor. Kittens, especially, are like little children and will taste almost anything. House cats, since they are deprived of outdoor greenery, are unusually fond of plants, some of which are poisonous. Garden cats (in fact, all cats) love the taste of antifreeze (which is especially poisonous) and will crawl right up under the hoods of cars for a sip.

Poisoning is one of the principal causes of pet deaths. In many localities it is second only to the automobile. Although deliberate poisonings are comparatively rare, it is good to be able to recognize the symptoms of the two most commonly used poisons—arsenic and strychnine. They are readily available as rat poisons and are so quick-acting that immediate attention is necessary to save the cat.

General Symptoms of Poisoning

☐ Crying
☐ Hard breathing
☐ Intense pain in the abdomen
☐ Salivation
☐ Trembling and perhaps convulsions
☐ Vomiting (usually)

209

General Emergency Treatment of Poisoning

At the first suspicion of poisoning you must act quickly; seconds may save the cat's life. If you can get the cat to vomit up the suspected poison before it is absorbed into the bloodstream, this may be sufficient to save its life. The quicker the chemical is released from the stomach, the easier the treatment and the better the results.

Emetics (to induce vomiting)

Hydrogen peroxide (3 percent). You can use it straight from the bottle or mix it with an equal amount of water.

Mustard powder. Use one tablespoon in a cup of warm water.

Table salt. Use one teaspoon in a cup of warm water.

Washing soda. Use a half teaspoon in a cup of warm water.

Administration

Don't get panicky and spill the liquid in quickly, as the cat might ingest it into the windpipe. Vomiting should occur in a few minutes. If it doesn't occur within ten to fifteen minutes, repeat.

Follow-up

Gather up some of the vomitus (if available) and take the cat to the veterinarian immediately. Do this even if the animal appears normal after vomiting.

Antidotes

If the poison is known, it is important to follow the emergency instructions on the bottle or can—and then get the cat immediately to a veterinarian.

If the poison is not known, there is a universal antidote which should be kept in every pet owner's medicine cabinet: two parts powdered charcoal (readily available at most drugstores) or burnt toast, one part milk of magnesia, and one part tannic acid or strong tea. Give half a tablespoon to a kitten and twice the amount to an adult cat.

Poisons

Acids, Alkalies

BENZOIC ACID

Benzoic acid can change a gentle cat into a wild, hard-to-handle, clawing animal. In severe cases, the cat will go into convulsions and die. Recently, at a cattery in London, 28 out of 70 cats died from an overdose of benzoic acid. It is widely used in preserving foods for both humans and animals and is harmless when used in proper proportions.

Emergency treatment: If the cat shows hyperactivity, a sedative should be given to calm the animal down until it gets to the veterinary hospital.

CARBOLIC ACID, MURIATIC ACID, AND ALKALIES SUCH AS LYE AND OTHER DRAIN CLEANERS

These caustic chemicals will burn the cat's mouth (the tongue and membranes) and any other membranes with which they come into contact. Unfortunately, cats will drink these (a sip is enough) if exposed to them. Often the tip of the tongue is lost.

One of the first symptoms is excessive salivation. The cat then becomes lethargic, refuses to eat (the mouth is too sore), becomes feverish (the mouth and tongue soon become infected), and unless treatment is instituted immediately the cat will starve to death. Also, there is often a bad odor from the mouth caused by the dying tissues. Glucose, saline, and antibiotics are desperately needed.

Emergency treatment: Quick medical care is required to save the cat's life. In the meantime, for *acid poisoning,* quickly give the cat bicarbonate of soda (one teaspoon). For *alkali poisoning,* pour vinegar or lemon juice into the side of the mouth to counteract the effects of the alkali.

Antifreeze

Cats love the taste of antifreeze, even though it is a deadly poison. Every spring and fall there are reports of cats dying because they crawled into the underparts of cars to get at antifreeze spilled from radiators or got into open containers of the lethal liquid. Symptoms include drowsiness, staggering, paralysis of the rear quarters, coma.

Emergency treatment: Before rushing the cat to a veterinarian, induce vomiting and then give the universal antidote. If there is any antifreeze on the cat's coat it should immediately be removed with lukewarm water and a mild soap and the pet should be wrapped in a towel.

Birds

It is possible for a cat to be poisoned by a bird who has feasted on greenery or insects sprayed with herbicides, insecticides, or pesticides. There is a special danger with pigeons in some localities, because of a poison put out to cut down the pigeon population. This particular poison affects the nervous system of the pigeon, and if the bird is devoured by a cat, there is severe pain, spasms, and convulsions, and the cat dies within twenty-four to thirty-six hours. (A cat may also contract coccidiosis by eating an infected bird; see page 202.)

Emergency treatment: Induce vomiting and then give the universal antidote. Rush the cat to a veterinary clinic.

Bleaches and Cleansers

Cats are exposed to many toxic materials every day, including a wide variety of household bleaches and cleansers. Especially toxic are detergents and disinfectants that contain coal-tar products such as creosote, carbolic acid, Lysol (in any form), petroleum distillates, phosphates, and pine oil. If these products are used when there is a cat in the house, extreme care should be taken.

If a container with a bleach, cleanser, or disinfectant breaks or tips over, the material should be thoroughly removed immediately. And if a cat should walk or roll in it, clean its paws and coat with lukewarm water and a mild soap.

When cleaning a floor, keep cats away until the floor has dried. Also, most floor waxes are very toxic.

Another danger is bathtubs, sinks, and toilets. Because cats are especially fond of drinking out of these fixtures, they should be thoroughly rinsed after an abrasive cleaning powder or deodorizer has been used. A small amount ingested or picked up on the paws could prove extremely toxic. When soaking clothes and dishes in bleaches and detergents, keep cats away, for the soaking solution is toxic. Animal food dishes should be rinsed well.

Also, dishwashers, washing machines, and clothes dryers should be kept out of bounds to cats, not only because of the danger of physical injury, but also because of the residues of bleaches and detergents which cats can get on their paws and fur and subsequently lick. The same applies to household scrubbing materials (brushes, mops, sponges).

The odor from bleaches (ammonia, Clorox) could cause distress in the cat. The same holds true for aerosol sprays (air fresheners and deodorizers, human deodorants and hair sprays, window cleaners, etc.).

Oven cleaners, as their directions state, are very toxic and must be used with caution.

Emergency treatment: Wash off as much of

the material as possible with lukewarm water and a mild soap. Induce vomiting. If available, follow the antidotal directions on the can or bottle from which the poison came.

Carbon Monoxide

Carbon monoxide, an odorless, colorless, and tasteless gas, is a deadly poison. Small doses may be received while warming up the engine of a car in a garage or when traveling for several hours with windows closed in a car with a faulty exhaust system. Such small doses will make humans only mildly ill with nausea, headache, and vomiting, but they can be fatal to a cat. When a cat becomes excessively sleepy while traveling, look for any leaks in the exhaust. Sometimes "car sickness" is really carbon monoxide poisoning. Many cases have been reported in which cats suffered carbon monoxide poisoning when traveling in car trunks or in station wagons with the air conditioning turned on, windows closed, and faulty exhaust systems leaking the toxic gas.

Emergency treatment: Fresh air and artificial respiration may save your cat's life. Quick action is needed to prevent the gas from destroying the brain cells.

Coal-Tar Products

These are abundant around the garage, garden, and house. They include creosote, fuel and motor oils, gasoline, anything containing benzine, many household, cleaning, and dry-cleaning products, petroleum distillates, turpentine.

Emergency Treatment: If any has been swallowed, induce vomiting immediately. On the skin surface, wash off as much as possible with lukewarm water and a mild soap. Then apply a mild oil such as baby oil or lanolin.

Cyanide

This is very deadly, but fortunately it has an extremely bad taste and even kittens are not likely to lick it. One of the symptoms of cyanide poisoning is heavy breathing which gets shorter and shorter—and then gasping for breath.

Emergency Treatment: Vomiting should be induced immediately. There is a specific antidote, methylene blue, which is found in bluing for washing. Mix 1 teaspoon bluing with 1 cup water, pour it in the side of the cat's mouth, and then rush the animal to the veterinarian.

Poisons in Food

Even though the cat's stomach is a strong organ which can digest many strange objects, cats are more sensititve to poisons than dogs and show toxic effects at much lower levels. Most cats can consume decayed and rotten food without suffering any ill consequences. Usually, the worse the food smells, the better the scavenger likes it. But their food can be contaminated in many ways. There may be high levels of *mercury* in fish; food or water can be contaminated with a bacteria called *Salmonella,* or meat can be contaminated with a bacteria called *Clostridium,* and both these bacteria cause food poisoning. Additionally, their food can contain insecticides, fungicides, and pesticides. Another form of contamination is by estrogen (female hormones), which are used in caponizing chickens and fattening steers.

Salmonella poisoning produces serious intestinal symptoms. In young animals, a severe case will be acute and sometimes end in death. The onset and termination are quick; within hours a kitten with severe vomiting and diarrhea can expire.

There can also be a prolonged intestinal infection which manifests itself in fever, vomiting, diarrhea, and after a while dehydration and weakness. There is acute diarrhea in these cases, and the animal may pass some blood when the intestines are badly irritated.

The chronic form, which shows no symptoms, is known as the "carrier stage"; it usually follows recovery from one of the other forms. The carrier cat, while itself appearing healthy, can pass the infection on to other cats.

Diagnosis requires the isolation of the bacteria by laboratory culture. Proper treatment would then be instituted by the veterinarian. Sanitation is by far the best means of preventing and controlling this type of poisoning. Feeding dishes should never come in contact with any fecal material.

Clostridium poisoning is characterized by partial to complete paralysis, for the bacteria give off a toxin which affects the nervous system. The cat can remain paralyzed for a period of a few days to two to three weeks. The animal needs to be fed intravenously and constant nursing care is needed to save it. The cat requires daily help in evacuation of both urine and feces, and must be turned from side to side at regular intervals to prevent lung congestion and bedsores.

Emergency treatment: If there is any reason to suspect food poisoning, the first step is to induce vomiting with hydrogen peroxide. This should be followed with a mild laxative such as milk of magnesia or mineral oil, and in extreme cases with an enema (see page 152). Evacuation of the bowels is imperative.

Herbicides, Insecticides, Weed Killers

Herbicides and insecticides are a growing danger to our pet population because of the increasing practice of spraying and dusting flowers, gardens, lawns, plants, shrubs, and trees. Insecticides used around the house, for killing cockroaches, flies, mosquitoes, and other insects, are also a hazard. It is important to realize that anything capable of killing insects or weeds can kill other living things as well. Cats delight in stalking and eating insects, and any poison so ingested can eventually build up to toxic symptoms. Even lawn sprays that are normally not toxic to cats can prove dangerous. It is wise to keep cats off treated lawns until the spray has dried. If your cat has been exposed to fresh spray, wash its feet with soap and water. Wipe the soles of your shoes after you have walked over contaminated ground so as not to take the material into the house. Herbicides and insecticides can be absorbed through the skin; if there is any question of an animal's exposure, get it into a sink and wash it thoroughly. Cats will also eat grass and plants and get poisoned in this way. Even Christmas trees that have been sprayed can be very toxic.

There is a "safe" weed killer, Varsol, which can be purchased at most gasoline stations. It is nontoxic to cats and is very effective on weeds. Varsol will not harm a cat if it walks across a sprayed driveway, lawn, or garden.

ARSENIC (SEE PESTICIDES)
This is commonly used in insect sprays for orchards. The symptoms of arsenic poisoning include vomiting and extreme pain.

CHLORINATED HYDROCARBONS
These are found in the most common group of insecticides (DDT, chlordane, lindane, etc.). The nervous system is affected, and the symptoms are drooling, foaming at the mouth, shaking, convulsions.

Emergency treatment: Try to induce vomiting with hydrogen peroxide, mustard, or salt water; then give the universal antidote. If the cat should have the poison on its body, wash it thoroughly. Then rush it to a veterinarian, as every second counts.

FLEA COLLARS, DIPS, POWDERS, SPRAYS
When you use flea collars, dips, powders, and sprays, be very careful that they are "for cats." Flea collars intended for dogs can be

toxic and can prove fatal to cats because of the strength and type of the chemical used. Powders containing DDT and lindane are lethal, especially for nursing mothers. Also bear in mind that there is always the possibility of an individual susceptibility and a bad reaction.

The flea collar, which is such an excellent addition to the feline world, cannot be worn by Persian cats and there are other cats who are sensitive to the chemicals the collar contains. Fortunately, reactions are rare, but the first time a cat wears a flea collar, it is a good idea to check the skin, especially at the neck, for a few days. Fastening the collar tightly could cause a reaction in some cats that might range from a light skin redness to purulent lesions. Falling hair has also been reported. For cats who are sensitive, the chemical is readily absorbed through the skin. It is transported through the body in the bloodstream and stored in the body fat. The liver is directly affected by this poison and can be badly damaged. I would definitely advise removing the flea collar under such conditions.

Occasionally, a sensitive person develops a mild poisoning-type rash after close contact with a pet wearing a flea collar. In households with young children, make sure they don't chew on the collar.

LIME
Lime is used on lawns and in orchard sprays. It will burn the mouth and tongue.

Emergency treatment: Thoroughly wash the mouth and give a half teaspoon of milk of magnesia. Then rush the cat to a veterinarian.

NICOTINE
This is commonly used in plant sprays and for spraying poultry houses. The symptoms of nicotine poisoning include vomiting, shaking and shivering, a staggering uncoordinated gait, and fits and convulsions.

Emergency treatment: Induce vomiting and get the cat to a veterinarian immediately for a transfusion and injections.

ORGANIC PHOSPHATES
These are found in many insecticides. The symptoms include drooling, excessive watering of the eyes, severe abdominal pain, and convulsions.

Emergency treatment: Get the animal to a veterinarian as quickly as possible. He has specific antidotes for this poison.

PYROPHOSPHATES
These compounds are used in insecticides, such as Malathion, and are lethal. They are found as residues on agricultural products as well as in flea and tick dips. The poison is absorbed through the skin and overexposure can be fatal. The symptoms are pinpoint pupils, watering of the eyes, salivation, respiratory spasms, violent abdominal cramps, vomiting, diarrhea, muscular twitching, and convulsions.

Emergency treatment: It must be administered promptly. If the animal has gotten into these chemicals, bathe it immediately and rush it to a veterinarian for oxygen and antidotes.

Household Products

Household products toxic to cats (in addition to those mentioned in other sections) include: camera film fixers; dry-cleaning preparations; dyes (both for clothes and for shoes); some glues and mucilages; lighter fluids (including those used for charcoal grills); all mothballs and moth sprays; many polishes (for floors, furniture, shoes, silver, etc.).

If the bottle or can recommends caution when the product is used around children, or gives an antidote, even more care should be taken when used around cats. Cats and children are both susceptible and sensitive to most chemicals.

Medicines

ANTIBIOTICS
Indiscriminate use of antibiotics can prove

toxic to some cats. These drugs should be used only on the advice of a veterinarian. Some beneficial drugs such as chloramphenicol (Chloromycetin) (which has saved many a cat from death) can be toxic if not used properly. Some drugs such as penicillin, Terramycin, and similar antibiotics can alter the bacterial balance of the stomach and intestines and thus lower an animal's resistance to fungal and other disease-producing germs.

ANTISEPTICS AND DISINFECTANTS (SEE ALSO BLEACHES AND CLEANSERS)
Antiseptics and disinfectants that are very toxic to cats include coal-tar products, the phenols, carbolic acid and derivatives. Lysol and pine-oil disinfectants are also derivatives, and none of these should be used around cats.

ASPIRIN
It has been proven that a single adult aspirin administered to a cat morning and evening for a week would likely result in poisoning and death. However, an occasional aspirin will not harm a cat.

BORIC ACID
Boric acid powder, which is widely used by humans as a mild antiseptic, can be highly toxic to cats when ingested.

Many cat owners use boric acid powder on white cats to counteract brown discoloration caused by tear stain. However, when there is more than one cat in the house, this can be dangerous, since animals tend to lick one another. Boric acid can cause hemorrhaging in the stomach and the intestinal tract and can prove fatal.

Emergency treatment: Contact your veterinarian immediately and give an emetic of powdered mustard until vomiting occurs.

CARBOLATED VASELINE
This contains phenol and is extremely poisonous to cats.

CASTOR OIL
Castor oil is not recommended for cats. It is too violent a cathartic and produces severe intestinal cramps.

HUMAN CONSTIPATION REMEDIES
Some of these contain deadly strychnine and should never be used for a cat.

NARCOTICS AND OPIATES
Cats are very sensitive to morphine and they go berserk instead of being sedated.

TRANQUILIZERS
These should be used only upon the advice of a veterinarian. Some are not predictable and induce wild behavior in some cats.

VITAMINS
An overdosage of vitamin D can cause an accumulation of calcium and possibly result in kidney stones. The same applies to cod-liver oil. Vitamin D is the only vitamin that is really toxic with overuse. Cats seem to be able to eliminate the others.

Paints

LEAD POISONING
Even paint fumes can make a cat very sick, so it is essential to have good ventilation while painting and to confine the cat to another part of the house or apartment. Poisoning usually comes about from licking or chewing on wet paint or drinking water out of paint cans or ingesting linoleum. Artists' oil paints are equally toxic.

Another common cause of lead poisoning is feeding from ceramic (glazed pottery) dishes. Although lead components are widely used in ceramic glazes, they are normally harmless when properly applied and fired. If they have not been fired long enough, acid in foods causes the lead to seep into the food, producing a toxic condition. The FDA has recently banned importation of certain pottery from Italy and Mexico because it is a lead-poisoning hazard.

Should a cat get paint on its fur or paws, *never, never* use turpentine to remove it. This is a coal-tar product and can severely burn the skin and mouth.

In chronic cases—a gradual exposure to lead—there is a bluish discoloration along the gum line. In large doses the acute symptoms are drooling, vomiting, and muscular twitching. When the poison is absorbed into the body, the cat will begin to walk in circles with the head down. After that, the cat will likely go into a corner and hold its head against a wall. Fast breathing and convulsions follow. Death will occur in twenty-four to thirty-six hours.

Emergency treatment: Immediately give an emetic and then the universal antidote. Get the cat to a veterinarian as quickly as possible, as he has specific medications.

Pesticides

To be poisoned by a pesticide, it is not necessary for a cat to directly ingest poison that has been put out in a container or on food for the purpose of killing rodents. A cat can be just as severely poisoned by catching and devouring a poisoned, dying mouse, rat, or squirrel. If this is a possibility, the cat owner should be on the constant lookout for symptoms.

ANTU

This deadly rat (and mouse) poison used by many exterminators kills both the rodent and the cat very quickly. It causes fluid leakage in the lungs, and the animal virtually drowns in its own fluids. Early symptoms include difficult breathing, intense coughing, and vomiting, and the animal experiences excruciating pain. There is very little hope of saving the cat because the body tissues are quickly destroyed.

Emergency treatment: Induce vomiting immediately, using mustard powder or a solution of soap and water, and pour the liquid into the side of the cat's mouth. Take the cat to a veterinarian.

ARSENIC

Arsenic causes severe abdominal pains, and the usual symptoms are watery and sometimes bloody diarrhea, salivation, vomiting, staggering, trembling, and convulsions. In the final stages there is a coldness of the extremities and paralysis of the body.

Emergency treatment: It is effective only in the early stages. As quickly as possible, attempt to induce vomiting with hydrogen peroxide. Also give the cat two or three teaspoons of milk of magnesia and strong tea. Then get the animal quickly to your veterinarian.

RED SQUILL

This is found in many rat poisons. The poisoned cat will show vomiting, weakness, dizziness, paralysis, and coma. Death soon follows. Unfortunately there is no specific treatment, but if started early enough symptomatic treatment will usually save the animal.

Emergency treatment: Give an emetic and rush the cat to a veterinarian.

SODIUM FLUOROACETATE (ALSO KNOWN AS *1080*)

Since this very potent poison is, unfortunately, odorless and tasteless, it can be eaten inadvertently. The symptoms show up quickly—crying in pain, then convulsions (it is quite violent, for the poison affects the brain and nervous system). As with several of these poisons, there is no known treatment.

STRYCHNINE

This is very commonly used in rat poisons, and with a large dose the cat will likely die before anything can be done to help. But if treatment is started early, the veterinarian can usually save the cat. The early symptoms are dilated pupils and twitching and stiffening of the neck muscles. In the later stages there are severe muscle spasms and usually convulsions. The limbs are extended and rigid; the neck is bent up and backward. At the slightest noise, such as the clapping of hands, the animal goes into severe convulsions. This hypersensitivity is diagnostic.

Emergency treatment: In the early stages you must administer an emetic—hydrogen peroxide or soapy or salty water. Then give strong tea to inactivate the strychnine. In the later stages when the animal is in convulsions, it needs sedation. Wrap the cat in a blanket, hold it until the convulsions subside, and get it to a veterinarian immediately. If nothing else is available, an aspirin tablet (up to three adult tablets) can sedate the cat and render it unconscious until veterinary treatment can be instituted. The veterinarian will intravenously inject a barbiturate agent and then wash out the stomach and intestines.

THALLIUM

This is a chemical used in rat poison, and in recent years many cases of thallium poisoning have been reported. It is an insidious type of poison, for although it is rapidly absorbed in the stomach, clinical signs don't always appear immediately; there may be a delay of several hours, even as much as two days. There are two forms of thallium poisoning—acute and chronic.

When the condition is acute, severe intestinal distress is noted. The animal vomits, and there is diarrhea with blood.

Among the characteristic signs of thallium poisoning are hair and skin changes. The superficial areas of the skin become reddened, the hair falls out, and the skin becomes necrotic, or death-like, in appearance. The skin between the toes shows these changes early. The skin around the muzzle becomes dry, cracked, and bloody, and then encrusted.

A significant sign of chronic poisoning is alopecia: hair begins to fall out twelve to fourteen days after ingestion of the poison. As the disease progresses there are respiratory infections, which can turn into pneumonia, and neurological signs, such as muscular tremors, incoordinated walking, and convulsions.

Emergency treatment: As soon as possible after ingestion, an emetic of salt and water should be given. Then the cat should be taken immediately to a veterinarian, as he has a specific antidote—dithizone—and can institute successful treatment.

WARFARIN

Although this rat poison is supposedly nontoxic to pets (and the label says so), it is the most popular rat poison on the market and one of the commonest sources of poisoning that we see today. One of the first symptoms is vomiting. In mild cases the vomitus is made up of gastric contents; in severe cases there is blood in the vomitus and the cat passes bloody, mucous stools. In milder cases there is weakness, sometimes lameness, and generally a bloody diarrhea. If the case is severe, the animal exhibits the same symptoms as those of shock—the blood pressure drops, the body becomes cool, breathing becomes shallow and weak, the pulse accelerates. Usually there is hemorrhaging in the body cavities and under the skin near the joints.

Emergency treatment: This poisoning requires immediate attention by your veterinarian for blood transfusions to restore clotting power. Injections with vitamin K are a specific for this poison.

Plants

There are many house and garden plants and weeds (variously, their bark, flowers, leaves, and limbs) which are poisonous to cats. If eaten by a pregnant cat they can cause serious birth defects such as cleft palate, dwarfism, harelip, twisted bones. It is especially important in the case of house cats, who crave greenery, to monitor the plants. The most common killer is *Larkspur*. Other plants and weeds poisonous to cats are:

Arrowgrass.

Azalea.

Bittersweet (the berries). A member of the deadly nightshade family.

Castor bean.

Cherry (ordinary and *Jerusalem).* Can give cyanide poisoning.

Dieffenbachia. This household plant causes a quick-acting poisoning. Within a few seconds after eating this plant a cat will begin to suffer severe abdominal pains, roll about on the floor, and salivate foam. Wrap the cat in a towel to keep it from thrashing about and induce vomiting as quickly as possible. Then rush the cat to a veterinarian so that it can be treated for this specific poison.

Elderberry. Can give cyanide poisoning.

Hemlock.

Jimson weed.

Laurel. If a cat eats laurel, it will show intense irritation, itchiness of the skin, running of the nose and eyes, severe abdominal pain, drooling and vomiting, and then convulsions and death. Since quick action is necessary, an emetic should be given, followed by a sedative. Then get the cat to a veterinarian.

Lily of the valley.

Locoweed.

Mistletoe.

Mushrooms and Toadstools. Cats like to eat them and are susceptible to some varieties just as people are. Drooling, vomiting, paralysis, and death are the consequences. If there is any suspicion, make the cat vomit immediately and then rush it to a veterinarian, as he has specific injections to counteract the poison.

Oleander.

Peach. The leaves can give cyanide poisoning.

Philodendron. A slow-acting posion. The cat ultimately becomes listless. There is a loss of appetite, loss of weight, and vomiting. If the posioning is discovered in time, the veterinarian can institute successful treatment. Otherwise enough poisons will have gotten into the body to destroy the organs.

Poinsettia (the leaves).

Rhubarb (the leaves).

Wisteria.

Emergency treatment: If poisoning is suspected, follow the procedures outlined on page 210.

Talcum Powder

It has recently been shown that "baby powder" can seriously affect infants and improper use has resulted in fatalities. It is an absolute poison to the baby's internal organs whether swallowed or inhaled into the lungs. This should caution the cat owner. Brain damage, pneumonia, and lung congestion are not uncommon results of powder inhalation.

Toads

Most of the poisonous toads are found in southern Florida and in the desert regions of the Southwest. There are at least nine different species capable of poisoning cats. The toxin in the toad is carried in wart-like lumps on the skin. The symptoms of toad poisoning include evidence of pain, diarrhea, blindness, and convulsions.

Emergency treatment: Irrigate the cat's mouth as soon as possible after contact with the toad. The cat should then be taken to a veterinarian for sedatives and tranquilizers to control pain and steroids to reduce inflammatory reaction.

Worm Medicine

Because worm medicine is strong enough to kill worms, under certain conditions it is strong enough to kill cats. There is no such thing as a 100 percent safe worm medicine. Any one of the medicines can be highly toxic if used incorrectly—either in overdosage or given to a sick cat.

Never, never give worm medicine to a cat with a fever. The fever likely signifies that the patient's body is not well enough to receive a jolt from a strong worm medicine. Since there are four or five types of worms and a specific medicine for each type, good judgment and caution must be exercised.

Emergency treatment: In any type of reaction to worm medicine, sugar in any form is an excellent antidote until you can get the cat to a veterinarian. After worming, if you see any wobbliness or incoordination, give Karo syrup or molasses.

18 · First Aid in Emergencies

Steps in First Aid to an Injured Cat

A hurt cat is terrified and confused, and if at all possible it will run off and try to hide. If too injured to move, the cat will attempt to bite or scratch; so keep your own safety in mind. Here are a few points to be followed when aiding an injured cat:

1. Approach the cat cautiously, speaking in a quiet and soothing voice. In any emergency situation, keeping yourself and the cat calm is the first order of business. Do not panic. That will frighten the cat and make matters worse.

2. If it is an outdoor accident, have your coat or shirt in readiness to wrap around the animal to restrain it. Gently—in case of internal injuries or broken bones—pick the cat up by the scruff of the neck (facing away from you to avoid clinging and scratching) and enclose the animal in the wrappings. If it is an indoor accident, a towel or pillowcase can be used for restraining purposes. If the cat is especially wild, adhesive tape can be wrapped around the back legs and around the muzzle (between the nostrils and eyes).

3. If the cat is bleeding, and fighting you, apply a pressure bandage to control the bleeding.

4. Then call a veterinarian for further instructions.

If Your Cat Is Struck by a Car

Since being hit by a moving vehicle is the most common of all emergency situations, I shall use it to illustrate the steps in first aid to an injured cat.

The main concern when a cat has been struck by a car must be whether shock and internal injuries are present. Broken legs and external injuries are relatively unimportant in the beginning. Saving the life of the animal comes first. X rays and broken bones can be taken care of later.

After a cat is hit, in its delirium it could hurt you, so approach it cautiously. The most important problems at this point are wrapping the cat in something (to restrain it and to keep it warm) and getting it to a veterinarian as quickly as possible.

Keeping the animal warm is imperative because shock almost always accompanies severe injuries. Usually the blood pressure drops, and if there is any loss of blood the body temperature does down quickly.

If there is apparent bleeding—and if the cat will allow it—it is a good idea to put a covering or pressure bandage over the injured area. If the wound is squirting blood, blood vessels have been ruptured, and a tourniquet should be applied to the points of pressure where the blood enters the area (see illustration). The less blood lost, the greater are the chances of recovery.

The next step is to rush the animal to a veterinary hospital. It will need injections, oxygen, and possibly blood transfusions to save its life.

Artificial Respiration

Artificial respiration is indicated whenever the animal's breathing has stopped but there is still a heartbeat. There are several traumatic experiences that can cause respiratory failure, such as drowning, electric shock, and anaphylactic shock due to snake bite, bee stings, and vaccination reactions.

The cat needs immediate attention because its body cells desperately require oxygen, and if the brain cells are without oxygen for ten to fifteen minutes, or even less, permanent brain damage results.

Artificial respiration should be given as follows:

The animal should be lying on its right side with the head and neck extended and the tongue as far out of the mouth as possible. Open the mouth, grasp the tongue, and gently extend it forward. It will hang out of the side of the cat's mouth.

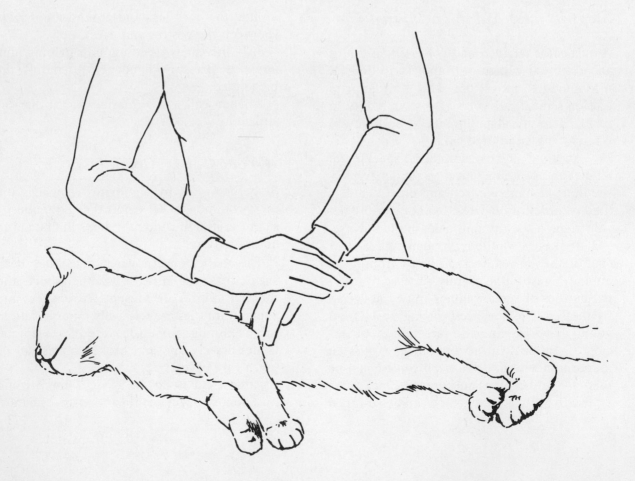

Place your two hands on the chest over the ribs, push down firmly, and squeeze the chest together to empty the lungs. Release the pressure of your hands (that is, pull up), and then squeeze again. Continue this procedure of down and up in a steady rhythm timed to the normal breathing rate of the cat, which is twenty to thirty times per minute. Do it gently but with strong pressure to the chest cavity. The pressure also massages the heart.

Don't give up quickly. You may have to work on the cat an hour or even longer. There's always hope of reviving an animal as long as a heartbeat is felt.

As soon as the cat starts breathing by itself, let it sniff some spirits of ammonia, and then treat it as a shock victim with stimulants and warmth. Professional help should be sought to treat the cause of the respiratory failure.

PRESSURE POINTS

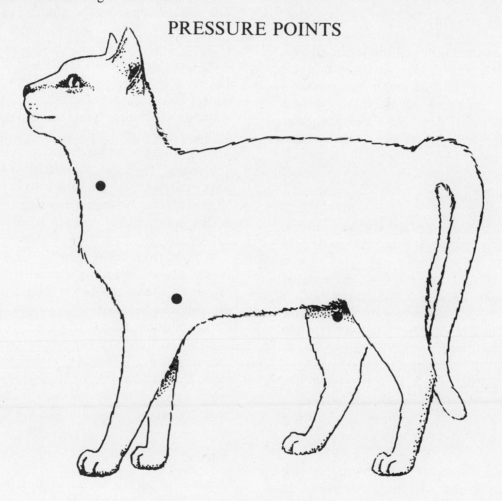

1. Pressure point near the jugular vein and carotid artery along the side of the neck controls hemorrhage on that side of the body.
2. Pressure point on the inside of the thigh where the femoral artery passes over the thighbone.
3. Pressure point is directly above the elbow on the front leg. Will stop bleeding in front leg.

Mouth-to-mouth resuscitation can also be administered if there are two of you. While one is applying artificial respiration, the other can be breathing directly into the cat's mouth, forcing air into the lungs. The hands should be cupped to form a cone over the cat's mouth and nostrils, and the breathing should be hard and continued until the cat begins to breathe for itself.

Hemorrhaging

Any sign of bleeding should be regarded as a critical emergency. The animal should be kept as still as possible and taken immediately to a veterinary clinic. For external bleeding, in the interim, cold water, ice packs, pressure, and tourniquets are the basic first-aid principles.

External Bleeding

Arterial. The severing of an artery is serious. The blood is bright red and spurts out in rhythm with the heartbeat.

Venous. When a vein has been severed, the blood is darker and seeps in a steady flow.

Capillary. This is an oozing of small surface blood vessels. It can be hazardous if the wound is extensive.

Bleeding can be stopped by direct pressure, either to the blood vessels or to the hemorrhaging area itself, by means of fingers or bandages, by use of a tourniquet, or by direct pressure to the pressure points on the cat's body.

To apply a tourniquet. Any emergency article that can be tied will do (a handkerchief, cord). Always tie the tourniquet above the wound between the wound and the heart. Loosen the tourniquet every five to eight minutes so that the area doesn't become deprived of the blood necessary to keep the tissues alive.

Internal Bleeding

Any internal bleeding should be regarded as serious. Injections by a veterinarian to help coagulate the blood are needed to stop the bleeding. If there is an extreme loss of blood, as the blood pressure drops the cat will go into shock.

Hemorrhaging from the eye is the result of a blow on the head or on the eyeball.

Blood coming from the mouth can indicate a broken jaw, a broken tooth, or a cut gum. Foreign objects such as bones and sharp sticks can cause various injuries to the mouth and the soft tissues of the throat. When a cat retches blood and it is frothy, it is mixed with air and is coming from the lungs. If it is darkish, it is mixed with gastric juices and is coming from the stomach.

Bleeding from both nostrils indicates a fractured bone in the sinuses or a foreign object in the nostrils. Bleeding from one nostril indicates an abscess or tumor in that one sinus.

If blood from the rectum is bright red, it is from the lower intestinal tract. If it is a darker brown or black, the blood is mingling with the digestive juices and is coming from the upper intestinal tract.

Bleeding from the urinary tract can indicate stones in the bladder or kidneys. If the cat is female and she is not in season, bleeding can signify tumors or cysts in the female passages or an infection in the uterus.

Shock

One way to tell if a cat is suffering from shock is to look at the gums. If they are pale and grayish, shock is indicated, and also possible internal bleeding. Other symptoms are weak and rapid heartbeat and a cold body, resulting in cold, bluish skin and pale mucous membranes (seen, for example, in the lips). The cat may be panting and showing hard breathing. It may go into a coma.

224

The management of shock should be understood, as it has wider application than mere fright. It covers most cases involving an unusual happening. The body—its organs and nervous system—seems to be so stunned that death may result from the shock and not from the injury itself. For instance, in cases of burns and other injuries, the shock condition rather than the accident itself may be the direct cause of death. Most often shock is a result of trauma, hemorrhage, intense pain, certain toxins, or severe fright.

When treating shock *never give liquids to an unconscious or semi-conscious animal,* except a drop or two of stimulant on the tongue, such as coffee or brandy. Inhalation of liquid can strangle the cat or produce a foreign-body pneumonia. If the animal is conscious and fights having the liquid administered, discontinue, as the excitement and distress are worse for its condition than any good to be derived from the stimulant.

In the case of a conscious cat, until it can be taken to the veterinary clinic, stimulants such as warm coffee or whiskey or brandy spilled into the corner of the mouth often help to save its life. They are good heart and blood stimulants in small doses. Spirits of ammonia or smelling salts can also be used. Another effective first-aid measure for shock is a mixture of one teaspoonful of salt and a half teaspoonful of baking soda in a pint of drinking water, given by mouth. This can also be given in place of ordinary drinking water for the first few days following injury or burns. The intense thirst associated with burn injury will make the patient receptive to the solution despite its unappealing taste. The salt and soda are helpful in restoring the essential elements the body loses during the shock syndrome.

When treating shock, keep the pet calm and warm; use blankets and hot-water bottles. Administer stimulants if the animal is conscious and able to swallow. Examine for injuries and stop any bleeding. Then rush the cat to a veterinarian. There is nothing more effective in shock than blood transfusions and oxygen.

Shock Formula

There is a very useful preparation to have on hand in your medicine chest, as it might save an animal who otherwise would have died of shock. It is prepared by putting four tablespoons of rock candy in a small covered jar and adding three tablespoons of whiskey or brandy (whichever the cat prefers). It takes several days for the candy to melt and form a thick syrup. This solution can be used in an emergency to prevent and treat shock.

Emergency Conditions
Abscesses (see also Bite Wounds)

An abscess is a large, painful, feverish swelling which can gather beneath the skin on almost any area of the body. It is an infection caused by a bruise or a puncture which closes up and therefore is prevented from draining. The animal is feverish, and reluctant to move because of the pain.

In the beginning the infection causes a swelling which is hard to the touch. At this stage hot Epsom salts or table salt compresses should be applied to bring the abscess to a head so that the core can be removed. The abscess should be lanced by a professional to avoid the dire results of punctured blood vessels.

Sometimes the abscess ruptures on its own and exudes a thick, foul-smelling, brownish-red mass. When this happens, the opening should be flushed out with hydrogen peroxide and then an antiseptic, such as boric acid solution or mild tincture of iodine, applied to the wound. Gradually the opening will close; but never allow the outside skin to close completely until all the pus has stopped draining.

225

Bee Stings and Insect Bites

I've seen many cats with terrible lumps on their heads and bodies caused by insect stings and bites. Usually, with a mild bite or two relief can be given with cold compresses of bicarbonate of soda (one tablespoon to a glass of water) and antihistamines to relieve the swelling. If the cause was bees, hornets, or wasps, the stinger can be removed with tweezers. Cold packs (ice water) are also helpful in reducing the pain and the swelling. Then a soothing ointment—zinc oxide or calamine lotion—can be applied. If the swelling remains, or increases, after twenty-four hours, consultation with a veterinarian is advised.

Some animals react violently to a sting or bite. As some humans do, they have an anaphylactic reaction and require immediate medical attention if they are to survive. They have to be treated as an animal in shock—kept warm and given stimulants—until they reach the veterinary clinic.

The stings of bees, hornets, wasps, and spiders produce violent reactions in cats sensitized by previous stings. After a sting a sensitive animal will feel pain at the site where the barb was inserted. This is followed by redness of skin, hives, and intense itching. Shortly thereafter the animal feels weakness and dizziness. Fainting, wheezing, shortness of breath, and choking may also be seen. These symptoms may all manifest themselves within a few minutes or may be delayed up to twenty-four hours. Call your veterinarian immediately; an injection of epinephrine or cortisone may be necessary.

Bite Wounds

One of the commonest wounds is a cat or dog bite. Cats enjoy fighting with one another—to show superiority, or to gain the affection of a female in heat, or two females will fight each other to vent their frustrations. The most dangerous bites are the deep puncture wounds that cats and dogs inflict with their long canine teeth. These bites usually enter the skin, go through the muscle. and puncture the bone. Often there will be hair and debris in the wound. A bite deep enough to hit the bone can cause osteomyelitis, an infection of the bone. In one chronic subterranean wound I worked on, none of the antibiotics had any effect and upon X ray we found the end of a cat's tooth embedded in the bone.

In first aid for a deep, penetrating bite wound, I recommend first dropping some hydrogen peroxide into the wound to prevent contamination. Next, any suitable antiseptic, such as Mercurochrome, should be used. Your veterinarian will treat the wound with an antibiotic ointment and prescribe a generalized antibiotic to prevent serious infection.

There is always the possibility that the bite wound was inflicted by a rabid animal and necessary precautions should be taken (see pages 182–183).

Broken Bones

When a broken bone is suspected a veterinarian is urgently needed. With X rays he will be able to pinpoint the fracture (or it may be a dislocated hip or shoulder, which he will also be able to ascertain) and undertake the proper therapy.

Burns

Many cats are burned each year, and in a variety of ways—on stoves, barbecue grills, with hot ashes, splattering oil, boiling water, and other hot substances, by electrical wiring and appliances, several kinds of chemicals, and even by lightning. The burns vary in degree from red skin, to singed fur, to badly scarred skin and fur.

If the burn is superficial, the cat can be washed with a bicarbonate of soda solution and then Vaseline or grease or a mild oil can be applied to the area to soothe and coat it and to keep it clean. If possible the area should be bandaged to prevent secondary infection.

No strong antiseptic with an alcohol base should be applied, or merthiolate or iodine, because these would further burn the skin.

If the cat is conscious and responding to your attention, mild cold tea applied to the burn area would be helpful. The tannic acid in the tea helps reduce pain and would offset the loss of fluids because it is an astringent and seals the pores.

When the burns are extensive or deep, all the necrotic (dead) skin and hair have to be removed by your veterinarian. The areas are then covered with Vaseline bandages, and your veterinarian gives antibiotic therapy. These burns are dangerous and require expert professional care to save the animal.

Burns caused by electrical wiring and chemicals are treated in the same way. However, if the burning chemical was an acid, you wash the wound with an alkali, such as bicarbonate of soda; if the burning agent was an alkali, such as lime or other garden products, you counter with an acid, such as vinegar.

Diarrhea

A sudden diarrhea, with or without blood, may be the result of poisoning. See Chapter 16 (Intestinal Disorders) and Chapter 17.

Drowning

The first thing to do for a cat who has been underwater too long is to hold it upside down (gently, by the hind legs) to allow the water to drain out of the lungs. In addition, gently pull the tongue out as far as possible. Then apply artificial respiration and also mouth-to-mouth resuscitation (if a second person is available). It may be necessary to continue for some time—half an hour or an hour, or as long as the heart continues beating.

When the cat begins to breathe, you must treat it for shock and keep it warm to prevent pneumonia. The animal may well develop a foreign-body pneumonia caused by water in the lungs. After it seems revived, it is best to get it to a veterinarian so that complications can be avoided.

Electric Shock

When a cat is knocked unconscious by stepping on or chewing into a live wire, be sure the current is turned off before you try to help. If it is not possible to get to the switch box—and time is of the utmost importance—don a pair of rubber gloves, or even a piece of wood will do, and pull out the plug, because you could receive a bad shock from the cat's body.

Then you must try to stimulate the cat's respiration. As long as the heart is beating, you have a good chance of reviving a cat who is not breathing. Give artificial respiration.

Fits and Convulsions

The best way to handle a cat having a fit or convulsions is to stay out of the way until it quiets down. It will likely run around and then end up in a dark corner. Let the cat stay there until it is relaxed. After the attack is over, give it a sedative and get it to your veterinarian.

Foreign Objects Swallowed

Curiosity *has* killed many a cat. And it has caused much distress to countless others. No object small enough to be swallowed or fascinating enough to be chewed upon can be discounted in the presence of a cat.

Many things—bone splinters, fish bones, needles, bits of wood—become wedged in the mouth between the teeth and gums or get stuck in the throat. If you notice your cat drooling and clawing at its mouth, try to dislodge only the superficial object with your fingers or tweezers. If you are unsuccessful the cat will likely have to be put under anesthesia and forceps used. If the cat is choking on a foreign object, such as a bone, pick it up by its hind legs and hold it upside down, shaking it slightly. This probably will cause the cat to cough up the object. Rush the animal to your veterinarian to make sure the object is gone and has not caused any injury to the throat. Do not try to dislodge the object with your finger. If the foreign body is down past the throat, leave it to your veterinarian. He has special instruments that go down into the esophagus and windpipe.

Needles are especially dangerous. They can become embedded in the roof of the mouth or in the throat and months later a big knot or swelling will appear in the cheek or neck. An X ray is definitely indicated.

Needles with thread attached, and such things as thread or string, cellophane, Christmas tinsel and icicles, will ball up in the stomach and intestines. The main symptom is vomiting and immediate help is necessary to save the animal. A laxative of mineral oil or milk of magnesia might dislodge the foreign object. An enema (see page 152) might be necessary. Otherwise, immediate professional help must be sought.

Many a cat has choked on a bead, a small rubber or plastic ball, bits of a catnip mouse or a toy. Sometimes these objects end up in the intestinal tract. Watch the toys carefully, and if a part should be missing and you have a sick cat, be suspicious.

If your cat has swallowed a unknown object, use a solution of hydrogen peroxide or table salt to make it regurgitate it.

Frostbite

Although a cat can stand an amazing amount of cold—its body adjusts to it—in certain areas of the country, should the animal be outdoors for a long period of time, its ears or toes could become frostbitten. The affected parts should be thawed out slowly with a minimum of abrasion, since they have little blood circulatory action and gangrene or necrosis can easily set in; they could slough off and be lost. After thawing, apply Vaseline or grease to the affected areas. When toes are frostbitten, the cat can be immersed in tepid (barely warm) water, and after the medication has been applied, the feet should be bandaged, but not tightly, so as not to interfere with the circulation.

Gunshot Wounds

The first thing in emergency treatment is to stop the bleeding. Then treat the cat for shock by wrapping it in a blanket and giving stimulants. Then rush it to your veterinarian.

Heart Attack

As with humans, a heart attack can occur while a cat is strenuously exerting itself out in the yard or relaxing in front of the fire. The animal will gasp for air and fall unconscious. The tongue may turn blue, indicating that the cat is not getting enough oxygen.

In emergency treatment give artificial respiration and a stimulant, such as warm coffee or brandy, to get the heart and respiration going again.

Applying pressure to the chest cavity does two things: it empties the lungs and it massages the heart (pressure on the chest cavity presses on the heart muscle and is almost like open-heart resuscitation). By pounding on the chest cavity firmly, but not roughly, the heart can sometimes be stimulated into beating.

When the animal regains consciousness, it should be treated as a shock case and kept warm, as its body temperature will drop rapidly if it is left uncovered. A veterinarian should be contacted, as the cat's heart needs

228

digitalization and other forms of stimulation that will have longer-lasting effects.

Heatstroke

This is a drastic condition seen during hot weather. Many of the cases occur because owners make the mistake of leaving their cats in parked automobiles while they go shopping for a "few moments." The causes of heatstroke in susceptible animals are high atmospheric temperatures, high humidity, and lack of ventilation.

The first signs of heatstroke are excessive panting, vomiting, weakness, inability to stand, and dilated pupils giving a blank expression. In later stages the tongue turns various shades of blue; it is difficult for the cat to get air and it becomes cyanotic.

Quick action is needed to save the animal. Move it into the fresh air or into a cool, ventilated area. Its temperature usually goes up to 106 degrees or more, so it has to be cooled as fast as possible. Cool water over the body is vital; it is preferable to soak the cat with wet towels to allow the heat to dissipate slowly. Ice packs can be applied to the head. Then rush your pet to the veterinarian for oxygen, intravenous saline and glucose injections, and general treatment for shock.

To prevent heatstroke when traveling in a car without air conditioning, it is best to have the cat in a carrier so that the windows can be kept open. At home a cat should not be cooped up in a hot room without adequate ventilation. The addition of salt to the diet during the summer months is advisable, as the cat's body loses salt rapidly in hot weather. A pinch in the dinner every night is all that is needed.

High-Rise Injury Syndrome

Falling accidents among urban cats living in apartment buildings have been steadily increasing, and veterinarians are seeing the results of such accidents with alarming frequency. A fall most commonly occurs when a screen or window is left open.

When cats fall, their efficient righting mechanism causes them to land in an upright position with the head down. The distances cats have fallen and survived are nothing short of amazing. At present, the record heights for survival are:

18 stories onto a hard surface (concrete, asphalt)

20 stories onto shrubbery

28 stories onto a canopy or awning

The most common injuries seen in cats that have fallen out of windows are head injuries resulting in nose bleeds, broken jaws, and pneumothorax (chest injuries). Also seen are broken teeth and broken legs. However, the most dangerous and fatal results are shock and internal bleeding. Quick professional help is a necessity.

Injuries

Body injuries such as occur when a cat tears its skin going through a barbed fence are frequent. To prevent infection, hydrogen peroxide should be applied to the wound, and for cosmetic reasons and good healing the wound will subsequently have to be sutured.

Ear injuries usually entail cuts and bruises on the ear flap received in a fight (in which case there may be punctures and tears) or in blows to the head (in which case there may be a hematoma or hemorrhaging). When there is a hematoma, the ear flap swells and a soft mass can be felt inside the ear. Because of the pain the cat shakes its head continually. The more the cat shakes its head, the greater the hemorrhaging and the greater the swelling. The best emergency treatment until you reach your veterinarian is cold packs to the ear.

Eye injuries should be treated with great care. Any injury to the outside covering of the eyeball (the cornea) should be looked upon as an emergency. Keep the eye moist with cold-water packs (gauze dipped in cold water, slightly wrung out) and keep it covered (the cat will try desperately to scratch it) until you get to your veterinarian.

Eyeball protrusion (ruptured eyeball) is not uncommon. A hard blow to the head can force the eyeball out of its socket. Quick action is necessary if the eyeball and eyesight are to be saved. Cold-water packs will keep the eyeball moist and control swelling. Rush the patient to the veterinarian, as each minute the eye is unattended reduces the possibility of getting it back into the socket.

Paw and *leg* injuries should be properly attended to immediately; if care is delayed, the cat might be lame for the rest of its life. At the first sign of limping the leg should be carefully examined from the pad up.

Although the cat's pad has a tough covering, it is vulnerable to penetration by such objects as glass, tacks and nails, and wood splinters. Any wound to the pad should be washed thoroughly with an antiseptic and then bandaged to keep dirt and debris away from it and to prevent it from opening further. Often wounds to the pad have to be sutured, and they are slow-healing because of the constant pressure of the cat's weight.

When dislocations, fractures, and sprains in the leg are not readily diagnosable, an X ray should be made. Heat should be applied and aspirin given to relieve the pain. If limping continues more than twenty-four hours or becomes more severe, the injury is more serious than a simple sprain. Even certain sprains, those in which the ligaments have been torn, require surgery to repair the ligaments and splints for immobilization.

Tail injuries are painful and tend to be difficult to treat because the cat's tail is constantly in motion. Antiseptics should be applied and the tail bandaged with a thick padding.

A broken tail is a common injury. It can occur when a cat's tail is stepped on or caught in a door or as the result of a cat fight or a run-in with an automobile. A broken tail will usually heal without complications, but you should have it attended to (your veterinarian will decide whether to splint it or not) because improper healing may result in infection and loss of part of the tail bone.

Paralysis

Paralysis is a disturbing sight. The cat is unable to move and sometimes it can't swallow. Paralysis can be due to a variety of causes, including cerebral hemorrhage and food poisoning. Spinal-disk rupture can cause a complete paralysis of the rear parts. A severe infestation of ticks can produce a generalized paralysis. For emergency treatment, move the cat carefully and get it to your veterinarian immediately.

Porcupine Quills

In certain parts of the country porcupine quills are a painful reality. The muzzle and head are generally affected most, as the cat is usually trying to attack the porcupine. Because removal of the quills is painful, the cat has to be given a general anesthetic. If at all possible, take the cat to a veterinarian, in a cat carrier or box preferably since the cat is in great pain. If you must remove the quills yourself, sedate the cat first and hold it down. Work each quill out individually, twisting gently, pushing it forward, then cutting it with an electrician's pliers. Swab the lacerations with an antiseptic after the quills are out.

Skunks

Encounters with skunks are more likely to happen with kittens, as most older cats tend to avoid skunks. The best thing you can do is wash the cat with water and a mild soap. You might also rub into the fur an old country remedy—tomato juice; there seems to be something in it that works as an antidote to skunk odor. Then you can rinse your pet with a 5 percent solution of ammonia, being careful not to get any into the eyes. You may have to repeat the washings several times.

There may be inflammation of the eyes because of irritation from the skunk spray. The eyes should be washed with warm water or a boric acid solution, and an eye ointment used (a human eye ointment will do). If the eyes are badly inflamed, a veterinarian should be consulted.

Snake Bite

During warm weather, should your pet come home with a large swollen mass around its face or neck or front leg, it is wise to suspect snake bite and get it treated immediately. If the cat is taken to a veterinarian within the first hour or two, it can usually be saved. In the meantime, the cat should be kept warm and quiet. Excitement will spread the venom through the body.

Other symptoms include intense pain, shortness of breath, vomiting, impaired vision, incoordination, and eventually paralysis.

Immediate first aid is the same as for humans. If the bite is on a leg, apply a tourniquet about two inches above the puncture and remove it for a short while every fifteen minutes. If you cut open the area with a blade (razor or knife) and squeeze out as much of the poison as possible, the cat will have a better chance. (I do not advise sucking out the venom, because there could be a lesion in your mouth which would expose you to the poison.)

If the bite is on the head or neck, apply ice packs to the area. If the cat will allow it (is not wriggling too much), attempt to cut over the fang marks so that you can squeeze out the poison.

Soap and water is the best detergent for a snake wound; then rush your cat to your veterinarian. With antitoxins and cortisone, most snake-bitten animals can be saved.

Stroke

A stroke, sometimes called apoplexy, is a sudden rupturing of a blood vessel in the brain. It may happen in a cat of any age but is usually seen in older animals.

The affected blood vessels may be on one side of the brain, or there may be a generalized hemorrhaging with total collapse and paralysis of the entire body. When one side of the brain is affected, the animal will usually show partial to complete paralysis of the limbs on the opposite side of the body.

Emergency treatment with stimulants, such as spirits of ammonia, whiskey, or brandy, is imperative. The animal should be rushed to a veterinarian.

Suffocation

It is not unknown for a cat owner to put his pet in the trunk of his car and upon arriving at his destination to find the animal unconscious. Not only can a cat suffocate for want of oxygen, but there is danger of carbon monoxide fumes seeping into the trunk.

Immediate artificial respiration may save the animal.

Unconsciousness, Coma

There is always the terrible prospect of finding a pet unconscious or in a coma. Unconsciousness has many causes. A heart attack is a common one; owing to circulatory failure, the animal faints. Shock, a brain injury (such as a concussion), a cerebral hemorrhage (as seen in strokes) can all cause a coma. Fits and convulsions can end in unconsciousness.

Emergency treatment should begin with stimulants. Use inhalants, such as spirits of ammonia or smelling salts; don't try to put anything in the cat's mouth. Artificial respiration and mouth-to-mouth resuscitation are indicated, but only if breathing has stopped. When the cat regains consciousness, you may drop whiskey or brandy into the side of its mouth. Your veterinarian should be consulted, since diagnosis is essential to prevent a recurrence. Unconsciousness causes a sudden drop in temperature, so wrap the cat in a blanket to keep it warm.

Vomiting

Until professional help is received and the cause for the vomiting found, symptomatic treatment should be used, such as Pepto-Bismol or Kaopectate given by eye dropper every hour until vomiting subsides.

For causes of vomiting, see page 245; for a recuperative diet, see page 137.

A cat who is vomiting is very thirsty, but the more water it drinks, the more it vomits. Take away all water and replace it with a few ice cubes in a dish. Remove all commercial cat food from the diet. The cat should be given no horsemeat and no milk. And no bones! Cooked cereals such as oatmeal and farina, and Pablum and other baby cereals and baby foods, are excellent.

Appendix I
Symptoms and Their Interpretation

This appendix is not intended as a guide to diagnosis or treatment, but as an index to the symptoms that signal a need for consultation with your veterinarian.

Even though your cat will never learn to open the medicine cabinet to seek out an aspirin tablet or laxative pill when it feels pain or constipation, it *can* communicate its needs, especially when it's ailing. For the health and welfare and often the *life* of your pet, the slightest symptom out of the ordinary, the slightest deviation from any of its normal habits or any change in its appearance, should be carefully watched.

Early treatment of any ailment or disease is much easier and less traumatic for your cat. And early diagnosis by the veterinarian is helped considerably by your early recognition that your pet is not up to par.

Since you know your cat, its responses and its actions can tell you a great deal about the state of its health—a little less enthusiasm in its welcome, less nimbleness in its step, less anticipation for its dinner . . .

In this appendix I discuss the various symptoms of illness that you can observe, their interpretation, and their causes. Even though your cat can't say, "I have an awful earache," it shows you it has an earache by shaking its head persistently and by tilting it to the side of the infected ear. By careful observation of the symptoms you should be able to determine what the next step should be. The ailment may be something simple that can easily be treated at home or can be watched at home for a few days. Or it may be something requiring early or immediate veterinary diagnosis and treatment.

Abdomen Tucked In (see Back Hunched Up)

Abdominal Enlargement (see also Bloat; Overweight)

If the cat is female and the swelling is not due to pregnancy, it may be infection of the uterus (metritis), which causes the uterus to fill with pus, giving a bloated or pregnant look. Severe impactions from constipation—with a lot of gas forming from the putrefactive material—will bloat the cat. In gastric bloat there is severe and dangerous enlargement of the stomach. Tumors of the abdominal cavity can be another cause. In older cats we sometimes see an enlargement of the abdomen due to a heart or kidney abnormality called dropsy; the abdominal cavity fills with fluid. The disease, peritonitis, caused by a virus, also gives an enlarged abdomen (see page 176).

Abdominal Straining

When your pet seems to be in distress, straining every few minutes while trying to have a bowel movement, the first thing to suspect is constipation. The problem could also be diarrhea, in which the animal strains because of the severe intestinal irritation. If the normal treatment (see pages 152 and 174) for either of these symptoms doesn't give relief and straining persists, professional help is indicated, as the cause can be impaction with bones or some other foreign body or even possibly a tumor in the intestinal tract.

Appetite, Lack of

When an animal misses more than one meal, start looking for causes. It is a symptom which can have many causes, beginning with an emotional one—strangers, a visiting or new cat or dog in the house. It can also be caused by an infection, such as sore throat or tonsillitis. Worms will cause intermittent appetite. In the case of a bad tooth or a gum infection, the cat will want to eat but won't pick up food because of the pain in its mouth. In the acute stage of any disease, appetite will be affected. As the temperature rises the cat begins to go off its normal routine. It will usually lack pep and sleep a lot. If it does go to its food, it will sniff it and walk away.

Occasionally a cat gets bored with one type of food. A variation in diet will often help; just change the brand and the appetite may pick up.

Appetite, Perverted (see page 111)

Appetite, Ravenous

When a cat starts to eat a lot more than normal, the cause may be internal parasites such as worms. Some females during their heat period have an immense surge in appetite without pathological significance. A happy cat will eat more than an unhappy cat; hand-fed cats tend to eat more than they need.

Back Hunched Up and Abdomen Tucked In

We usually see a cat in this position when it has abdominal pain. It walks laboriously, slow and stiff-legged, with the back hunched up and the abdomen tucked in. The condition is caused by kidney disease (nephritis), or in the female it can also be caused by metritis. In addition, it manifests itself in any painful condition in the abdominal cavity, such as severe constipation, foreign-body impactions, diarrhea, and bladder infections. This hunching condition could also indicate a spinal abnormality—a spinal injury, a slipped disk, spinal arthritis.

Bad Breath (see also Odor)

The odor emanating from the cat's mouth can be putrid at times. It is caused most often by tartar on the teeth or by infected teeth and gums. Also there is a fungal infection of the lips (similar to trench mouth) which gives a bad odor. These conditions must be treated because without proper care the animal will lose its teeth and be forced to eat chopped and homogenized food the rest of its life.

234

In severe kidney diseases the breath smells like urine; this signifies uremia. A foul odor can be caused by digestive disturbances, infection of the stomach or pancreas, or worms.

Bald or Bare Spots (see page 190)

Behavior, Change In

Any deviation in behavior should be regarded with suspicion; there is always a physiological or psychological cause. (See Chapter 11.)

Bleeding

This is a symptom which requires prompt action because any loss of blood can be critical. In all accident cases, it is of primary importance to stop the hemorrhaging (see page 224).

The causative agents of bleeding *from the rectum* can be worms, foreign bodies, tumors, and poisoning.

Bleeding *from the urinary tract* signifies kidney or bladder stones, cystitis, or some other kidney infection.

Bleeding *from the ear* can mean either infection of the ear or brain concussion.

Bleeding *from the mouth* can be caused by blood coming from the stomach or lungs. If the blood is from the stomach, it is usually mixed with stomach juices and there will be vomiting. If the blood is frothy or bubbly, there may be hemorrhaging in the lungs and drastic treatment is needed immediately.

Bleeding *from the nostrils* indicates a ruptured abscess in the sinus cavity, a tumor in the nasal passages, or an abscessed tooth.

Bleeding *from the vaginal tract* means a miscarriage or a female infection.

Bloat (see also Abdominal Enlargement; Overweight)

Bloat is a serious condition, and immediate professional care is needed to save the animal. The earliest symptoms are extreme restlessness and swelling of the abdomen. The swelling is rapid and acute; the stomach will stretch to two or three times its normal size within an hour. This is an emergency condition since the stomach may rupture.

Bowels, Lack of Control (Fecal Incontinence) (see also Diarrhea)

There are times when a cat can't control its bowel movements. We see this condition in older animals suffering from a partial paralysis of the nerves controlling the rectal muscles. It also occurs following a cerebral hemorrhage; an automobile accident in which the spine or the anal ring has been damaged; or a cat fight in which the anal ring has been injured, bitten, or badly torn. Another cause of fecal incontinence is tumors inside the rectum.

Breathing, Fast (see also Coughing; Panting)

The cat's normal respiratory rate is 30 breaths per minute while at rest. Anytime there is an increase in respiration at rest, some abnormality is indicated. Of course, after exercise or excitement or on a hot day a cat can breathe rapidly, 60 to 90 breaths per minute, without pathological significance. Persistent fast breathing while at rest, when accompanied by a rapid, weak pulse and dilated pupils, means the cat is in shock. Fast breathing is present in pneumonia and in the case of a ruptured diaphragm, which is a hernia caused by an injury—usually an automobile accident or a severe blow to the midsection. It is present in the early stages of some poisonings.

Breathing, Slow

A lessening in the rate of respiration is found in narcotic poisoning, diseases of the brain, and in later stages of infectious ailments and diseases.

Colds (see also Eyes, Running; Sneezing)

Colds are as common in cats as they are in human beings, and the symptoms are similar: running nose, red and running eyes, red throat, and fever. The cat will also sneeze and have difficulty breathing.

Circling

If your cat is circling to one side—either left or right—and possibly even continuing to the point of exhaustion and prostration, this indicates most probably an ear disorder; there may be an infection in the middle or inner ear. Or circling might indicate antifreeze toxicity (see page 211). Cerebellar ataxia, a virus infection of the brain in young kittens, can also cause incoordination and circling.

Convulsions (see also Fits; Frothing at the mouth)

Convulsions are a condition of generalized, severe, spasmodic jerkings of the entire body. While having these seizures, the animal is usually semi-conscious or in severe cases completely unconscious. The convulsions usually last from two to three minutes to ten minutes, with periods of quiescence in between. Other symptoms include "chewing-gum fits" (rapid chomping of the jaws), lying on one side with the mouth twitching rapidly, and moving the feet as if running. When the animal comes out of the convulsive attack, it usually staggers for ten or fifteen minutes and appears blind—walking into objects and snapping at anything that comes near it.

Convulsions have many causes. Certain brain diseases cause convulsions—some types of brain tumors and epilepsy. Cats with very high fevers can go into convulsions, and sunstroke can be included in this category. Poisons are another cause, the most notable being strychnine, which is very quick-acting and sends the victim into a severe and prolonged type of convulsion. The hookworm, during migration through the bloodstream, may end up in the cerebral vessels, produce pressure on the brain, and then convulsions. Eclampsia (milk fever) in the nursing queen may cause severe convulsions, although it is not as common as in the dog. Overexcitement or apoplexy, in some extreme cases, can bring on convulsions.

Coughing (see also Wheezing)

Coughing is a symptom of a respiratory affliction. It can be symptomatic of something as simple as a too tight collar pressing on the windpipe or something as serious as a severe lung infection. Of all the causes of coughing, one of the mildest is laryngitis. Tonsillitis is a common cause as well. The cough in these ailments—dry and hacking—is intensified by exercise and excitement. The lower down the infection is, the deeper the cough. Tracheobronchitis, an infection of the lower respiratory tract, is accompanied by a deep cough which produces a white frothy matter from the bronchial tubes. If not treated it can develop into pneumonia or pleurisy, and labored breathing will accompany the cough. Coughing can also be symptomatic of hookworms and roundworms. Lung tumors will produce a cough, as will chronic sinus infection (sinusitis). Cats can have, but not commonly, tuberculosis, with its typical hacking cough. If a cat swallows a foreign object, it can end up penetrating the esophagus wall and pressing on the windpipe. This causes a cough of emergency proportions.

Crying

When a cat cries persistently it usually means pain, which shouldn't be ignored. In kittens crying usually indicates colic. Any digestive disturbance will cause crying. But it can be caused by many painful abnormalities or any physical discomfort.

Deafness

Deafness is often seen in older cats as the nerve controlling hearing degenerates. Excessive wax in the ear canal will partially block hearing. Some kittens are born deaf. Congenital deafness is quite common in white cats with blue eyes.

Diarrhea

In this condition the bowel movements are loose, varying in color from light tan to dark brown to a black, tarry mass. The color of the stool often indicates the nature of the dysfunction. In many diseases (e.g., enteritis) diarrhea is but one of the symptoms. In chronic tonsillitis the swallowed discharge seems to infect the intestines and cause diarrhea. In simple diarrhea, although the movements are watery and loose, they are normal in color. This can be caused by overeating, a sudden change in diet, or an emotional disturbance. But a change in stool color is usually symptomatic of a more serious condition. A black, tarry mass most often means that there is bleeding in the upper intestinal tract, while bright-colored blood in the feces means bleeding in the lower intestinal tract. A bloody, mucous stool usually signifies extreme irritation in the upper or lower intestinal tract, or both. This kind of stool can be caused by infection, certain poisons, sharp foreign bodies, and by worms: the hookworm is the most common culprit, followed by the roundworm and tapeworm. Coccidiosis, strongyles, and giardia—protozoan-type parasites—also cause bloody, mucous stools. Over-eating of bones sometimes produces a white or light-colored stool. Black stools can be caused by the iron in such foods as liver. Because the condition of the stool is helpful in diagnosis, bring a sample when you take the cat with you to the veterinarian.

Drooling, Excessive

When we notice our pet salivating excessively, we should immediately look into its mouth for one of several causes. A foreign body such as a bone or a wood splinter may be causing irritation, or an infected tooth or a gum infection may be involved. Nausea from an irritated stomach can also cause excessive salivation. Some cats merely have to be presented with a tasty tidbit to set them drooling, and I have noticed cats in my clinic drooling excessively due to emotional trauma. Drooling can also be caused by distasteful medicine or by tonsillitis.

Ear, Drooping

Drooping ear pinna is a rather common condition among cats who are out of doors for long periods of time in severe winter weather. It is similar to frostbite in humans. Dark-colored or Siamese cats may have white hair growth at the tips of the ear after a period of denudation. Treatment of the condition is futile.

Ear-Flap Enlargement

This can vary in size from a dime to a half-dollar. Called a hematoma (a cyst filled with blood), it is the result of a ruptured blood vessel in the ear flap. Usually it is due to an injury to the ear or is brought about by excessive headshaking or scratching. It can also be caused by ear-mite infestation, or a bee sting, insect bite, or snake bite, and will be aggravated by headshaking.

Ear Discharge

Varying in color from a light-colored pus to a fetid blackish color. Usually caused by a secondary infection due to ear mites.

Ear Mites (see pages 168 and 207)

Eyes, Blinking

The eye is a sensitive organ, and excessive blinking usually means pain caused by a foreign body, an ulcer, a scratch on the cornea, an abscess or sty on the eyelid, or a simple irritation caused by a speck of dust in the eye (see page 169).

Eyes, Bulging of Eyeball

Usually an enlargement of the eye is due to an injury or caused by glaucoma. Sometimes an abscess or infection behind the eye will push the eyeball outward.

Eyes, Color Change

When the normal color of the eye turns to a grayish or bluish white, this signifies an infection or inflammation of the outer covering of the eye (the cornea).

Eyes, Film Over

When the inner eyelid (third eyelid, nictitating membrane) appears over part or most of the eye, it is usually a sign of sickness. The most common cause is a case of worms. However, a fever or an infected eye will also produce this symptom.

Eyes, Red

Sometimes called "pink eye," this condition, conjunctivitis, is an inflammation and infection of the conjunctiva, the inner covering of the eyelid. It can be caused by dirt or dust, or by bacterial infection.

Eyes, Running (see also Colds; Sneezing)

There is normally a small amount of a clear-looking discharge in the eyes. When the discharge becomes a yellowish matter which gathers in the corners of the eyes, there is some abnormality. This may be caused by a foreign body or by an infection.

Any slight irritation of the eye caused by dust, dirt, extremely cold air, etc., will produce watering. This secretion will go down the tear duct into the nasal passages, producing a nasal discharge with subsequent sneezing. If the tear duct becomes clogged, the discharge from the eyes will spill over the side of the face and cause staining of the fur and skin.

Feet, Tender (see also Limping)

When your pet holds up its paws or walks gingerly, look for trouble on the bottom of its pads. There may be a fungus infection, an embedded foreign body, a wound, or even too long or split claws. Some cats have thin pads, and even strenuous exercise can produce bleeding and irritation.

Fits (see also Convulsions; Frothing at the Mouth)

A fit is not quite so severe as a convulsion. In "running fits" (hysteria), the cat appears very nervous; it looks frantically every way and runs blindly—bumping into things and crying. It may be a calmed down by talking to it quietly and soothingly; the symptoms will gradually subside. Running fits can be caused by a heavy infestation of worms producing cramps and pain in the intestinal tract or depriving the body or normal nutrients, especially minerals and calcium. Kittens sometimes have fits when they are cutting their teeth and the blood calcium level drops.

The other type of fit is similar to apoplexy in humans, and can occur in excitable cats. They seem to be cracking up, taking off in circles for no apparent reason. They are best left alone to calm down by themselves, as they tend to bite and scratch. When the cat is back to normal, it is wise to seek professional help to prevent recurrence.

Frothing at the Mouth (see also Convulsions; Fits)

Unfortunately, the first thing many people think when they see a cat frothing at the mouth is that it has rabies and has gone mad. This is an age-old misconception, and countless non-rabid pets have been wrongly destroyed. An irritation of the mouth caused by eating something distasteful, or cuts, foreign bodies, and bruises, can cause frothing. An upset stomach can cause excessive salivation and frothing. Teething kittens, with their sore and tender gums, will often drool and froth at the mouth. If the cat shows other signs of illness along with the frothing, professional help should be sought immediately.

Gas (Flatulence)

Excessive gas is usually caused by a digestive disturbance in the alimentary tract, generally due to an improper diet or scavenging. A diet composed exclusively of meat, without enough roughage, can cause this condition, as well as certain types of food, such as hard-boiled eggs, cabbage, cauliflower, onions, peppers, turnips, and certain brands of cat food. High-strung animals also have this problem. As a cat gets older you can expect more digestive disorders and more interference with assimilation of certain foods, and it will pass more wind.

Gums, Fiery Red

When the normal gum color turns fiery red, it usually signifies a gum infection. The gums are swollen and bleed easily. The condition should be treated as soon as possible; neglect can result in the loosening and premature loss of the teeth.

Gums, Pale

When the gums look pale—whitish or grayish—anemia is indicated. The foremost cause of anemia is worms; parasites such as hookworms feed on the blood. Feline infectious anemia is a common cause of pale gums. Other causes are disease, malignant tumors, and blood loss in the intestinal cavity due to foreign bodies or poisoning.

Hair Balls, Vomiting of

All cats are fastidious about keeping themselves clean, and regularly lick themselves. Consequently, large amounts of hair are often ingested, especially in the long-haired breeds. These wads of hair collect in the stomach and intestines and can cause constipation and other more complicated illness unless the cat regurgitates the hair or passes it in its bowel movements. Therefore, if your cat has vomited hair balls, it should not alarm you; it is a normal process of elimination. But it should serve to remind you to brush your cat more thoroughly and often.

In severe cases, the hair balls can cause intestinal blockage and your veterinarian has to dislodge them by means of enemas or, in extreme cases, surgery.

Head, Swollen

It is disturbing to see one's pet with part or all of its head swollen to an astonishing size. Sometimes the eyes are swollen shut. The condition can be caused by several things, the most common being an allergy similar to hives in humans and brought about by the eating of something that doesn't agree with the cat's system—generally from a garbage can, or table scraps given as a treat. Crab and lobster meat seem to be especially common culprits. Another common cause of head swelling is an encounter with a snake or a bee or a spider.

Headshaking

This symptom indicates ear distress. The cat also scratches at its ear and cries with pain when it hits a tender spot. In the beginning the head scratching is mild, but as the infection progresses the cat walks with its head tilted on the same side as the ear infection. Ear infection can be caused by ear mites, bacteria, or fungi, and all three can occur at the same time. Parasites such as fleas and ticks can work their way into the ear canal. Also, a child may have stuck a foreign body into the cat's ear. Because of proximity to the brain, if the infection is allowed to progress to the middle ear or inner ear the consequences can be serious, with high fever and convulsions. Headshaking can also be caused by fly-bite infection at the tip of the ear.

Hives

These are bumps on the cat's body, appearing most often on the head. The bumps are accompanied by intense itching, and the cause is usually, as in humans, an allergic response to food or drink. Occasionally an anaphylactic reaction to an injected drug or vaccine is responsible.

Incoordination (see also Paralysis)

This is any deviation from the normal gait of the animal. Sometimes it will hold its head to one side and walk in circles. The cause can be a head injury, a brain injury, an inner-ear infection, or a brain tumor.

Limping (see also Feet, Tender)

When a cat limps, there are several possible causes. The most likely one, and the first thing the cat should be examined for, is an injury to the pad of its foot, possibly caused by a foreign body such as glass, metal, or wood splinters. Although the pad has a tough covering, it is not invulnerable.

Sometimes cockleburs or matted hair balls get lodged between the toes.

Dislocations, sprains, and fractures are common causes of limping. In the simple sprain the symptoms should abate in a day or two. With a fracture the symptoms will depend on the severity of the break—whether it is a simple hairline crack in the bone or a compound fracture with pieces of bone penetrating the skin.

Dislocations and fractures can occur even in the toes—phalangeal fracture or dislocation. In each toe there are three phalanges—three parts, three bones. Sometimes a running cat will take a wrong step, stumble, or step into a hole, and one of these tiny bones will be fractured or dislocated, causing a lameness.

Bursitis, arthritis, and rheumatism can also be responsible for limping. In bursitis and arthritis the joints usually get quite feverish. Rheumatism is often seen in middle-aged and older cats, and on cold, damp days the signs are more pronounced.

Bone infections can cause lameness and are usually the result of injuries, bite wounds, or gunshot wounds. In rare cases limping can be caused by bone tumors. Rickets can cause a kitten to limp

If limping continues more than twenty-four hours, or if it steadily worsens, medical care is indicated.

Lumps

Most growths are soft hairless lumps in the skin, and are usually seen in cats over the age of six. They vary in size from a pea to a walnut. They are sometimes referred to as "old-age tumors," and are generally benign but occasionally may prove to be malignant, as in mast-cell tumors.

Another type of lump is a sebaceous cyst. Its appearance and size are similar to the tumor, but it contains a cheesy substance. Sometimes the cysts rupture and then fill up again.

Any lump on the body of your cat should be brought to the attention of your veterinarian. If it turns out to be malignant, fast removal can save your pet's life.

Mouth, Ulcerated (Trench Mouth)

Infection of gums and lips can cause an unpleasant odor. Badly decomposed teeth can also cause an ulceration of the mouth. Although this ailment is also called trench mouth, it is not the same as the infection in humans and is not contagious to humans.

Nose: Cold, Dry, Hot (see also Temperature)

Although the cat normally has a moist nose, a dry nose doesn't necessarily mean illness. Nor does a hot nose signify a fever. I've seen cats with cold noses and temperatures of 105 degrees. That the nose is an indicator of the cat's health is one of the most common myths about cats. Actually, the temperature of the nose varies with the temperature and humidity of the cat's immediate environment.

Nose, Running (Nasal Discharge)

A clear watery discharge from the nostrils is not necessarily significant, and can be normal. If the discharge is excessive, or turns to thick mucus or a yellow pus-like secretion, there is an infection present. A running nose, with purulent matter, can be a symptom of distemper, pneumonia, pneumonitis, rhinotracheitis, and other respiratory diseases.

Any eye irritation or infection is accompanied by nasal discharge because the eye drains down the tear duct into the nostril.

Sinus infections can cause a running nose. Also, the sinuses can become clogged, infected (sinusitis), or abscessed (caused by an infected tooth); a nasal worm occasionally gets into the frontal sinuses.

Foreign bodies are another cause of nasal discharge. I have removed all kinds of objects, including pieces of straw, wood, and even needles.

Odor (see also Bad Breath)

An unpleasant odor emanating from the cat's body can be due to several causes, and sometimes a tenative diagnosis can be made just from the odor.

Among skin diseases, sarcoptic mange has a typical musty odor; fungus infection has a sour odor. Some ear infections give rise to a putrid odor. An anal gland infection can produce a discharge which has a distinctive unpleasant odor (the reason why the anal glands are sometimes called skunk glands).

Overweight (see also Abdominal Enlargement; Bloat)

Lack of exercise is a major cause of obesity in cats. In spayed and castrated animals the lack of hormones sometimes causes obesity. A cat with a hypoactive (underactive) thyroid is listless and rapidly gains excessive weight. If an older cat shows a distinct increase in weight, fluids may be collecting in the body due to congestive heart failure or inadequate kidney functioning.

Panting (see also Breathing, Fast; Coughing)

Normally a cat pants after exercise, and in hot weather, since this is one of the only two ways it has to perspire (the other is through the pads of the feet).

Excessive panting usually signifies an abnormality. In such pathological conditions as fever, lung disease, and heart disease, there is increased panting, and also a blueness or paleness to the tongue if not enough oxygen is reaching the lungs.

Paralysis (see also Incoordination)

Usually paralysis starts in the rear legs, and the animal drags itself, unable to walk. It is generally caused by disease, poison, or an injury to the brain or spinal cord. There is also paralysis with a slipped disk and more seriously with a ruptured disk. The symptoms come on gradually, starting with a slight incoordination in the rear legs, reluctance to move, an arched back, and pain when the back is touched.

Tetanus, or lockjaw, can cause paralysis or stiffening of the body. It is a rare disease in cats and is usually caused by a puncture wound infected with the tetanus germ.

An injury to the nerves of the front leg can cause a paralysis, and the cat will drag its toes. This, called radial paralysis, may be seen after a cat is hit by a car.

Tick paralysis is a completely generalized paralysis caused by tick infestation. A single tick which attaches itself to the skin over the spinal cord can be responsible for paralysis.

Penis, Discharge From

Dripping blood from the penis requires close scrutiny to determine if the blood is coming from inside the penis—through the urethra—or is external. Inside, it generally means infection or stones in the bladder of kidney. Outside, it usually means an injury—a bite or a foreign body embedded in the sheath.

Rectal Growths

Occasionally tumors are seen growing on the outside of the anus. Male cats are more prone to this condition than females. As the tumors are usually malignant, they should be treated immediately.

There is a condition called prolapse of the rectum—a large mass of intestine protrudes from the anus because the tissue holding the rectum in place has broken down. It is usually caused by a severe case of diarrhea in which there is continuous straining.

Rubbing Rear Along Ground

When an animal drags its rear along the ground, it doesn't always mean worms, as many people think. Ninety percent of the time infected anal glands are responsible. Certain types of worms, notably the tapeworm, can sometimes be the cause. Segments of the tapeworm will often crawl out of the anus, and the cat will slide itself along the ground to relieve the irritation. The cat will also lick the anus to get relief.

Rumbling or Noisy Intestines

When the cat's intestinal tract rumbles and growls, it is usually due to an intestinal upset. Both infection and chronic colitis can bring on the noisy spells. If the cat apparently is not sick and the attacks are only intermittent, the cause could be worms.

Scratching

Observe where the cat is concentrating its scratching. External parasites—fleas and lice—are the commonest skin irritants. Skin diseases are also a common cause—eczema, dry skin—and can be brought on by many things, including too much bathing with strong soaps, inadequate diet, and allergies. Scratching is associated, as well, with any skin lesion.

Scratching at the head or vicinity of ears usually means ear-mite infection. (See page 207.)

Shedding

Normally cats shed twice a year, in the spring and in the fall, when they're changing their coats. Some cats who live in warm houses shed profusely the year round because the heat dries out their skin and fur. Too much bathing with strong soaps can cause abnormal shedding. So can worm infestation.

During disease, with high fever, the animal will begin to lose fur, and the shedding will continue after recovery. Cats can shed after any severe traumatic or emotional experience.

Shivering and Trembling

Most often these symptoms mean that the cat has a fever. Almost any type of ailment that causes a fever brings on shivering and trembling. Certain types of poisons, both external and internal, produce a nervous reaction and trembling. Insecticide powders, lawn sprays, and fertilizers elicit a toxic reaction. A nursing queen can show signs of trembling and shaking in the early stages of eclampsia (milk fever).

Sneezing (see also Colds; Eyes, Running)

The cat will have spasmodic sneezing when trying to rid its nostrils and sinus passages of certain secretions. Allergies are a common cause of sneezing: in spring, plant pollens, and in the house, dust and wool rugs, are commonly responsible. Drainage from an eye infection will cause a cat to sneeze. So will infections of the sinuses. Pneumonitis and rhino-tracheitis produce severe and persistent sneezing.

Snoring

This is not very common in cats. If present, it usually indicates an infection or enlargement of the throat. In upper respiratory diseases, the nostrils become clogged with a purulent mass and breathing becomes more difficult.

Sores

Sores can appear on any part of the body, and the term covers a multitude of infections. They can be caused by insect bites, bites from lice, fleas, and ticks, eczemas, and other skin infections, such as ringworm.

Self-mutilation will greatly magnify a simple sore. The old saying that a cat's tongue can heal its wounds is not correct. Although a cat can keep a wound clean by licking it, it can also make it much worse by biting and scratching it.

Spraying

Tomcats will usually start spraying at the beginning of puberty. This is a form of territorial instinct; he is marking the house (unfortunately) with his urine to make sure that other tomcats will know that "Kilroy was here."

Castration will usually clear up this problem. For further discussion of problem cases, see Chapter 11.

Stiff-Leggedness (see also Back Hunched Up)

In the male this condition is usually caused by an injured testicle. We also see stiff-leggedness in older cats who are arthritic or rheumatic.

Tail Biting (see page 111)

Temperature

The temperature is a sensitive indicator of the normal or abnormal metabolism of the body. The normal body temperature of cats is 100 to 101 degrees. In kittens, the temperature may go up to 102 degrees without cause for alarm. And in the adult cat, temperatures ranging from 101 to 102 degrees are not necessarily disturbing, since there can be variation with room temperature, exercise, and excitement. But anything over 102 degrees should be considered abnormal. Although the insides of the ears and thighs will indicate if there is a fever, the best way to find out a cat's temperature is with a rectal thermometer (see page 151).

Any temperature reading under 100 degrees should also be considered abnormal. When the temperature begins to drop, the body is weakening, and emergency measures should be taken immediately (see page 151). The exception is the whelping queen, who gives fair notice of the event when her temperature drops under 100 degrees twenty-four hours before delivery of her first kitten.

Testicles, Enlarged

Often when a male cat fights, the scrotum or testicles are injured. There can be severe swelling, with pain and stiff-leggedness. If the swelling continues, in either or both testicles, inflammation develops which requires professional treatment. An enlargement can also mean a tumorous growth of the testicle.

Thirst

Cats normally drink more water in hot weather and after exercise. But, at any time, a dramatic increase in water consumption is a danger signal. Excessive thirst is a symptom of some kidney diseases, one type of diabetes, and fever. With any inflammation of the stomach, such as gastritis, the cat will try to drink water but will vomit it immediately. In all cases of extreme thirst your veterinarian should be consulted as quickly as possible.

Urinary Abnormalities

Dribbling urine. This is common in the spayed female as she approaches middle or old age and is due to a female hormone deficiency. In older cats, male and female, there is a relaxing of the muscle tone in the bladder and urethra, and consequent leaking, over which the animal has no control. This condition can be helped by hormones. When a completely housebroken cat starts urinating in the house, there is a medical or psychological cause. Usually a urinary tract infection is involved. Some animals do it out of spite or jealousy and develop a psychosomatic urinary tract infection.

Frequent urination. Several urinary disorders can be involved in this symptom. It can signify an inflammation of the bladder known as cystitis. Because of a burning sensation the animal feels the need to urinate often, and sometimes there is no urine. After a prolonged attack there is blood from the irritation to the lining of the bladder wall. The animal is in extreme pain and usually walks with a hunched-up back and cries when touched. It is seen more often in females and is sometimes caused by getting wet and chilled, and lying in damp places.

Straining and blood. This is the opposite of the dribbling syndrome. The animal does a lot of straining, and pain is evident. Only a few drops of urine appear, usually accompanied by blood. This is a symptom of bladder or kidney stones.

Vaginal Discharge

After whelping, a queen may have a slight, spotty reddish discharge for about a week under normal conditions. If the normal red color turns either to a purulent or black or greenish color, this is always a danger symptom of infection, retained afterbirth, or a dead kitten inside the uterus.

A large mass of the uterus protruding from the vagina is known as prolapse of the uterus. This is caused by a breakdown of the musculature of the vagina and uterus, either from undue straining or from tumors.

Vomiting

Vomiting commonly occurs in all cats and is due to many varieties of ailments and diseases, from simple to serious. The cat vomits frequently because it can regurgitate at will. We often see our pet eating grass and then vomiting. This is its way of relieving its indigestion. We also see cats regurgitating food immediately after eating it and then eating the vomited mass. This is not a pretty sight, but it is their way of predigesting their food. Often the mother cat will regurgitate her food so that her kittens can eat it—softened, warmed, and homogenized. Occasionally a cat will vomit in the morning before breakfast. It will be a yellow, frothy mass, like beaten egg yolk. Generally this means simply that the cat is hungry and empty; the yellow vomitus is bile. Simple vomiting can be due to hair balls, eating food that is too cold, eating too fast, eating fried or greasy food. The cat usually does not appear sickly, is not physically depressed or feverish.

Vomiting can be caused by the following:
□ Brain injuries.
□ Car sickness.
□ Constipation or impaction.
□ Constricted stomach (pyloric stenosis). This occurs in kittens and is characterized by vomiting shortly after eating. After persistent vomiting the kitten becomes weak and dehydrated.
□ Diseases. Among them are distemper (enteritis), hepatitis, leptospirosis, metritis, nephritis, and pancreatitis.
□ Emotionalism (psychogenic vomiting).

Highly nervous cats often vomit when they get excited. Cats have been known to vomit when jealous or wanting attention. They are usually cats who are overindulged and undertrained.
□ Fatigue. Caused by strenuous play, and exercise after eating.
□ Foreign bodies.
□ Gastritis. Caused by eating spoiled, greasy, fried foods, or by overeating improper food or too many bones.
□ Heatstroke, overheating.
□ Intestinal infections in enteritis.
□ Obstruction or interception of the bowels. This is caused by a twisting of the intestines and the symptoms are acute. The animal is in severe pain, and your veterinarian is needed immediately.
□ Poisons. The symptoms are severe—fast breathing, twitching, severe cramps, diarrhea sometimes with blood—and immediate emergency treatment is necessary (see Chapter 17).
□ Tonsillitis.
□ Worms.

In all cases of vomiting, if it is persistent, examination is needed for the cause. Examine the substance that is regurgitated to see if it contains blood.

Weight Loss

Along with loss of weight, the animal usually becomes rough-coated (dull-looking) and begins to lose fur. Loss of weight is serious, and the cause must be ascertained as soon as possible. As the cat loses weight it will likely develop anemia; it will be tired and listless. The first thing to suspect is one of the following diseases: diabetes, enteritis, hepatitis, leptospirosis, nephritis.

If the cat has diarrhea of any extent, there is loss of weight. If this persists, the cause of the diarrhea must be discovered.

Other causes of weight loss are:
□ Chronic colitis. With this condition there is a persistent and intermittent diarrhea from a

variety of causes. The animal is not assimilating food properly, so that part of what it is eating is being wasted—passing through the body undigested.

☐ Chronic tonsillitis. This condition keeps the animal from eating properly.

☐ Dental problems. Because of an abnormality—abscessed tooth, loose tooth or teeth, gum infection, etc.—the cat cannot eat properly.

☐ Emotional disturbances can cause "hunger strikes." Excitable cats often use up so much energy running and jumping that their weight stays at a minimum.

☐ External parasites. Animals become emaciated when heavily infested with ticks, fleas, or lice, as the parasites feed on their blood.

☐ Inadequate diet.

☐ Intestinal worms.

☐ Malignant tumors.

Wetting (see also Urinary Abnormalities)

Some kittens when they get excited will have an involuntary urination.

Wheezing (see also Coughing)

This is almost like an asthmatic condition in humans. The wheeze is a sound made on inspiration, whereas the cough is made on expiration. Wheezing is caused by allergies or bronchial diseases.

Yellowness (Jaundice)

When the animal appears yellow—skin, membranes of the eyes, mouth—it is a serious problem. It signifies a dysfunction of the liver and can also mean an obstruction in the bile duct due to stones or growths. It is seen in hepatitis and leptospirosis. Certain poisons can affect the liver in such a way that the cat exhibits jaundice. An overdose of worm medicine can affect the liver. For jaundice, quick professional care is recommended.

Appendix II
A List of Hazards in House and Garden

I have listed here the common household and garden items (including poisons that are discussed in Chapter 17) that pose a danger to your pet's well-being. The list is intended only as a reminder to the cat owner that many commonplace objects and substances can be dangerous to a cat with a free run of the premises.

Items marked with an asterisk indicate both a potential poison and objects (such as sinks and washing machines) that will often contain residues of toxic substances (such as bleaches and cleansers).

Index